Private International Law: A Hungarian Perspective

Law in Eastern Europe

A SERIES PUBLISHED IN COOPERATION WITH LEIDEN UNIVERSITY AND THE UNIVERSITIES OF TARTU AND GRAZ

VOLUME 71

The titles published in this series are listed at *brill.com/laee*

Private International Law: A Hungarian Perspective

By

Csongor István Nagy

BRILL | NIJHOFF

LEIDEN | BOSTON

The publication of this book was generously supported by the HUN-REN Hungarian Research Network (earlier: Eötvös Loránd Research Network).

Some parts of the book draw on the results of the multiyear CEPIL project (Cross-Border Litigation in Central-Europe: EU Private International Law Before National Courts) carried out with the generous support of the European Commission's Directorate General for Justice and Consumers (European Union's Justice Programme (2014-2020), 800789–CEPIL–JUST-AG-2017/JUST-JCOO-AG-2017). The CEPIL project's research findings were published in Nagy, Cs.I. (ed.), *Cross-border litigation in Central-Europe: EU private international law before national courts* (Kluwer Law International, The Hague, 2022). The content of this book represents the views of the author only and is his sole responsibility. The European Commission does not accept any responsibility for use that may be made of the information it contains.

The author is indebted to Tamás Szabados for thoroughly reviewing the manuscript. Of course, all views and any errors remain the author's own.

Library of Congress Cataloging-in-Publication Data

Names: Nagy, Csongor István, 1979- editor.
Title: Private international law : a Hungarian perspective / [edited] by Csongor István Nagy.
Description: Leiden ; Boston : Brill/Nijhoff, 2024. | Series: Law in Eastern Europe, 0075-823X ; volume 71 | Includes bibliographical references and index.
Identifiers: LCCN 2024002977 (print) | LCCN 2024002978 (ebook) | ISBN 9789004690837 (hardback) | ISBN 9789004694569 (ebook)
Subjects: LCSH: Conflict of laws–Hungary. | Judicial assistance–Hungary.
Classification: LCC KKF480 .P75 2024 (print) | LCC KKF480 (ebook) | DDC 346.439–dc23/eng/20240129
LC record available at https://lccn.loc.gov/2024002977
LC ebook record available at https://lccn.loc.gov/2024002978

Typeface for the Latin, Greek, and Cyrillic scripts: "Brill". See and download: brill.com/brill-typeface.

ISSN 0075-823X
ISBN 978-90-04-69083-7 (hardback)
ISBN 978-90-04-69456-9 (e-book)
DOI 10.1163/9789004694569

This book is printed on acid-free paper and produced in a sustainable manner.

To Abigél, Nimród and Zsófia for their patience, encouragement and support

Contents

Abbreviations

1954 Hague Convention	Hague Convention on Civil Procedure, The Hague, March 1, 1954.
1958 New York Convention	United Nations Convention on the Recognition and Enforcement of Foreign Arbitral Awards, New York, June 10, 1958.
1961 Geneva Convention	European Convention on International Commercial Arbitration, Geneva, April 21, 1961.
1961 Hague Convention	Convention on the Conflicts of Laws Relating to the Form of Testamentary Dispositions, The Hague, October 5, 1961.
1961 Vienna Convention	Vienna Convention on Diplomatic Relations, Vienna, April 18, 1961.
1963 Vienna Convention	Convention on Civil Liability for Nuclear Damage, Vienna, May 21, 1963.
1971 Hague Convention	Convention on the Recognition and Enforcement of Foreign Judgments in Civil and Commercial Matters, The Hague, February 1, 1971.
1973 Hague Convention	Convention on the Law Applicable to Products Liability, The Hague, October 2, 1973.
1980 Hague Convention	Convention on the Civil Aspects of International Child Abduction, The Hague, October 25, 1980.
1980 Rome Convention	80/934/EEC: Convention on the law applicable to contractual obligations opened for signature in Rome on 19 June 1980. Consolidated version. OJ L 266, 9.10.1980, pp. 1–19.
1996 Hague Convention	Convention on Jurisdiction, Applicable Law, Recognition, Enforcement and Co-operation in Respect of Parental Responsibility and Measures for the Protection of Children, The Hague, October 19, 1996.
1999 Montréal Convention	Convention for the Unification of Certain Rules for International Carriage by Air, Montreal, May 28, 1999.
2000 Hague Convention	Convention on the International Protection of Adults, The Hague, January 13, 2000.

2000 Brussels II Regulation	Council Regulation (EC) No 1347/2000 of 29 May 2000 on jurisdiction and the recognition and enforcement of judgments in matrimonial matters and in matters of parental responsibility for children of both spouses. OJ L 160, 30.6.2000, pp. 19–36.
2000 Insolvency Regulation	Council Regulation (EC) No 1346/2000 of 29 May 2000 on insolvency proceedings. OJ L 160, 30.6.2000, pp. 1–18.
2001 Brussels I Regulation	Council Regulation (EC) No 44/2001 of 22 December 2000 on jurisdiction and the recognition and enforcement of judgments in civil and commercial matters. OJ L 12, 16.1.2001, pp. 1–23.
2003 Brussels II Regulation	Council Regulation (EC) No 2201/2003 of 27 November 2003 concerning jurisdiction and the recognition and enforcement of judgments in matrimonial matters and the matters of parental responsibility, repealing Regulation (EC) No 1347/2000. OJ L 338, 23.12.2003, pp. 1–29.
2007 Hague Protocol	2009/941/EC: Council Decision of 30 November 2009 on the conclusion by the European Community of the Hague Protocol of 23 November 2007 on the Law Applicable to Maintenance Obligations. OJ L 331, 16.12.2009, pp. 17–23.
2007 Lugano Convention	Convention on jurisdiction and the recognition and enforcement of judgments in civil and commercial matters, Lugano, 30 October 2007. OJ L 339, 21.12.2007, pp. 3–41.
2012 Brussels I Regulation	Regulation (EU) No 1215/2012 of the European Parliament and of the Council of 12 December 2012 on jurisdiction and the recognition and enforcement of judgments in civil and commercial matters. OJ L 351, 20.12.2012, pp. 1–32.
2015 Insolvency Regulation	Regulation (EU) No 2015/848 of the European Parliament and of the Council of 20 May 2015 on insolvency proceedings. OJ L 141, 5.6.2015, pp. 19–72.

2019 Brussels II Regulation	Council Regulation (EU) 2019/1111 of 25 June 2019 on jurisdiction, the recognition and enforcement of decisions in matrimonial matters and the matters of parental responsibility, and on international child abduction. OJ L 178, 2.7.2019, pp. 1–115.
Act on Authors' Rights	Act LXXVI of 1999 on Authors' Rights (in Hungarian: '*1999. évi LXXVI. törvény a szerzői jogról*').
APIL	Act XXVIII of 2017 on Private International Law (in Hungarian: '*2017. évi XXVIII. törvény a nemzetközi magánjogról*'). This monograph relies on the following translation of the APIL: T. Szabados, "Hungary: Act XXVIII of 2017 on Private International Law," 82(4) *Rabels Zeitschrift für Ausländisches und Internationales Privatrecht* (2018), 1004–1045. Accordingly, quotations from the APIL are from this source.
Arbitration Act	Act LX of 2017 on Arbitration (in Hungarian: '*2017. évi LX. törvény a választottbíráskodásról*').
Bankruptcy Act	Act XLIX of 1991 on Liquidation and Bankruptcy Procedure (in Hungarian: '*1991. évi XLIX. törvény a csődeljárásról és a felszámolási eljárásról*')
Brussels I Regulation	The 2001 Brussels I Regulation and the 2012 Brussels I Regulation jointly, and, if not specified otherwise, article numbers refer to the 2012 Brussels I Regulation.
Brussels II Regulation	The 2000 Brussels II Regulation, the 2003 Brussels II Regulation, and the 2019 Brussels II Regulation jointly; article numbers refer to the 2019 Brussels II Regulation.
Budapest-Capital Regional Court	In Hungarian: '*Fővárosi Törvényszék*', before January 1, 2012: '*Fővárosi Bíróság*'.
CIM	Appendix B to COTIF: Uniform Rules concerning the Contract of International Carriage of Goods by Rail (CIM).
CISG	United Nations Convention on Contracts for the International Sale of Goods, Vienna, April 11, 1980.

Citizenship Act	Act LV of 1993 on Hungarian Citizenship (in Hungarian: '*1993. évi LV. törvény a magyar állampolgárságról*').
CIV	Appendix A to COTIF: Uniform Rules concerning the Contract of International Carriage of Passengers by Rail (CIV).
Civil Code	Act V of 2013 on the Civil Code (in Hungarian: '*2013. évi V. törvény a Polgári Törvénykönyvről*').
CJEU	Court of Justice of the European Union.
CMR	Convention on the Contract for the International Carriage of Goods by Road (CMR), Geneva, May 19, 1956.
Code of Civil Procedure	Act CXXX of 2016 on Civil Procedure (in Hungarian: '*2016. évi CXXX. törvény a polgári perrendtartásról*').
Code on Criminal Procedure	Act XC of 2017 on Criminal Procedure (in Hungarian: '*2017. évi XC. törvény a büntetőeljárásról*').
Company Court	In Hungarian: '*cégbíróság*'.
Constitution	Fundamental Law of Hungary (in Hungarian: '*Magyarország Alaptörvénye*').
COTIF	Convention concerning International Carriage by Rail, Berne, May 9, 1980.
ECHR	European Convention on Human Rights.
ECJ	European Court of Justice.
ECtHR	European Court of Human Rights.
EEA	European Economic Area.
EEO Regulation	Regulation (EC) No 805/2004 of the European Parliament and of the Council of 21 April 2004 creating a European Enforcement Order for uncontested claims. OJ L 143, 30.4.2004, pp. 15–39.
Enforcement Act	Act LVIII of 1994 on Judicial Enforcement (in Hungarian: '*1994. évi LIII. törvény a bírósági végrehajtásról*').
EPO Regulation	Regulation (EC) No 1896/2006 of the European Parliament and of the Council of 12 December 2006 creating a European order for payment procedure. OJ L 399, 30.12.2006, pp. 1–32.

ESCP Regulation	Regulation (EC) No 861/2007 of the European Parliament and of the Council of 11 July 2007 establishing a European Small Claims Procedure. OJ L 199, 31.7.2007, pp. 1–22.
EU	European Union.
EU courts	Court of Justice of the European Union (including the General Court and the European Court of Justice).
EU PIL	EU private international law.
EU private international law instruments	EU legal acts dealing with private international law: Brussels I Regulation, Brussels II Regulation, Insolvency Regulation, Maintenance Regulation, Matrimonial Property Regulation, Rome I Regulation, Rome II Regulation, Rome III Regulation, Succession Regulation, and the Regulation on the Property Consequences of Registered Partnerships.
European Commission	Commission of the European Union.
GC	General Court.
High Court of Appeal	In Hungarian: '*Ítélőtábla*'.
Hungarian Chamber of Commerce and Industry (HCCI)	In Hungarian: '*Magyar Kereskedelmi és Iparkamara*'.
Insolvency Regulation	The 2000 Insolvency Regulation and the 2015 Insolvency Regulation jointly; article numbers refer to the 2015 Insolvency Regulation.
Judiciary Act	Act LXVI of 1997 on the Organization and Administration of Courts (in Hungarian: '*1997. évi LXVI. törvény a bíróságok szervezetéről és igazgatásáról*').
Labour Code	Act I of 2012 on the Labour Code (in Hungarian: '*2012. évi I. törvény a munka törvénykönyvéről*').
Land Registry Act	Act CXLI of 1997 on Land Registry (in Hungary: '*1997. évi CXLI. törvény az ingatlan-nyilvántartásról*').
Maintenance Regulation	Regulation (EC) No 4/2009 of 18 December 2008 on jurisdiction, applicable law, recognition and enforcement of decisions and cooperation in matters relating to maintenance obligations. OJ L 7, 10.1.2009, pp. 1–79.

Matrimonial Property Regulation	Council Regulation (EU) No 2016/1103 of 24 June 2016 implementing enhanced cooperation in the area of jurisdiction, applicable law and the recognition and enforcement of decisions in matters of matrimonial property regimes. OJ L 183, 8.7.2016, pp. 1–29.
old APIL	Law-Decree (Act) 13 of 1979 on Private International Law (in Hungarian: '*1979. évi 13. törvényerejű rendelet a nemzetközi magánjogról*').
old Civil Code	Act IV of 1959 on the Civil Code (in Hungarian: '*1959. évi IV. törvénya Polgári Törvénykönyvről*').
PIL	Private international law.
Regulation on the Property Consequences of Registered Partnerships	Council Regulation (EU) No 2016/1104 of 24 June 2016 implementing enhanced cooperation in the area of jurisdiction, applicable law and the recognition and enforcement of decisions in matters of the property consequences of registered partnerships. OJ L 183, 8.7.2016, pp. 30–56.
Rome I Regulation	Regulation (EC) No 593/2008 of the European Parliament and of the Council of 17 June 2008 on the law applicable to contractual obligations (Rome I). OJ L 177, 4.7.2008, pp. 6–16.
Rome II Regulation	Regulation (EC) No 864/2007 of the European Parliament and of the Council of 11 July 2007 on the law applicable to non-contractual obligations (Rome II). OJ L 199, 31.7.2007, pp. 40–49.
Rome III Regulation	Council Regulation (EU) No 1259/2010 of 20 December 2010 implementing enhanced cooperation in the area of the law applicable to divorce and legal separation. OJ L 343, 29.12.2010, pp. 10–16.
Service Regulation	Regulation (EC) No 1393/2007 of the European Parliament and of the Council of 13 November 2007 on the service in the Member States of judicial and extrajudicial documents in civil or commercial matters (service of documents), and repealing Council Regulation (EC) No 1348/2000. OJ L 324, 10.12.2007, pp. 79–120.

Succession Regulation	Regulation (EU) No 650/2012 of the European Parliament and of the Council of 4 July 2012 on jurisdiction, applicable law, recognition and enforcement of decisions and acceptance and enforcement of authentic instruments in matters of succession and on the creation of a European Certificate of Succession. OJ L 201, 27.7.2012, pp. 107–134.
Supreme Court	Supreme Court of Hungary (in Hungarian: *'Kúria'*, before January 1, 2012: *'Magyar Köztársaság Legfelsőbb Bírósága'*).
Taking-of-Evidence Regulation	Council Regulation (EC) No 1206/2001 of 28 May 2001 on cooperation between the courts of the Member States in the taking of evidence in civil or commercial matters. OJ L 174, 27.6.2001, pp. 1–24.
TEU	Treaty on the European Union: Consolidated versions of the Treaty on European Union and the Treaty on the Functioning of the European Union. OJ C 83 of 30.3.2010.
TFEU	Treaty on the Functioning of the European Union: Consolidated versions of the Treaty on European Union and the Treaty on the Functioning of the European Union. OJ C 83 of 30.3.2010.

CHAPTER 1

General Introduction

1 Historical Development

The Hungarian legal system belongs to the civil-law family. Hungarian private law has Roman law roots, and statutory law plays a central role. The application and interpretation of the law are mainly based on the construction of a statute or other regulation.

The first written sources of Hungarian law are to be found in the early 11th century law books of Saint Stephen (in Hungarian: '*Szent István*'), the founder of the Kingdom of Hungary. Subsequent kings also enacted law books (e.g., Saint Ladislaus, in Hungarian: '*Szent László*', Coloman I the Booklover, in Hungarian: '*Könyves Kálmán*', Louis the Great, in Hungarian: '*Nagy Lajos*'). The Golden Bull of 1222 (in Hungarian: 'Aranybulla'), adopted by Andrew II, is particularly noteworthy as this was Hungary's first written constitutional document, playing a role in Hungarian legal history like the Magna Charta of 1215 in England or the German Golden Bull of 1356 in Germany. It established, among others, the right to personal freedom and a fair trial: the first rule of the Hungarian Golden Bull provided that no nobleman could be arrested unless he or she had been convicted in accordance with the law.

In 1514, István Werbőczi wrote a remarkable compilation of Hungarian customary law, entitled '*Tripartitum opus iuris consuetudinarii inclyti regni Hungariae*'. The compilation's abbreviated name was '*Tripartitum*' or Triplebook (in Hungarian: '*Hármaskönyv*') as it consisted of three books. Though enacted by the parliament and signed by the king, the compilation was not promulgated. Nevertheless, it was applied in judicial practice as the law of the land.

In 1848, several laws were adopted (the so-called laws of April) in order to transform Hungary into a constitutional monarchy. Although the revolution and war of independence of 1848 were repressed by the Austrian and Russian armies and the democratic achievements were abolished, in 1867 a settlement (in Hungarian: '*kiegyezés*', in German: '*Ausgleich*') was reached between the Austrian royal court and Hungary which began the period of prosperity and development ended by the First World War. In this period of dualism (Austro-Hungarian Empire) Hungary experienced an economic boom. Legal development also kept pace with this economic progress, entailing the adoption of several modern codes of law, e.g., the commercial code of 1875, the criminal

 | DOI:10.1163/9789004694569_002

code of 1878 (Code of Csemegi), the code on criminal procedure of 1896, the code on civil procedure of 1911.

In the 20th century Hungary experienced two reversals of fortune. First, as a result of the peace treaty of Trianon at the end of the First World War, the country lost two-thirds of its territory. Second, after the Second World War, Hungary became part of the Soviet sphere of influence and the communist party seized power, introducing the system of planned economy (the name of the country was changed to 'People's Republic of Hungary', in Hungarian: 'Magyar Népköztársaság'). The consequence was that Hungarian law was heavily impregnated with socialist-communist ideology, and this had a palpable impact also on the concepts of private law.

In 1989, the socialist regime collapsed, and several laws were adopted to transform the country into a liberal democracy and market economy. Interestingly, the reform in the domain of private and economic law had started some years before the socialist regime collapsed and the 'system change' was accomplished. For instance, the company act was adopted already in 1988 (Act VI of 1988).

The history of Hungarian private international law dates back to the second part of the 19th century. In this period, several judgments of the then Hungarian supreme court (in Hungarian: '*Kúria*') dealt with issues of private international law and international civil procedure. This field of law was first codified in 1979, followed by the adoption of the currently effective APIL in 2017.

2 Private International Law: Choice of Law and International Civil Procedure

The term 'private international law' (in Hungarian: '*nemzetközi magánjog*') has a different meaning in the various legal systems. In a wider sense, it embraces three questions: first, the determination of the applicable law, i.e., the law applicable to a particular legal question ('choice of law'); second, the selection of the court or courts that have power to entertain a lawsuit (jurisdiction); third, the determination of the conditions and the procedure applicable to the recognition and enforcement of foreign judgments. The latter two questions make up the field of 'international civil procedural law'. In a narrower sense, 'private international law' embraces only those rules that designate the applicable law. For instance, in Austrian and German law a strict conceptual delimitation prevails between private international law (in German: '*internationales Privatrecht*') and international civil procedural law (in German: '*internationales Zivilprozessrecht*'), while in English, French, and US law these fields (choice of law and international civil procedural law) are normally conceived as a single unit.

In Hungary, the term 'private international law' may be used in both a narrow and a wide sense. It may refer to the question of the applicable law but may also be used widely to refer to all three questions of conflict of laws, that is, civil jurisdiction, applicable law, and recognition and enforcement of foreign judgments. Hungarian PIL textbooks, while acknowledging the notional difference between the two fields, consistently deal with both choice of law and international civil procedural law. Some authors regard jurisdiction and choice of law as part of private international law,[1] while others do not use the term 'private international law' but prefer 'private conflict of laws' (in Hungarian: '*kollíziós magánjog*').[2] Some scholars regard jurisdiction, choice of law, and recognition and enforcement as part of private international law.[3]

This much is certain that choice-of-law rules and international civil procedural rules are different in nature. While the former use an indirect method and determine the law applicable to a particular case, the latter use the traditional methods of procedural law to determine the state whose courts can entertain a lawsuit and to determine the legal effects of foreign judgments (recognition and enforcement). In traditional civil law characterization, these two fields cannot be part of the same 'branch of law' (in German: '*Rechtszweig*'), since they employ different regulatory methods. On the other hand, their virtual interrelation is obvious, and these two fields merit joint consideration due to practical reasons. Furthermore, the term 'private international law' is not consistent anyway, since these rules are neither 'private', nor 'international'. Choice-of-law rules have no private-law nature as they do not regulate legal relations directly, but determine the applicable private law, thus solving the case indirectly; in other words, private law and choice of law use different regulatory methods. Furthermore, most PIL norms, while they deal with international fact patterns, are not international in terms of source; quite the contrary, most conflict norms are included in national legislation. The developments in EU law have modulated this landscape; nevertheless, EU legal acts are also not international but 'European', meaning that they are part of a *sui generis* legal order.

1 L. Kecskés, "A civilisztikai jogalkotást érintő újabb EU jogalkotással kapcsolatos néhány elméleti kérdés," (5) *Európai Jog* (2006), 3–13.

2 L. Burián, D.T. Czigler, L. Kecskés & I. Vörös, *Európai és magyar nemzetközi kollíziós magánjog* (Krim Bt., Budapest, 2010).

3 Cs. I. Nagy, *Nemzetközi magánjog* (HVG-Orac, Budapest, 2017), 23–24.

In this book the term 'private international law' (and its synonym: 'conflict of laws') is used in a wider sense. The question of applicable law is referred to as 'choice of law'. The term 'international civil procedural law' (or 'international civil procedure') refers to the rules on jurisdiction (i.e., which state's courts have the power to entertain a case) and recognition and enforcement (i.e. under which conditions and according to which procedure can a decision have legal effects in a foreign country).

3 Sources of Private International Law

The main source of Hungarian private international law is the APIL. Nonetheless, lately, EU law has taken over the field and replaced national conflict-of-laws rules. Certain fields were, in essence, 'Europeanized'. Furthermore, Section 2 of the APIL gives automatic precedence to international treaties.

3.1 *National Law*

In Hungary the hierarchy of legal sources is the following. The legal system is headed by the constitution. The old constitution was adopted in Act XX of 1949 and completely amended in 1989.[4] The Hungarian Parliament adopted Hungary's new constitution (Fundamental Law, in Hungarian: '*Alaptörvény*') on April 18, 2011; the new constitution entered into force on January 1, 2012. The acts (statutes) of the Parliament follow in rank. The parliament adopts acts normally with a simple majority, but if it enacts a law amending the constitution a two-thirds majority is required. Furthermore, there are certain fields defined in the constitution where a two-thirds majority is required.

Explanatory memoranda are attached to the bills submitted to the Parliament by the government. These are important sources of information and courts regulary rely on them. Article 28 of the Constitution requires courts to base their interpretation of the law primarily on the pertinent explanatory memoranda. An explanatory memorandum explains, on the one hand, why the government submitted the given bill and the reasons that justify its enactment and, on the other, presents the provisions of the bill. Accordingly, they reveal the legislative intent and, at times, the interpretation the legislative attributed to the diffent provisions of the bill.

4 Act XX of 1949 on the Constitution of the Republic of Hungary (in Hungarian: '*1949. évi XX. törvény A Magyar Köztársaság Alkotmánya*').

Law-decrees are also legal sources which have the same rank in the hierarchy of norms as acts of parliament; in fact, they can be regarded as statutes. Law-decrees cannot be issued anymore; the power to adopt them was abolished in 1989; however, several law-decrees adopted before this date are still in force. Law-decrees were adopted by the Presidential Council of the People's Republic in the period when the Parliament was not sitting; the Presidential Council could regulate any matter except for an amendment to the constitution. This scheme ran counter to the principle of separation of powers and was abolished in 1989. At the same time, several important laws were enacted in this form. For instance, the old APIL was adopted as a law-decree. Furthermore, numerous international treaties were promulgated in law-decrees.

The next layer of the system of legal sources is represented by government decrees, followed by ministerial decrees issued by individual ministers. These decrees normally deal with sectoral issues and execute rules included in acts. Decrees contain, accordingly, rather concrete provisions.

The bottom layer of the legal system consists of the ordinances of local self-governmening entities (in Hungarian: '*önkormányzat*'), such as towns and municipalities. These sources of law deal with local issues.

The most important source of Hungarian civil law is the Civil Code, which was enacted in 2013 (Act V of 2013) and replaced the old Civil Code adopted in 1959 (Act IV of 1959). The Civil Code covers all fields of civil law broadly conceived, including company and family law. Procedural rules are included in the Code of Civil Procedure, which was enacted in 2016 (Act CXXX of 2016 on the Civil Procedure) and replaced the old Code of Civil Procedure adopted in 1952 (Act III of 1952).

In Hungarian law there is no commercial code and Hungarian law does not distinguish between commercial and ordinary civil law (contrary to German and French law), albeit that, normally, special rules apply to consumer contracts and some provisions apply only to business-to-business transactions.

Private international law is regulated by Act XXVIII of 2017 on Private International Law (APIL).[5] This replaced Law-Decree (Act) 13 of 1979 on private international law (old APIL). The APIL, as the code of Hungarian private international law, contains the Hungarian choice-of-law rules and provisions on international civil procedural law, including jurisdiction, recognition and enforcement, and judicial cooperation. The APIL's explanatory memorandum

5 In Hungarian: "2017. évi XXVIII. törvény a nemzetközi magánjogról." This monograph relies on the translation of APIL provided by Tamás Szabados and, hence, quotations are from his translation. See T. Szabados, "Hungary: Act XXVIII of 2017 on Private International Law," 82(4) *Rabels Zeitschrift für Ausländisches und Internationales Privatrecht* (2018), 1004–1045.

introduces the various provisions of the APIL in detail and is an important source of interpretation in the application of Hungarian PIL.

Case law plays a central role in the application of the law, and Supreme Court judgments have precedential force if published in the 'Collection of Judicial Decisions' ('*Bírósági Határozatok Gyűjteménye*'). This force implies that if a court wishes to depart from a Supreme Court judgment published in the 'Collection of Judicial Decisions', it needs to justify this in its judgment.[6]

Furthermore, there is a special mechanism in Hungarian law that is meant to ensure the consistency of judicial practice: this is the 'procedure for the consistency of the case law' ('*jogegységi eljárás*'), at the end of which a 'decision for the consistency of the case law' ('*jogegységi határozat*') is delivered. The Supreme Court is obliged to ensure the consistency of the case law, and 'decisions for the consistency of the case law' are binding on the courts. It is very important that these decisions are not judgments, in the sense that they do not adjudicate on a particular matter; they simply decide questions of interpretation of the law.

Other court judgments have no formal precedential value but are usually followed in practice. Court judgments are published after having been anonymized and are freely available at the courts' website (www.birosag.hu). However, court orders are not published and are publicly accessible only if they are selected by one of the court reports (collections) and published by them.

Legal scholarship (doctrine) plays a role in the application of PIL rules (both EU and national). Commentaries and legal periodicals provide an important input in this regard. However, Hungarian courts, as part of their general drafting style, rarely cite scholarly works; hence, it is difficult to ascertain the impact of academic works on day-to-day practice.

Customary law as such is not a source of Hungarian law.

3.2 *EU Law*

Hungary is a member of the EU and, hence, EU private international law (EU PIL) takes precedence over national rules and is regularly applied by Hungarian courts.

EU law is, increasingly, taking over the fields of national private international law. Two decades ago, the proposition that private international law is not international as far as its sources are concerned but is essentially national, although its subject matter is, indeed, international in nature, was still valid.[7]

6 Section 346(5) of the Code of Civil Procedure.

7 *See* para 27.

Nowadays, this proposition is losing weight. Nevertheless, developments at the EU level do not refute the traditional proposition as, first, these instruments are European (i.e., regional) and not international (i.e. global) and, second, these are the fruits of EU law, a *sui generis* legal order that diverges from traditional public international law.[8]

In the realm of choice-of-law rules, with some exceptions, the field of obligations was taken over by EU legislation. The Rome I Regulation is applicable as from December 17, 2009 and determines the law applicable to contractual obligations. The Rome II Regulation is applicable as from January 11, 2009[9] and regulates the choice-of-law issues relating to non-contractual obligations (i.e., delicts (torts), unjust enrichment, *negotiorum gestio* and *culpa in contrahendo*).

From the two EU PIL instruments adopted in the frame of enhanced cooperation, Hungary takes part in the Rome III Regulation, hence, the law applicable to divorce and legal separation is not determined by the Hungarian rules but by this EU legal act. At the same time, Hungary does not take part in the enhanced cooperation concering the Matrimonial Property Regulation and the Regulation on the Property Consequences of Registered Partnerships; hence, these EU legal acts do not apply in Hungary. The conflicts aspects of matrimonial property and the property consequences of registered partnerships are regulated by the APIL (Sections 27–29 and 37 of the APIL).

As far as international civil procedural law is concerned, the EU extensively legislated in the fields of jurisdiction, recognition, and enforcement, as well as judicial cooperation (service of documents and taking of evidence). The Brussels I Regulation establishes rules on jurisdiction, as well as recognition and enforcement in civil and commercial matters. The Brussels II Regulation regulates the same questions in respect of divorce, marriage annulment, separation, and parental responsibility, as well as international child abduction.

Some of the EU legal instruments establish both international civil procedural and choice-of-law rules. The Insolvency Regulation regulates all three aspects of insolvency and reorganization proceedings (jurisdiction, applicable law and recognition and enforcement). The Maintenance Regulation deals with the questions of jurisdiction, applicable law, recognition and enforcement, and cooperation in matters relating to maintenance obligations. The Succession Regulation establishes rules on jurisdiction, applicable law, recognition and enforcement, and the acceptance and enforcement of authentic

8 *See* para 27.

9 ECJ, Case C-412/10, *Deo Antoine Homawoo v GMF Assurances SA* (2014) EU:C:2011:546.

instruments in matters of succession and creates a European Certificate of succession.

Hungarian courts have been active in terms of referring private international law cases to the ECJ[10] and have contributed via quite a few preliminary rulings to the development of EU conflict of laws.

EU private international law has also had an impact on the handling of matters falling outside the scope of EU PIL rules. On the one hand, national PIL rules governing matters outside the scope of EU legal instruments were significantly influenced by EU PIL.[11] On the other hand, mutual trust was enhanced by the emergence of EU PIL, which facilitated recognition and enforcement also in matters not covered by EU legislation. For instance, while, under Hungarian law, recognition and enforcement presupposed reciprocity, in Case *Pf.20218/2013/8*[12] the High Court of Appeal of Debrecen disregarded this requirement when it had to decide on the recognition of the judgment of another Member State in an area not covered by any EU PIL instrument at the relevant time (matrimonial property).[13] Absent an international treaty providing otherwise, foreign judgments in pecuniary matters can be recognized and enforced in Hungary only if there is reciprocity.[14] However, the court seems to have disregarded this requirement as to a judgment of a sister-state, stressing that due to the principle of mutual trust the recognition court may, in principle, not review the jurisdiction of the court delivering the judgment and recognition may be rejected only exceptionally.

3.3 *International Treaties*

Private international law questions are also dealt with in multilateral and bilateral treaties, which have precedence over the APIL (Section 2 of the APIL). Hungarian law employs a mixed system as far as the relationship between international and domestic law is concerned. The monist approach is used

10 See e.g. ECJ, Case C-527/10, *ERSTE Bank Hungary Nyrt v Magyar Állam and Others* (2012) EU:C:2012:417; ECJ, Case C-519/12, *OTP Bank* (2013) EU:C:2013:674; ECJ, Case C-210/06, *CARTESIO* (2008) EU:C:2008:723; ECJ, Case C-378/10, *VALE* (2012) EU:C:2012:440; ECJ, Case C-94/14, *Flight Refund Ltd v Deutsche Lufthansa AG* (2016) EU:C:2016:148; ECJ, Case C-102/15, *Gazdasági Versenyhivatal v Siemens* (2016) EU:C:2016:607.

11 See Cs. I. Nagy, *Nemzetközi magánjog* (HVG-Orac, Budapest, 2017).

12 Appealed from P.21966/2011/49 (Miskolc Regional Court).

13 Hungary does not take part in the enhanced cooperation concerning the Matrimonial Property Regulation and the Regulation on the Property Consequences of Registered Partnerships.
Section 113 of the APIL.

14 Section 113 of the APIL.

in respect of *ius cogens*,[15] while a dualist system applies to all other norms of international law.[16] Section 2 of the APIL gives precedence to international treaties, thus ruling out the potential clash between PIL rules embedded in international treaties and the provision of the APIL.

The relationship between EU PIL instruments and international treaties is regulated by each EU legal instrument individually.[17]

Hungary is party to some 20 multilateral treaties with a PIL content, four of which are in force through Hungary's EU membership and has about 45 bilateral international treaties with other countries on legal assistance in judicial matters which also cover civil cases. These treaties regulate various private international law matters.[18]

4 Courts and Authorities Applying Private International Law

PIL is applied predominantly by courts, which are the only authentic interpreters of the law. Nonetheless, there are various non-judicial bodies and entites which deal with civil law matters and, as such, apply PIL. A significant number of family law issues concerning children, such as certain issues related to the exercise of access rights, are handled by the Guardianship and Child Protection Office ('*gyámhivatal*'). Another important example is public notaries, which are responsible for probate procedures and need to identify the applicable succession law.

The Hungarian judicial system is four-tiered, comprising local courts ('*járásbíróság*'), regional courts ('*törvényszék*'), high courts of appeal ('*ítélőtábla*'), and the Supreme Court (*Kúria*). The general courts (first instance courts) are the local courts (in Budapest: district courts) and the regional courts, in Budapest the Budapest-Capital Regional Court (in Hungarian: *Fővárosi Törvényszék*). There are five high courts of appeal seated in Győr, Budapest, Debrecen, Szeged, and Pécs.

15 Article P of the Hungarian Constitution; Section 7(1) of the old Hungarian constitution.

16 Act L of 2005 on the procedure concerning international treaties (in Hungarian: '*2005. évi L. törvény a nemzetközi szerződésekkel kapcsolatos eljárásról*').

17 See. e.g. Brussels I Regulation, Articles 67–73; Brussels II Regulation, 59–63; Rome I Regulation, Article 25; Rome II Regulation, Article 28; Succession Regulation, Article 75.

18 See the compilation of the Department of Private International Law of the Ministry of Justice of Hungary, available at https://igazsagugyiinformaciok.kormany.hu/download/b/ac/c2000/%C3%A1llamok%20%C3%A9s%20egyezm%C3%A9nyek%20t%C3%A1j%C3%A9koztat%C3%B3%202021_07_22.pdf.

The rules on international jurisdiction (*'joghatóság'*) merely identify the state whose courts have the power to entertain the case, but they do not identify a specific court within this state's judicial system. This task is left to the domestic rules of procedure. Accordingly, if Hungarian courts have jurisdiction, the next step is to ascertain the Hungarian court or courts under Sections 21–31 of the Code of Civil Procedure competent to hear the case. This is based on two coordinates. Venue (territorial competence) is the geographic allocation of cases among the different courts and follows rules similar to those for international jurisdiction, including the *actor sequitur forum rei* principle and *prorogatio fori*. While the rules on venue allocate cases among the different territorial judicial units, subject-matter competence allocates them within the judicial hierarchy.

Regional courts are general (first instance) courts, which handle all disputes except for those that fall under the general competence of local courts. Regional courts also act as labor courts. Local courts handle low-value claims, except for certain matters which fall under the original (subject-matter) competence of regional courts irrespective of the claims' value (e.g., copyright, international carriage of goods), actions concerning personal status and enforcement disputes.[19] Cross-border matters may come under the competence of both local and regional courts. Company registrars are run by the company court, which is part of the regional court. In Hungary, there are no special courts. Regional courts act as both general and appellate courts: they hear the disputes that do not fall within the competence of local courts and appeals against judgments of the latter. High courts of appeal are high appellate courts adjudicating on appeals against county court judgments. Parties have one appeal as of right: local court judgments can be appealed to regional courts, while regional court judgments can be appealed to the courts of appeal. The judicial system is headed by the Supreme Court, which hears extraordinary appeals on points of law. This is the supervision procedure (in Hungarian: *'felülvizsgálati eljárás'*), initiated through a plea of supervision (in Hungarian: *'felülvizsgálati kérelem'*).

19 Section 20 of the Code on Civil Procedure.

CHAPTER 2

General Questions and Principles of Choice of Law

1 Scope of Private International Law

The scope of the APIL covers 'private international law matters' (in Hungarian: '*nemzetközi magánjogi tényállás*'), i.e., fact patterns that contain a substantial international element. The purpose of the APIL is to determine the applicable law, the jurisdictional and procedural rules, and the conditions of recognition and enforcement of foreign judgments in private law matters having a foreign element.[1] Accordingly, the APIL does not apply to purely domestic matters, irrespective of whether the case is purely Hungarian or related exclusively to a single foreign country.

The concept of 'private international law matter' has a real legal function. In a case between two Russian companies, the Supreme Court held that the APIL was not applicable since there was no foreign (or rather international) element in the controversy. Since it was the APIL that contained the rules on international jurisdiction, the Court concluded that those rules included in the APIL were not applicable and, hence, Hungarian courts had no jurisdiction.[2]

The notion of 'private international law matter' had a pivotal role also in a case before the Permanent Arbitration Court attached to the Hungarian Chamber of Commerce and Industry, where two Hungarian firms subjected their contract with no foreign element to English law. The arbitral tribunal refused to apply English law. It held that the case was not a 'private international law matter', as it involved no substantial foreign element; hence, the rules of the APIL were not applicable. Unfortunately, the tribunal treated the choice-of-law clause as invalid and did not examine whether English law could be applied in place of the non-mandatory rules (*ius dispositivum*) of Hungarian law, similarly to a case where a contract refers to a set of standard contractual terms.[3]

In Case *Gf.II.20.176/2007/5*, the first defendant was a Hungarian limited liability company that was in liquidation; the liquidator sold the first defendant's real estate located in Hungary to the second and third defendants (both

1 Section 2 of the APIL.

2 Court judgment published under number EBH2004. 1047. and BH2004. 376.

3 Decision of the Arbitral Tribunal attached to the Hungarian Chamber of Commerce and Industry published under number VB1998. 3.

 | DOI:10.1163/9789004694569_003

Hungarian companies). The plaintiff, an Austrian firm and the sole shareholder in the limited liability company under liquidation, sued the company and the two purchasers for a judicial declaration of the invalidity of the sales contract. The High Court of Appeal of Győr held that the legal relationship at stake contained no international element: the sales contract was concluded by Hungarian parties in the context of Hungarian bankruptcy proceedings against a domestic debtor concerning real estate located in Hungary, and the parties also did not choose a foreign law. The Court held that the mere circumstance that the plaintiff was an Austrian company did not warrant the application of the PIL rules and, hence, Hungarian law was to be applied exclusively.

In Case *Pf.IV.20.352/2007/4*, the plaintiffs were passengers in a Hungarian bus, which had a collision in Austria. They claimed compensation from the tortfeasor's liability insurer (a Hungarian company). The High Court of Appeal of Győr held that the APIL was not applicable because the motor-vehicle-liability insurance relationship contained no foreign element. The circumstance that the damages were sustained abroad did not qualify as a substantial foreign element. Unfortunately, the High Court of Appeal failed to consider that the legal relationship between the injured party and the liability insurer (the motor-vehicle-liability insurance relationship) is accessory to the delictual relationship between the injured person and the wrongdoer. It is to be noted that in this case the court, at the end of the day, applied Austrian law due to one of the then effective and since repealed provisions of the government decree on motor-vehicle-liability insurance, which provided that in case of damage caused abroad, the insurer's payment obligation is governed by the law of the place where the loss occurred.

The same question of scope emerges in the application of the EU PIL instruments, which are applicable to 'situations involving a conflict of laws'.[4]

2 State Law, Non-state Law

The rules of the APIL deal with state law and with matters where there is a need to choose between two or more different state laws. Non-state law, including religious law and *lex mercatoria*, plays no role in the application of PIL unless it is transformed into law by a state (which implies that it becomes state law). For instance, Hungarian courts are not mandated to apply sharia as religious

4 See, e.g., Article 1(1) of the Rome I Regulation, Article 1(1) of the Rome II Regulation, Article 1(1) of the Rome III Regulation.

law, but if they have to apply the law of a country that incporates sharia, by applying the law of that state they apply sharia. Furthermore, non-state law may play a role in the adjudication of legal disputes as a fact or contractual stipulation. The parties may subject themselves to the rules of non-state law by explicitly or implicitly incorporating it into their contractual relationship.

3 Choice-of-Law Rules

3.1 *Taxonomy of Choice-of-Law Rules*

Hungarian PIL, in accordance with international practice, distinguishes between unilateral and multilateral choice-of-law norms. Unilateral rules do not determine the applicable law at large, but prescribe those cases a Hungarian substantive rule is applicable to. On the other hand, multilateral choice-of-law norms contain a mechanism for the determination of the applicable law, which may be either Hungarian or foreign law. Hungarian PIL is predominantly made up of multilateral choice-of-law norms; unilateral rules are exceptional.

According to Hungarian PIL, multilateral choice-of-law rules have two layers: the hypothesis and the disposition. The hypothesis contains legal notions (such as contract, delictual liability, unjust enrichment, *in rem* rights), while the disposition contains connecting factors (such as nationality, habitual residence, the place where the damages occurred). Choice of law does not deal with facts but determines the law applicable to legal concepts and legal questions.

It is unsettled whether choice-of-law norms contain a third element, i.e., sanction. The majority position is that they contain no sanction and have, hence, only two elements (hypothesis and disposition), since the legal consequences (sanction) are embedded in the law invoked.[5] Accordingly, choice-of-law rules are considered to have no legal consequences in terms of sanction, aside from the duty to apply the law determined by them. This duty is, however, generally not considered to be a legal consequence but merely the bare consequence of linking the legal question to a particular legal system. This is an important *differentia specifica* of choice-of-law rules: contrary to substantive norms, which naturally involve legal consequences as a conceptual element, choice-of-law rules do not directly provide for a legal consequence (though

5 F. Mádl & L. Vékás, *Nemzetközi magánjog, nemzetközi gazdasági kapcsolatok joga* (Akadémiai Kiadó, Budapest, 2004), 85; Cs.I. Nagy, *Nemzetközi magánjog* (HVG-Orac, Budapest, 2017), 32–33.

they entail legal consequences indirectly, through pointing to a legal system that provides for a legal consequence). According to the alternative position, the term 'sanction' should be grasped as a legal consequence in general and not as a punishment or detrimental consequence. A legal norm may have both favorable and detrimental consequences. The 'sanction' of a choice-of-law norm is the legislator's command to apply the foreign law (or Hungarian law if the choice-of-law rule points to Hungarian law).

Hypothesis	Disposition	Sanction
Legal notion, concept, institution	Connecting factor	No sanction. / The command to apply the law determined by the choice-of-law rule.

Given that choice-of-law rules solve legal problems indirectly, by reference to a legal system, they are 'blind' and normally contain no value judgement. This principle is, however, not without exception and choice of law, at times, gives way to substantive considerations, such as *favor testamenti* or the application of the law more favorable to the child.

3.2 *Connecting Factors*

The heart of the choice-of-law rule is the connecting factor, which links the legal question to a legal system. Most choice-of-law rules use objective connecting factors, which embed circumstances that are not dependent (at least not directly) on the will of the parties. Party autonomy, i.e., the right to choose the applicable law, is conceived as a subjective connecting factor, given that it is based on a subjective element (the will of the parties or the party). Circumstances that can be influenced by the parties indirectly are considered objective connecting factors. For instance, although a party may be relatively free to choose his place of living or habitual residence, these are considered objective connecting factors. The choice about the place of living or habitual residence indirectly determines the applicable law and it is usually influenced by considerations that go beyond the issue of the applicable law.

3.3 *Combination of Connecting Factors*

In numerous fields the APIL uses a set of connecting factors to determine the applicable law. These provisions can be taxonomized as follows.

The most often used method of combining different connecting factors is subsidiarity, where the subsidiary connecting factor comes into play if the higher-ranked one fails to determine the applicable law. In this case, the APIL establishes a general connecting factor and supplements this with a set of subsidiary connecting factors in case the *lex causae* cannot be determined by means of the general connecting factor. For instance, the personal law of natural persons (Section 15 of the APIL) is determined by their citizenship (*lex patriae*); however, if this fails to determine the applicable law, the law of the habitual residence must be applied. If habitual residence fails to determine the applicable law, the *lex fori* applies. The law applicable to personal and property relations between spouses follows the same scheme: the general connecting factor is the spouses' common citizenship, supplemented by their habitual residence (last habitual residence) and the *lex fori* as the connecting factor of last resort (Section 27 of the APIL). The same method of subsidiarity is used concerning the personal law of legal persons, where the APIL provides for the application of the law of incorporation, the law of the registered seat, and the law of the real seat (Section 22 of the APIL).

Cumulative connecting factors are used in cases where an act must be judged on the basis of more than one legal system (and, hence, has to comply with the requirements of more than one legal system). The reason for using cumulative connecting factors is to obviate the risk of limping legal relations. For instance, according to Section 26 of the APIL, the substantive validity of a marriage is governed by the personal laws of the two spouses. The marriage is invalid if it fails to comply with the substantive requirements under either law. In the same vein, according to Section 33 of the APIL, the validity of an adoption is subject to the cumulative conditions under the personal laws of the adoptive parent and the person to be adopted.

Alternative connecting factors are used in cases where PIL has substantive considerations. In this case the substantive law result is recognized if it is recognized under any of the laws indicated by the listed connecting factors. For instance, inspired by the principle of *favor testamenti*, Section 64 of the APIL provides that an oral will is formally valid if it complies with Hungarian law, the *lex loci actus*, the personal law, the law of the place of living, or the habitual residence of the deceased or, in the case of immovable property, the *lex rei sitae*. As a further example, Section 34 of the APIL establishes, as a general rule, that the legal relationship between parent and child is governed by the *lex fori*, but the court may take into account the law of another, closely connected state, if this is justified by the interests of the child.

3.4 *Party Autonomy*

The APIL gives the parties broad freedom to choose the applicable law, though it establishes no such right in general. The parties can choose the law only where the APIL specifically authorizes them to and it contains such rules in various fields ranging from contracts and torts to matrimonial property and property law. Section 9 of the APIL establishes general rules for party choice (but, as noted, not a general right to choose the applicable law).

In Hungarian scholarship, in accordance with international practice, two theories of party autonomy are recognized, depending on the residual role of the law that would be applicable in the absence of the parties' choice: 'choice in the substantive sense' (in Hungarian: '*anyagi jogi jogválasztás*', in German: '*materiellrechtliche Rechtswahl*') and 'choice in conflict sense' (in Hungarian: '*kollíziós jogválasztás*', in German: '*kollisionsrechtliche Rechtswahl*'). 'Choice in the conflict sense' implies that the rules of the chosen law are to be applied irrespective of the mandatory rules of the law that would otherwise be applicable in the absence of the parties' choice. The concept of 'choice in the substantive sense' implies that the law chosen by the parties can be applied only within the limits of the mandatory rules of the law that would otherwise be applicable. In other words, under this concept the parties have no more freedom than under substantive law; they can derogate from non-mandatory rules (*ius dispositivum*) but cannot go against mandatory norms (*ius cogens*). In this sense, the parties' choice of law works in the same way as a contractual reference to standard terms or to commercial customs and usages.

The APIL generally follows the approach of 'choice in the conflict sense'; if the parties choose the law to be applied to the contract, that law governs the agreement irrespective of the norms of the law that would be applicable in the absence of the parties' choice. Of course, the imperative rules (overriding mandatory rules) of that law might be applicable.

Exceptions to the prevalence of 'choice in the conflict sense' can be found in the field of contractual and non-contractual obligations in respect of matters that have no (or no relevant) international element (Sections 50(4) and 63(3) of the APIL). If the contractual or non-contractual legal relationship is connected to the law of a single state, the parties' choice cannot interfere with the application of the mandatory rules of the law of that state. The APIL contains no exceptions to the 'choice in the conflict sense' principle outside the field of contracts and non-contractual legal relationships. The reason is that outside the law of obligations the parties do not have the liberty to choose whichever law they please, but their freedom of choice is limited, that is, they can choose only from a list of laws that are statutorily considered to be connected. This implies that if the parties choose the law in accordance with a connecting factor on the statutory list and this connecting factor points to a foreign law, it cannot be claimed that the case has no (relevant) international element.

The APIL's rules on party autonomy may be taxonomized from three aspects: is the choice of the applicable law based on a unilateral decision or on an agreement; may the applicable law be chosen implicitly or only explicitly (by express declaration); can the parties choose any law, even an unconnected law, or is their choice limited to a list provided by the law? Along these lines there is an important difference between party autonomy in the field of obligations (contracts and torts) and that in other fields, such as family and succession law. In the former case, the parties may, both explicitly and implicitly, choose the law of any state (including unconnected states).[6] On the other hand, in other fields (such as matrimonial property, name, property law), the parties' choice may only be explicit (the law does not recognize the parties' implicit choice) and they can choose only from the options set out in the APIL (that is, the APIL determines a set of laws the parties may choose from). In none of these cases may the parties' choice interfere with the rights of third parties (Section 9(2) of the APIL).

The choice of the applicable law may be unilateral or bi-or multilateral. While the law applicable to the contract is chosen by the parties, in numerous cases it is chosen by means of a unilateral declaration. This cluster of cases embraces not only matters where there is no opposing party (such as names), but also adversarial proceedings (such as the violations of personality rights).

The parties can choose the applicable law by agreement in the realm of contracts (Section 50(1) of the APIL), non-contractual oblitgations (Section 63(1) of the APIL), matrimonial property and the property relations between registered partners and cohabitants (Sections 28(1), 36 and 37(1) of the APIL), and some other property rights (Sections 44(3), 45 (1) and (2) of the APIL).

A party can unilaterally choose the law applicable to his name (Section 16 of the APIL), the legal declaration made for the case in which he or she is placed under guardianship or protective measures (Section 19 of the APIL), and personality rights (Section 23 of the APIL).

The choice can be either explicit or implicit. According to Section 9(1) of the APIL, as a general principle, the choice must be explicit, unless a special provision of the APIL expressly allows an implicit choice. The APIL contains such special provisions permitting implicit choice only as regards contractual (Section 50(1) of the APIL) and non-contractual obligations (Section 63(1) of

6 Section 9 of the APIL provides that, unless the APIL provides otherwise, the parties' choice has to be explicit. However, the rules on contracts and torts (in Sections 50(1) and 63 (1) of the APIL) recognize the parties' right to make implicit choices.

the APIL). Outside these fields the general principle prevails, and only explicit choices are legally valid.

The freedom of choice can be either complete (authorizing the parties to choose any law) or *à la carte* (allowing them to choose only one of the laws listed by the APIL). In the field of contractual and non-contractual obligations, the choice is free in the sense that the parties can choose any law, including those of legal systems that are completely unconnected to the case. Beyond this, however, the choice is restricted to the laws that are linked to the matter by way of a listed connecting factor. As regards names, a person may choose Hungarian law, and a citizen of multiple jurisdictions, as to the birth name, can choose the law of any of his citizenships (Section 16 of the APIL). As regards the existence, validity, scope, modification, and withdrawal of a declaration made by an adult with the capacity for the case of the future limitation of his disposing capacity or the absence of his capacity to protect his interests, the person may choose the law of any of his citizenships or habitual residence(s) or the *lex rei sitae* (Section 19 of the APIL). As regards personality rights, a person may choose the law of his center of interests, the law of the wrongdoer's habitual residence, or Hungarian law. Where matrimonial property and the property consequences of registered partnerships and cohabitations are concerned, the spouses (partners, cohabitants) may choose the law of a state of which one of the spouses is a citizen or is habitually resident in or Hungarian law (Sections 28(1) and 36–37 of the APIL). In the case of a sale with reservation of title, the law of the state of destination may be chosen as regards the property law aspects (Section 44(3) of the APIL); in the case of transfer of title, the parties may choose between the *lex rei sitae* and the law of the state of destination (Section 45(1) of the APIL); in the case of the transfer of an undertaking (business), although not of real estates, the personal law of the legal predecessor may be chosen (Section 45(2) of the APIL).

3.5 *Dépeçage*

When it comes to choice of law, it is not the law applicable to the matter at large, but that applicable to a particular legal question, that must be sought. A matter may contain numerous questions coming under different legal headings. The legal capacity of one of the contracting parties is an issue of personal law, the question whether that person was the author of a copyright work is an intellectual property law issue, while the conclusion and validity of a license agreement is a contractual question. The laws applicable to these questions are to be determined separately.

4 Application of the Choice-of-Law Rule

4.1 *Characterization (Classification)*

As the hypothesis of the choice-of-law rule is made up of legal notions and not statutory fact patterns applicable to real-life cases, the very first question to be asked concerning its application is how these legal notions are defined. The application of a choice-of-law rule presupposes the identification of a legal notion that necessitates the application of the rule and calls for characterization, that is, the issue at stake must be classified as coming under a legal concept.

Under the APIL, characterization, in principle, must be done on the basis of the *lex fori* (Hungarian law), but, exceptionally, the putative *lex causae* may also be taken into account. Section 4 of the APIL adopts the *lex fori* approach as a general principle; it provides that the characterization of facts and legal issues is governed by the concepts and notions of Hungarian law. Nevertheless, it also takes account of cases where a legal institution is unknown to Hungarian law or is known but understood as having a different content or different designation. If a legal institution in unknown to Hungarian law, characterization must be carried out based on the foreign law that contains it. In this case, the function and purpose of the legal institution in the foreign law must be taken into account. If the legal institution is not unknown to Hungarian law but has a different function or purpose than in the foreign legal system, the latter must be taken into consideration during characterization. Accordingly, in principle, the *lex fori* must be applied to the question of characterization,[7] but, as an exception, the presumptive *lex causae* may also be taken into consideration. Characterization is to be done based on the notions, structure, and thinking of Hungarian law.

For example, in civil law jurisdictions, including Hungary, prescription is a substantive-law question, but in most US states it is a procedural issue. A similar divergence exists regarding the quantum of damages: in English and Scottish law this has traditionally been considered a procedural issue,[8] whereas in Hungarian civil law it is, for the most part, a question of substantive law. In some cases, a legal institution, such as the institution of separation (*separatio a thoro et mensa*), is completely unknown to Hungarian law.

Section 4 of the APIL grants the court the ability to investigate the presumptive *lex causae* when carrying out the characterization. The APIL's explanatory

---

7 See Case *8. G. 40.160/2008/46.* (Budapest-Capital Regional Court).

8 *Boys v Chaplin* [1971] A.C. 356.; *McElroy v McAllister* [1949] S.C. 110.; *Harding v Wealands* [2006] UKHL 32, HL, 66–67.

memorandum provides an example in this regard. Same-sex couples may register their relationship in both Hungary and the Netherlands. Hungarian law distinguishes between same-sex registered partnership, which constitutes a *quasi* marital status, and cohabitation, which does not. Cohabitation may be registered, however, this merely serves evidentiary purposes and does not grant any rights. From a substantive-law perspective, registered and non-registered cohabitations have the same status, though the registration may make proof easier. By contrast, the registration of same-sex couples under Dutch law is similar to Hungarian law's notion of registered partnership: it has a constitutive effect, entails legal consequences similar to those of marriage, and also amounts to a marriage impediment. In this case characterization is carried out under Hungarian law, but the relevant foreign law must also be taken into account.

In Case *Gpkf.II.26.269/2008/2*, the plaintiff, in a matter where the parties stipulated the application of English law, moved for a *Mareva* injunction, arguing that this remedy is a substantive-law concept under English law, and so English law had to be applied. It is to be noted that, according to Section 66 of the APIL, the procedure of Hungarian courts and authorities is governed by Hungarian law. The High Court of Appeal of Győr held, based on Article 4 of the APIL, that the *Mareva* injunction addressed a question of procedural law, and procedure was governed by Hungarian law.

Since EU choice-of-law rules have largely replaced national provisions, the question of characterization raises novel and interesting dilemmas, which are to be tackled autonomously in the different EU law instruments (e.g., Rome I Regulation, Rome II Regulation). The terms in the EU PIL instruments must be given an autonomous meaning and be construed uniformly and in a coherent manner.[9]

While the problem of preliminary question is well known in scholarship, it is not specifically regulated by the APIL and has not given rise to any case law.

4.2 *Time Dimension and Change of the Applicable Law*

The applicable law is, in essence, determined by the circumstances and the rules in place at the time when the facts occurred. The APIL does not specify this principle; nonetheless, it can be deduced from its general approach and special rules. For instance, Section 39 of the APIL provides for the application of the *lex rei sitae* in respect of property rights and other *in rem* rights, and

9 See Cs. I. Nagy, "Az egységes fogalomértelmezés követelménye a formálódó közösségi nemzetközi magánjogban, különös tekintettel a polgári és kereskedelmi ügy, a szerződés és a szerződésen kívüli kötelem fogalmára," (2) *Európai Jog* (2008), 3–12.

provides that the law of the *situs* is the law of the state in which the thing is situated at the time the facts giving rise to the legal effect arise.

In the same vein, as a general principle, Section 14 of the APIL rules out the negative retrospective effects of the applicable law and results in the accumulation of the applicable laws. This implies that, in principle, PIL cases must be judged on the basis of the circumstances prevailing at the time when the facts emerged. Section 14 of the APIL provides that the change in circumstances that determine the applicable law affects the legal relationships that have validly come into existence only if the APIL specifically provides so. This implies that the applicable law has no retrospective effects, or at least no negative ones, and the applicable law must be determined based on the circumstances that prevailed at the time the facts giving rise to the legal effect emerged. If the applicable law changes because the circumstances underlying the connecting factor change (place of living, citizenship, etc.), the new applicable law will be applicable only for the future and will not affect the validity of the legal relationships that have already occurred. Accordingly, Section 14 of the APIL implies the acumulation of the applicable law.

This means, for instance, that if the law applicable to matrimonial property changes, the property effects that emerged under the previously applicable law remain notwithstanding the change of the *lex causae*. Put another way, the earlier applicable law remains applicable to the facts that emerged before the applicable law changed. For instance, if an English husband and an Italian wife have lived in Hungary since 2019, as they have no common citizenship, their personal and property relations are governed by Hungarian law (last common place of living). If, in 2021, the Italian wife acquires English citizenship and abandons her Italian citizenship, the applicable law changes to English law (common citizenship). In this case, Section 14 of the APIL implies that the Hungarian court should apply Hungarian and English law cumulatively and English law will not invalidate the property law consequences (marriage contract, acquisition of property) that arose before the Italian wife acquired English citizenship. Note that Hungarian law follows the principle of community of matrimonial property, while English law features the separation of property. If, in 2022, the Hungarian court dissolved the marriage and the matrimonial property, at the time of the court proceedings the applicable law (due to the common citizenship) would be English law; however, the validly effected property law consequences that emerged before 2021 (before the wife acquired English citizenship) under the then applicable Hungarian law are respected. If, in 2020, the husband purchased an apartment out of the income he earned during the marriage, this qualifies as common property under Hungarian law (unless there is a marriage contract providing otherwise). When the Hungarian court decides whether the apartment qualifies as separate or community property, it applies English law (since the spouses' common citizenship is English) but, due to Section 14 of the APIL, it has to respect the validly effected property law consequences under Hungarian law. The fact that the apartment became the spouses' common property would amount to such a consequence. As a matter of practice, this implies that the property effects that occurred before the Italian wife's acquisition of English citizenship in 2021 are, in fact, governed by Hungarian law.

4.3 *Fraudulent Connection (Evasion of the Law)*

The connecting factor embedded in the choice-of-law rule determines the connection relevant for the determination of the applicable law. Contrary to the old APIL,[10] the currently effective APIL contains no specific rule on fraudulent connection (evasion of the law). Hence, as a general principle, the court does not investigate how and why the fact referred to in the choice-of-law rule's connecting factor came into existence and what the parties' motivation was. The general escape clause may, however, be used to address the issues raised by cases where the parties endeavor to have a law applied with the help of an artificial or sham foreign element created by them in order to circumvent the otherwise applicable law.

4.4 *Reference to the Law of States with Multiple Legal Orders*

Section 6 of the APIL deals with the application of the law of states with more than one legal system. It provides that where the state whose law is invoked has multiple legal systems, the applicable law shall be determined by its interterritorial choice-of-law rules. The same principle applies if the state applies different rules to different groups of persons (e.g., religious groups): the internal (interpersonal) choice-of-law rules apply. In the absence of interterritorial or interpersonal rules, including where their content cannot be ascertained or they do not lead to a single law, the principle of closest connection governs the determination of the applicable law.

10 Section 8 of the old APIL defined fraudulent connection as the parties' endeavor to have a foreign law applied with the help of an artificial or sham foreign element created by them in order to circumvent the otherwise applicable Hungarian law. Interestingly, the rules on fraudulent connection were applicable only if the parties endeavored to evade Hungarian law and to have foreign law applied; the purview of the above provisions did not cover the situation where they strove for Hungarian law. Hence, in a case of fraudulent connection Hungarian law had to be applied, as the evasion of a foreign law did not amount to fraudulent connection.

5 Application of the Designated Law

5.1 *Judicial Notice and Proof of Foreign Law*

The application of foreign law is not contingent on reciprocity (that is, the requirement that the foreign state whose law is supposed to be applied also applies Hungarian law). Contrary to the old APIL,[11] the currently effective APIL contains no specific provision on this question, but it is generally understood that reciprocity is not a requirement of the application of foreign law.

The starting point for Hungarian choice of law is that the law to be applied is the one that has the closest connection with the case, i.e., the proper law, because this is the law that provides the adequate answer for the legal question raised. The application of foreign law is not a matter of comity; hence, it cannot depend on whether the other sovereign is also ready to apply Hungarian law.

Although EU PIL instruments are silent on the question of reciprocity, Hungarian courts apply the law determined by these instruments without inquiring whether there is reciprocity.

One of the pivotal questions of choice of law is the determination of the content of foreign law. According to Hungarian private international law, foreign law is to be applied as it is applied in the foreign country by the foreign court, i.e., not only the statutory language but also judicial practice and social context are to be considered.[12]

The forum is assumed to be *ex officio* familiar with its own law and to be its most authentic interpreter (*iura novit curia*). Nonetheless, with respect to foreign law, this may not be the case. Moreover, the application and identification of the foreign law might be burdensome. The question is who should bear the burden and risk of ascertaining the content of foreign law. The answer to this question depends on whether foreign law is considered to be a factual or a legal issue. Facts are, in principle, to be proved by the parties and it is, normally, the plaintiff who bears the burden of proof. On the other hand, it is not the parties' duty to prove what the law is, it is the court's business to know

---

11 Section 6 of the old APIL established that the application of foreign law, in principle, did not depend on reciprocity: Hungarian courts applied the foreign law even if the foreign sovereign refused to apply Hungarian law. Nevertheless, Section 6 of the old APIL also provided that a piece of legislation could make the application of foreign law dependent on reciprocity; in this case, until the contrary was proved, it was to be presumed that there was reciprocity. Finally, Section 6 of the old APIL also provided that if a piece of legislation expressly required that the existence of reciprocity be proved, the court had to contact the minister of justice, who had the power to make a binding declaration in this regard.

12 Cs. I. Nagy, *Nemzetközi magánjog* (HVG-Orac, Budapest, 2017), 39.

and interpret the law. Hungarian law is clear in this regard: foreign law is not a factual issue. Hungarian courts have to apply foreign law of their own motion (*ex officio*), and they bear the burden of ascertaining it.

Sections 7–8 of the APIL deal with the determination of foreign law and provide for different tools, which are meant to help the court or administrative authority to determine the content of foreign law. The court has to apply foreign law of its own motion (*ex officio*). If the court is familiar with the foreign law it can rely on its own knowledge. The court may appoint an expert[13] and consider the allegations made and evidence submitted by the parties. The court may also contact the minister of justice, who provides information about the foreign law. Although this is supposed to be a tool of last resort, it is normally used automatically in judicial practice. The minister of justice contacts the state concerned for information. Hungary is party to the 1968 European Convention on Information on Foreign Law (London) and to its Strasbourg Protocol of 1978, so the minister may seek information based on the Convention.[14] Information about the foreign law may also be obtained via the European Judicial Network.[15]

In Case *Pf.VI.26.608/2001/6*, the Supreme Court vacated the first instance judgment and remanded the case because the first instance court had failed to realize that there was an international element in the matter. It had applied Hungarian instead of German law, which was applicable in this case according to the old APIL. The judgment stressed that the court must apply foreign law of its own motion and, hence, the failure to apply the *lex causae* is a ground that necessitates the repetition of the entire evidentiary procedure.

In Case *Gf.4.30.112/2006/5*, in a case decided under the old APIL, the High Court of Appeal of Debrecen held that the court has to determine the content of foreign law of its own motion. Hence, it cannot establish the content of foreign law solely on the basis of the plaintiff's submission; the court is not relieved of the obligation to determine the content of foreign law *ex officio*, even if there is no dispute between the parties as to the question of the applicable law. The High Court of Appeal stressed that the determination of the content of the foreign law is not the parties' but the court's task.

It is hoped that this practice will change under the currently effective APIL, whose language gives more discretion to the court. This may be taken as an

13 Note that Hungarian civil procedural law follows the model of court-appointed experts, contrary to the common law notion of expert witness.

14 Promulgated by Government Regulation 140 of 1992.

15 Decision 2001/470/EC establishing a European Judicial Network in civil and commercial matters, [2001] OJ L 174/25, as amended by Decision 568/2009/EC, [2009] OJ L 168/35.

authorization for the court to rely more intensively on the submissions of the parties. While the old APIL allowed the court to 'take into account' the evidence submitted by a party, the currently effective APIL makes it clear that the court may use any means to ascertain the content of the foreign law and this discretion extends to the submissions of the parties. The APIL's explanatory memorandum confirms this approach. It provides that although it is the duty of the court to determine the content of the foreign law, the judge has a margin of appreciation in choosing the means of doing so and may take the submissions of the parties into account.

In Case *Gfv.VII.30.130/2016*,[16] in relation to a claim that was submitted in the context of insolvency proceedings, the Supreme Court established that it was the party's duty to refer to any eventual choice-of-law agreement and submit the relevant evidence. This implies that if the procedural rules do not allow a party to raise new facts, that party is barred from referring to the choice-of-law agreement. According to the facts of the case, the creditor submitted a claim to the liquidator, which was rejected. The creditor attacked the decision before the court, which also rejected the claim. The creditor appealed and, in the appeal, referred to the parties' choice of Austrian law and attached the pertinent contractual documentation. The Supreme Court affirmed the appeal court's refusal to consider this evidence. According to the rules of civil procedure, no new facts may be raised in the appeal unless the party learned the new fact or obtained the new evidence after the first instance decision was made. The fact that, instead of the law of the seller (Hungarian law), Austrian law was applicable due to the parties' choice qualified as such a new fact. The Supreme Court noted that the court can acquire knowledge of the choice only from the parties' submissions, and it is the parties' duty to inform the court that the case is governed by a law different from that applicable under the general rules.[17]

Section 8(3) of the APIL provides that if the content of the foreign law cannot be established within a reasonable time, Hungarian law must be applied. Section 8(3) also provides that if the case cannot be adjudicated based on Hungarian law, the court has to apply the law closest to the *lex causae*. The latter is a law that is akin to the applicable law and, hence, is based on similar principles. By way of example, if a contract is governed by Lebanese law but the provisions of Lebanese law cannot be ascertained, Section 8(3) allows the court to adjudicate on the contractual dispute on the basis of French law, given the similarities between the two sytems. It ought to be noted that the APIL's

16 Reported as BH 2017.3.97.

17 Para. 23.

explanatory memorandum confirms that the term 'cannot be adjudicated' should be interpreted as 'cannot be [properly] adjudicated' under Hungarian law. The legislative intent was not to address cases where Hungarian law contained no provision on the question at all, but to deal with cases where the court considers that Hungarian law would not provide an appropriate answer.

5.2 *Renvoi* (*Remission, Transmission*)

When choice-of-law rules lead to the application of foreign law, the question emerges whether the foreign legal system is invoked in its entirety, or the choice-of-law rule refers solely to the substantive law of the foreign legal system. In the former case the reference is to be understood widely (i.e., the foreign legal system is invoked in its entirety), while in the latter case the reference is to be understood narrowly (i.e. only the substantive law of the foreign legal system is invoked, with the exclusion of the choice-of-law rules).

If the choice-of-law rules invoke the foreign legal system in its entirety, including the foreign rules that determine the applicable law, the choice-of-law problem re-emerges, in this case on the basis of foreign choice-of-law rules. Foreign choice-of-law rules may refer to themselves, may refer back to the law of the forum (remission), or may point to the law of a third country (transmission).

The problem of *renvoi* is to be solved on the basis of the requirement of international decisional harmony. There is harmony between the legal systems concerned if the choice-of-law rules of the forum and those of the law invoked by the former lead to the application of the same law. Nevertheless, the problem of *renvoi* can essentially be resolved only if the two legal systems follow different approaches in respect of this question, i.e., one of them precludes remission, while the other permits it, or *vice versa*. If the two legal systems adopt the same approach, no international harmony can be reached.

Assume that Peter International is the citizen of country 'B' and has his habitual residence in country 'A'; country 'A' follows the principle of citizenship (nationality) and country 'B' follows that of habitual residence when determining the *lex personae*. In this case, the law of country 'A' points to the law of country 'B' (*lex patriae*), and the law of country 'B' points to the law of country 'A' (habitual residence).

If both systems preclude remission, the courts of the two countries apply different laws. The courts of country 'A', applying their choice-of-law rules, will apply the law of citizenship without accepting remission, which is the law of country 'B', while the courts of country 'B', applying their choice-of-law rules, will apply the law of habitual residence without accepting remission, which is the law of country 'A'. The same international disharmony emerges if both systems accept remission. The courts of country 'A', applying their choice-of-law rules, will, first, apply the law of citizenship, which is the law of country 'B'; however, as the latter points back to the law of country 'A', they will apply their own domestic law. On the other hand, the courts of country 'B', applying their choice-of-law rules, will, first, apply the law of habitual residence, which is the law of country 'A'; however, as the latter points back to the law of country 'B', they will apply their own domestic law. If the two choice-of-law systems follow different models, international harmony can be reached. For example, if country 'A' accepts remission, while country 'B' does not, the courts of the two countries will apply the same law. The law of country 'A' will refer to the law of country 'B' but, as the latter refers back to the law of country 'A', the courts of country 'A' accept the remission and apply their own law. At the same time, the courts of country 'B' will apply the law of country 'A' as the law of habitual residence, disregarding the fact that the choice-of-law rules of country 'A' point back to country 'B'. A perfectly harmonious outcome: the courts of both countries apply the law of country 'A'.

Accordingly, it seems to be impossible to find a generally applicable solution that could serve as a panacea for *renvoi* situations. The approach of English courts (foreign court doctrine) may at first glance seem to be such a solution; nevertheless, this method works only as long as a single country applies it. According to the foreign court doctrine, the English judge puts himself in the foreign judge's shoes and tries to identify the law the foreign court would apply and then, applies that law.[18]

Hungarian private international law has a simple solution concerning the problem of *renvoi*: it accepts remission and transmission only where the reference to foreign law is based on citizenship.

Section 5 of the APIL provides that if the APIL points to a foreign law, this is a reference to the substantive rules of the legal system invoked. Nevertheless, if the reference to foreign law is based on citizenship and the foreign law refers back to Hungarian law or to the law of the third country, the remission and transmission have to be taken into account. Accordingly, in this case, if the foreign law refers back to Hungarian law, Hungarian law has to be applied; if it refers to the law of a third country, the law of that country has to be applied. In this case, the substantive law of Hungary (remission) or that of the third country invoked (transmission) has to be applied, with the exclusion of their choice-of-law rules. Nonethless, this exception works only if the reference to foreign law is based on citizenship. In all other cases the general rule applies,

18 J.G. Collier, *Conflict of Laws* (CUP, Cambridge, 2004), 21.

and this precludes both remission and transmission and provides for the application of the substantive rules of the legal system invoked.

EU choice-of-law instruments, with the exception of the Succession Regulation,[19] exclude *renvoi* and point to the substantive rules of the *lex causae*.[20]

5.3 *Application and Adaptation*

Foreign law has to be applied as law and not as fact. According to Sections 7–8 of the APIL, the applicable foreign law has to be applied *ex officio* and the court has to ascertain its content *ex officio*. The foreign law has to be applied and interpreted in the way it is applied and interpreted in the foreign jurisdiction. Any error in applying the foreign law amounts to a legal error.

The fragmentation of the applicable law resulting from the principle that choice of law determines the law applicable to individual legal questions and not to the case at large may lead to unjust or unintended consequences. The individual rules of a legal system interact with each other. Legal institutions are created in the context of a given legal system, taking into account the contextual legal notions. In terms of practice, the law of a country may be very generous in the field of spousal maintenance because it follows the principle of separation in the field of matrimonial property. Here, maintenance may serve the purpose of compensating one of the spouses for the loss of their matrimonial status, while in community-of-property systems there is normally nothing to be compensated for, since the spouses normally end up with half of the gains. Moreover, inheritance rules may also be shaped by matrimonial property considerations. For example, the surviving spouse may inherit one part of a legacy to counterbalance the division of property in marriage law, while in systems featuring the community of matrimonial property the surviving spouse may inherit not ownership but merely some kind of life interest (usufruct). If the rules of different legal systems are taken out of their context and mixed in their application, this could lead to over-or under-compensation: although under most substantive laws there is no rose without thorns, choice of law may lead to situations where the spouse gets only the roses or only the thorns.

The APIL contains no provision on assimilation or adaptation. However, the rules on characterization may be used to correct the unjust or unintended consequences of the fragmentation of the applicable law. The rules

---

19 Article 34 of the Succession Regulation.

20 See Article 20 of the Rome I Regulation, Article 24 of the Rome II Regulation, Article 11 of the Rome III Regulation. \ For the Insolvency Regulation see paragraph 87 of the Virgos-Schmit Report; for the Maintenance Regulation see Article 12 of the 2007 Hague Protocol.

on characterization may be used to recharacterize or reconceptualize foreign legal institutions, taking into account their function and regulatory purpose. Section 4 of the APIL adopts the *lex fori* approach, but also provides that where a legal institution is unknown to Hungarian law, or is known but with a different content or different designation, the foreign law that regulates it may be taken into consideration. In this case, the function and purpose of the legal institution in the foreign legal system have to be taken into account. If the legal institution is not unknown to Hungarian law but has a different function or purpose in the foreign legal system, the latter has to be taken into consideration in the course of characterization.

5.4 *Ordre Public* (*Public Policy*) *and Imperative Rules* (*Overriding Mandatory Rules*)

Public policy (in French: '*ordre public*', in German: '*öffentliche Ordnung*', in Hungarian: '*közrend*') is a traditional concept of PIL which has an important role in both choice of law and international civil procedural law. Public policy and imperative (overriding mandatory) rules have the same roots: the former is a negative, the latter are positive expressions of the same consideration. The forum always gives precedence to its own public policy and imperative norms and may, in some cases, give consideration to the imperative rules of third countries.

The starting point in choice of law is that the forum recognizes foreign law as equivalent to its own law (even if the two are different) and endeavors to identify the legal system that is most closely related to the case (or, more precisely, to the legal question), since this will provide the appropriate answer. This is, however, a very generous rule, since the law mandates the application of foreign law without knowing its content. The court usually learns the content of the foreign law after identifying it as applicable. Due to the 'blindness' of choice of law, the application of foreign law is, in fact, a 'leap in the dark'.[21] It is possible for the foreign law not only to differ from the law of the forum, but for the extent of divergence to be intolerable for the court.

Public policy is relevant in different fields of PIL. First, in choice of law: if the application of the foreign law breaches the forum's public policy, it cannot be applied. Second, with respect to the recognition and enforcement of foreign judgments and arbitral awards: a foreign judgment or award that is contrary to Hungarian public policy cannot be recognized and enforced in Hungary.

21 L. Raape, *Internationales Privatrecht* (Franz Vahlen Verlag, Berlin u. Fankfurt am Main, 1961), 90.

Third, public policy also plays an important role in the field of judicial cooperation: no legal assistance is provided if it goes against Hungarian public policy.

Public policy is a traditionally indefinable term. Section 12 of the APIL provides that foreign law cannot be applied if the result of its application in the given case manifestly and gravely infringes the fundamental values and constitutional principles of the Hungarian legal system ('if the result thereof in the given case obviously and seriously violated the fundamental values and constitutional principles of the Hungarian legal system').

Recourse to the public policy clause is highly exceptional in Hungary and is reserved for cases where the application of the foreign law would be manifestly contrary to the fundamental principles of Hungarian law.[22] Here, it is not the foreign law as such that is measured, but its application in the concrete case. Textbook examples of breach of Hungarian public policy include polygamy, discrimination based on gender, and punitive damages, as well as the failure adequately to protect the weaker party (such as an employee or consumer).

Pursuant to Section 12(2) of the APIL, in the event that the application of the foreign law is found to infringe Hungarian public policy and there are no means of avoiding the infringement, Hungarian law is to be applied instead. Accordingly, the application of Hungarian law is not automatic in cases where the application of the foreign law is contrary to Hungarian public policy. Hungarian law steps in only if the matter cannot be resolved otherwise. For instance, if foreign law discriminates on the basis of gender, its application may breach Hungarian public policy in the given case. However, this does not necessarily mean that Hungarian law has to be applied instead. The court may simply ignore the discriminatory provision and apply the general rules of the foreign law without it to avoid a discriminatory outcome.

Imperative rules (overriding mandatory rules) are provisions that are to be applied unconditionally. They have a public policy character, are applicable irrespective of the *lex causae,* and override any eventual conflicting provisions. Section 13(1) of the APIL provides that a provision of Hungarian law is imperative if it can be clearly established on the basis of its content and purpose that it needs to be applied unconditionally to the legal relationsips coming within the scope of the APIL. While in most cases the imperative nature of a norm can be established only on the basis of the above factors, some rules are explicitly stated by the law to be imperative. For instance, according to Section 26(4) of the APIL, the Hungarian rules on unavoidable marriage impediments are imperative and, irrespective of the applicable law, a marriage cannot be

22 See Case *Gf.II.20.304/2005/4.* (High Court of Appeal of Győr).

concluded in Hungary if it flouts an unavoidable marriage impediment under Hungarian law.

Section 13(2) of the APIL authorizes the court to consider the imperative rules of foreign countries if they are closely connected to the case and have decisive importance in its resolution.

In Case *17.P.22.503/2004/107*, the Budapest-Capital Regional Court examined the rules of Iranian law, which provide that the husband has an unqualified right to terminate the marriage via a unilateral declaration without giving any reasons (*talaq* divorce), while the wife may request the dissolution of the marriage only under certain conditions (e.g. if the husband does not maintain her, the marriage causes hardship or inconvenience to her, etc.). The Budapest-Capital Regional Court held that these provisions of the Iranian Civil Code discriminate on the basis of gender as to the right to institute divorce proceedings and, hence, violate Hungarian public policy.

EU PIL instruments authorize courts to refuse to apply a foreign law if to do so would violate the forum's public policy[23] or imperative norms.[24] Article 9(3) of the Rome I Regulation allows (but does not oblige) the court to take into consideration the imperative norms of the place of performance of the contract 'in so far as those overriding mandatory provisions render the performance of the contract unlawful'. In considering whether to give effect to those provisions, the court shall take into consideration their nature and purpose and the consequences of their application or non-application. Article 30 of the Succession Regulation provides for the application of the imperative norms of the situs of certain assets ('immovable property, certain enterprises or other special categories of assets'). In both cases, the imperative rules of the third country are relevant also from the perspective of practical enforceability. The contract's place of performance may easily be the place of enforcement, and ignorance of the local imperative rules may thwart the judgment's enforcement in that country. In the same vein, to have practical legal effects a decision under succession law needs to be recognized in the country where the real estate is located. This recognition is, however, dubious if the decision is incompatible with the local imperative rules.

In Case *Gf.20062/2015/8*,[25] the 1980 Rome Convention was applied but the High Court of Appeal of Győr also referred to the Rome I Regulation when interpreting the Convention, and specifically to the concept of imperative

---

23 Article 21 of the Rome I Regulation; Article 26 of the Rome II Regulation; Article 12 of the Rome III Regulation; Article 35 of the Succession Regulation.

24 Article 9 of the Rome I Regulation; Article 16 of the Rome II Regulation.

25 Appealed from Case G.20918/2011/115 (Győr Regional Court).

norms. The parties concluded a loan contract and chose Austrian law. Contrary to the defendants' allegations, the court established that the Hungarian rules on the coming into existence, form, validity, substantive elements, rights and obligations, performance, and termination of the legal relationship did not meet the requirements of Article 9(1) of the Rome I Regulation. Furthermore, the court also held that the application of imperative rules is warranted chiefly in cases where the parties choose the law of a state the fact pattern has no connection with. This condition was not met either, since the fact pattern, through the plaintiff and its business activity, was connected to Austria.

In Case *Gfv.V.30.045/2019/9.*,[26] the plaintiff bank sought a declaratory judgment establishing that, due to the civil war in Libya and the embargo measures adopted by the European Union against it, it was freed from the duties consequent on the bank guarantee it had issued. Although, in the declaration the bank chose Libyan law to be applied to the bank guarantee, in its statement of claim it relied exclusively on the European embargo measures without any reference to Libyan law and argued that the latter was irrelevant in relation to its request for a declaratory judgment.

The Budapest-Capital Regional Court decided for the plaintiff on the basis of the Embargo Regulation[27] without ascertaining the content of Libyan law.

The High Court of Appeal of Budapest overturned the judgment. It held that although the provisions of the Embargo Regulation qualified as imperative norms under Article 9 of the Rome I Regulation and, as such, replaced the rules of the applicable law, the impact of these rules on the plaintiff's contractual obligations could be established only on the basis of the joint interpretation of these imperative norms and the rules of *lex causae*. According to the Court, the provisions of the Embargo Regulation affected the execution of contracts but did not change the substantive law, because, as far as unconditional application was concerned, it interfered with civil law relationships only as regards the performance, in order provisionally to prevent an increase in the pecuniary assets of the persons concerned. The rules of the embargo regulated the performance of the contract but were not relevant to the legal effects of the fact that underlay the legal relationship. The High Court of Appeal of Budapest also held that the public policy exception enshrined in Article 21 of the Rome I Regulation does not rule out the application of the *lex causae* in its totality; it merely excludes its application to specific facts. It may not be reasonably

26 Appealed from Case *Gf.40608/2017/12* (High Court of Appeal of Budapest), appealed from Case 29.G.42.778/2016/38 (Budapest-Capital Regional Court).

27 Regulation 204/2011 of 2 March 2011 concerning restrictive measures in view of the situation in Libya. OJ L 58, 3.3.2011, pp. 1–13.

supposed that the Libyan rules applicable to the legal relationship based on the bank guarantee would, due to the prevailing political situation, clearly violate Hungarian public policy.

On appeal, the Supreme Court reversed the High Court of Appeal of Budapest's judgment and reinstated that of the Budapest-Capital Regional Court. The Supreme Court established that the scope of the imperative norms is not affected by the choice-of-law norms and, hence, they impact substantive law relationships.[28] The payment of the bank guarantee came under the prohibition of the imperative norm and, hence, the latter not only had paramount importance in the case[29] but, according to the Supreme Court, it was not essential to ascertain the content of Libyan law in order to adjudicate on the plaintiff's petition. Because of the Embargo Regulation, no payment could be made during the time the bank guarantee was open and the payment obligation could not linger on after that, as the embargo did not aim to extend the legal relationships concerned. Hence, the Court could establish that the bank guarantee had expired, and the bank had no payment obligations anymore.[30] As to the ascertainment of the content of foreign law, the Supreme Court noted that this was the responsibility not of the parties but of the court, which had to apply the foreign law *ex officio*. While the parties may certainly make submissions and submit evidence, this does not relieve the court of its responsibility. In the event of a civil war in the country concerned, which complicates intercourse with the foreign state and hinders the ascertainment of the content of foreign law, the court may conclude, with reference to Section 5(3) of the APIL, that the content of the foreign law cannot be determined and, hence, Hungarian law must be applied.[31]

28 Para. 49.
29 Para. 52.
30 Para. 64.
31 Paras 53–54.

CHAPTER 3

Choice-of-Law Rules

1 The Pervasive Principle of Closest Connection

The principle of closest connections plays two important roles in Hungarian private international law. First, choice-of-law rules are, for the most part, inspired by this principle and convert it into specific norms. Second, the principle of closest connection also has a normative role. The APIL contains a general fallback rule (Section 11) that determines, with reference to the principle of closest connection, the law applicable to matters not covered by a specific choice-of-law rule. Furthermore, the APIL also contains a general escape clause (Section 10) which, again with reference to the principle of closest connection, empowers the judge to apply a law different from the one pointed to by the specific rules of the APIL.

Section 11 of the APIL contains an all-embracing and pervasive choice-of-law rule: if the APIL contains no specific provision as to a legal relationship that comes within its scope (that is, a private international law case), the law of the most closely connected country has to be applied. This is a general fallback rule and not an escape clause. Section 11 of the APIL applies only if the APIL contains no specific choice-of-law rule concerning a given case. Contrary to the general escape clause included in Section 10 of the APIL and discussed below, Section 11 does not authorize the court to depart from a specific choice-of-law rule set out in the APIL.

According to Section 10 of the APIL, if, in the light of its facts, it is obvious that the case is substantially more closely connected to a law different from that determined by the APIL's specific provisions, by way of exception, the court can apply this more closely connected law. Accordingly, the principle of closest connection can be considered a general rule behind all the choice-of-law rules of the APIL also in the sense that the judge always has the right, on the basis of the general escape clause embedded in Section 10 of the APIL, to set aside a specific choice-of-law norm and to apply the law that is manifestly more closely connected with the case.

The general escape clause does not apply if the parties chose the applicable law, that is, the court may not rely on Section 10 of the APIL to disapply the law chosen by the parties.

It is an important requirement that the court has to make the decision on the applicability of the general escape clause within 30 days after receiving the

 | DOI:10.1163/9789004694569_004

defendant's defense. The tight deadline makes the practical application of the general escape clause nearly unfeasible.

Section 10 of the APIL may be of help in cases where the court does not find the applicable law appropriate. The court's approach to the property relations between the spouses and the treatment of the marriage contract in Case *Pfv.II.21.240/2007/4* may provide an example of this. The matter was adjudicated on the basis of the old APIL, which contained no general escape clause. The court could not find a choice-of-law solution but tried to correct the inappropriateness of the applicable law by means of the leeway it had under substantive law. Here, the plaintiff was a Swedish-Iranian dual citizen and, at the time of the court proceedings, lived in Sweden, while the defendant had only Iranian citizenship. On the basis of Section 11 of the old APIL, the plaintiff's personal law was Swedish law (she had dual citizenship, neither of which was Hungarian, and thus the personal law was determined by the place of living). On the other hand, the defendant's personal law was Iranian law. Since the spouses had no common personal law, the court applied the law of the last common place of living, which was Hungary. Nonetheless, the Supreme Court noted in its judgment that, although Hungarian law was to be applied to the personal and property relationships between the spouses, when examining under Hungarian law whether the marriage contract was contrary to good morals, the traditions and principles of Iranian law (as the law of the country both spouses stemmed from) also had to be taken into account as part of the court's balancing. That is, the foregoing element was a circumstance that had relevance also in the application of Hungarian substantive law. Under the currently effective APIL, the court could rely on Section 10 to apply Iranian instead of Hungarian law.

Given the tight deadline set by Section 10 of the APIL for the application of the general escape clause, it is assumed that it may be mainly used in cases where the parties jointly request the court to apply a law different from the *lex causae*. If the parties have the right to choose the applicable law, they may make use of party autonomy. However, if they have no such right in a given case but find the law set out by the APIL to be inappropriate, they may jointly request the court to apply Section 10 of the APIL.

2 Personal Law

The meaning of personal law (*lex personae*) is twofold: it has both a substantive-law and a choice-of-law face; *lex personae* (personal law) is both a bundle of substantive-law issues and a set of connecting factors. On the one hand, the *lex personae* embraces those questions of substantive law that are personal, i.e., that are connected to the person; these include, by way of example, legal capacity and contractual capacity. On the other hand, the *lex personae* also designates the connecting factor or factors that are used to find the law applicable to these 'personal' questions, e.g., citizenship, domicile.

2.1 *Natural Persons*

According to Section 15(1) of the APIL, natural persons' personal law encompasses legal capacity, capacity to act, and personality rights.

'Legal capacity' is used as the translation of the Hungarian concept of '*jogképesség*', which is the equivalent of the German concept of '*Rechtsfähigkeit*'. A person having legal capacity can be the holder of rights and obligations; legal capacity implies the quality of being a legal subject. Nevertheless, it is not all those with legal capacity who can enter into commitments, but only those that have 'capacity to act'[1] (in Hungarian: '*cselekvőképesség*'; in German: '*Geschäftsfähigkeit*'). 'Capacity to act' implies the legal faculty to make decisions amending the person's rights and obligations. Only persons (or entities) having legal capacity can have capacity to act. On the other hand, not all persons who are legal subjects, i.e., have legal capacity, have capacity to act. Minors or mentally disabled persons have no or restricted capacity to act. Nonetheless, it has to be noted that, in Hungarian law, 'capacity to act' is different from and does not extend to 'delictual capacity', which is a tort law question.

Section 15 of the APIL determines the personal law of natural persons by means of three subsidiary connecting factors: citizenship (nationality), habitual residence, and *lex fori*. Domicile plays no role in this regard.

The principal connecting factor used by the APIL for determining a natural person's *lex personae* is citizenship (*lex patriae*). If a person has multiple citizenships, the applicable law is determined by the citizenship to which, considering the circumstances of the matter, he or she has the closest connection. Where one of the multiple citizenships is Hungarian, there is a rebuttable presumption that the person is most closely connected to Hungary. If the person has multiple citizenships none of which is Hungarian and has no closer connection to any of them, or if the person's citizenship cannot be identified, as well as in the case of stateless persons, personal law is determined by the habitual residence. If the applicable law cannot be identified on the basis of the foregoing rules, Hungarian law has to be applied.

1 An alternative translation of the Hungarian term could be 'disposing capacity'.

Section 3 of the APIL provides a statutory definition of the terms 'place of living' (domicile) and 'habitual residence'. The former refers to 'the place where a person lives permanently or with the intention of settling there definitively', and the latter to 'the place where, taking all the circumstances of the given legal relationship into account, the actual center of his life is located; in determining this, the facts referring to the intention of the person concerned must be also taken into consideration'.

The place of living is the place where someone lives permanently or with the purpose of settling down. On the other hand, habitual residence refers to the place where the person has the center of his life; the circumstances revealing the person's intentions need to be taken into account in this regard. Accordingly, subjective elements need to be taken into account as to both the 'place of living' and 'habitual residence'; however, 'habitual residence' is more a factual than a subjective issue.

The APIL sets out two cases where the *lex fori* (Hungarian law) is used as an alternative connecting factor to protect legitimate expectations. Section 17 of the APIL provides that in respect of transactions concerning Hungary the person shall be regarded as having capacity to act if he or she has such capacity under Hungarian law. In respect to everyday transactions of minor importance that are concluded and performed in Hungary, as well as all transactions whose legal consequences arise in Hungary, a person's capacity to act can be established on the basis of Hungarian law if he or she has no or restricted disposing capacity under his personal law.

Furthermore, Hungarian law has to be applied to the question of death and the presumption of death of a missing person if a domestic legal interest warrants this. Such interest can be the settling of the legal status of property located in Hungary, such as where the person concerned has property located in Hungary and the adjudication of the property's legal fate (from the point of view of inheritance law) necessitates a decision on the question of death or the presumption of death of a missing person.[2]

Hungarian law uses different terms for guardianship over minors (in Hungarian: '*gyámság*') and guardianship over adults (in Hungarian: '*gondnokság*').

Guardianship over minors is governed by the law of the hearing court, but if the interests of the child warrant, a closely connected law may exceptionally be applied or taken into account.[3] Given that the APIL is applied solely

2 Section 21 of the APIL.

3 Section 34 of the APIL.

by Hungarian courts and administrative authorities, the foregoing provision implies that, in principle, Hungarian law has to be applied in matters concerning guardianship over minors.

Guardianship over adults and other protective measures that do not affect the person's capacity to act are not governed by the personal law but by the law of habitual residence of the person concerned. However, if the interests of the adult concerned warrant it, the court may exceptionally apply or take into account the law of a state to which the case is more closely connected.[4]

The law of the habitual residence also applies to the legal declarations an adult makes for the situation in which he or she would be placed under guardianship or protective measures would be adopted to protect these interests; however, in his written declaration, he or she may also choose the law of his citizenship, earlier habitual residence, or the *situs* of the assets.[5]

The law of the appointing court applies to the legal representation of a person restricted in managing his own affairs and to the *ad hoc* guardianship of adults.[6]

The personal law of stateless persons is determined by their habitual residence.[7]

The personal law of refugees is Hungarian law. The rationale of this rule is that it would be inappropriate to keep such persons subjected to the law of the country of origin they fled from. At the same time, the rights and obligations acquired remain intact.[8]

2.2 *Names of Natural Persons*

The name of a natural person is governed by their personal law, but the application of Hungarian law may be requested. In addition to this, with respect to their birth name, Section 16(2) of the APIL grants natural persons having multiple citizenships the ability to choose the law of any country whose citizenship they have. As regards married names, Section 16(3) of the APIL provides that the parties may jointly request the application of the law of the citizenship of either spouse. In the absence of a joint request, the married name is governed by the law applicable to the spouses' personal and property relations, which is determined by Section 27 of the APIL. The law that served as the basis

4 Section 18 of the APIL.
5 Section 19 of the APIL.
6 Section 20 of the APIL.
7 Section 15 of the APIL.
8 Section 15 of the APIL.

for establishing the married name continues to apply where the marriage is dissolved or annulled.

Section 16 was inserted in the APIL with the desire to comply with the CJEU's judgment in *Carlos Garcia Avello*.[9] In this case, the legal dispute arose out of Belgium's refusal to change, in accordance with Spanish customs, the surnames of the two children of a Spanish father and a Belgian mother, who had dual citizenship. Under Belgian law, the children acquire the surname of their father, while under Spanish law the children take the first surnames of the parents. In this ruling, the CJEU, essentially, established that a dual citizen who is the citizen of two Member States is entitled to choose a name that complies with the law or customs of either Member State. It held that Articles 18 (prohibition of discrimination based on nationality) and 20 (Union citizenship) TFEU preclude Member States from 'refusing to grant an application for a change of surname made on behalf of minor children resident in that State and having dual nationality of that State and of another Member State, in the case where the purpose of that application is to enable those children to bear the surname to which they are entitled according to the law and tradition of the second Member State'.[10]

In the absence of Section 16 the question of name would come under personal law, which is presumed to be Hungarian law, if the person has multiple citizenships but is also a citizen of Hungary. Although this rebuttable presumption is maintained, as to name, the person is granted the right to choose the law of any country he or she is a citizen of. In this regard, Section 16 goes beyond the judgment in *Carlos Garcia Avello*. Under the APIL, the right to choose between the various laws applies irrespective of whether the person concerned chooses the law of a Member State or not; what is more, the person has the right to choose irrespective of whether the matter has any link to the EU at all. For instance, a person having dual Hungarian-Russian citizenship can opt for the latter when registering his name (or rather his parents would do that acting as statutory representatives); a US-Canadian citizen would also have the right to choose, although such a case, absent additional circumstances, would probably not be an EU matter and, thus, would fall outside the scope of the judgment in *Carlos Garcia Avello*.

---

9 ECJ, Case C-148/02, *Carlos Garcia Avello v Belgian State* (2003) EU:C:2003:539.

10 Para. 45.

2.3 *Legal Persons*

The personal law of legal persons (*lex societas*), according to Section 22(4) of the APIL, embraces the legal person's legal capacity, coming into existence, representation, personality rights, and organizational and internal matters, and the responsibility of the legal person, its members, and officers.

In general, there are two approaches to connecting a legal person to a particular legal system. Common law systems normally follow the principle of incorporation (registration, in German: '*Gründungstheorie*'), while civil-law legal systems traditionally follow the principle of seat (in German: '*Sitztheorie*').

Section 22 of the APIL sets out three subsidiary connecting factors with regard to the *lex societas*. Although Hungary is a continental system, it follows the principle of incorporation. If the place of incorporation fails to determine the applicable law because the organization was incorporated under the laws of more than one state, the law of the registered seat must be applied. If the registered seat also fails to determine the applicable law because the organization has no or more than one registered seat and is not incorporated in any of those states, the legal person's actual seat (central administration/management) determines the applicable law.[11]

In Case *Cgf.11.32.573/1997/7*, the Company Court interpreted the concept of legal capacity in the context of proceedings for company registration. According to the facts, the Company Court refused to register a company because one of its founders, which was a company, was not registered at the time when the articles of association were signed. In the relevant period, the concept of 'pre-company', i.e., the notion that a company is granted limited legal capacity before its final registration, was unknown in Hungarian company law (this was introduced only by the Company Act of 1997), and the court considered the company taking part in the process of foundation to be 'non-existent'. On appeal, the appellate court held that the question whether the German company had legal capacity was to be adjudicated upon according to German law, as this was the company's personal law. According to German law, the company, as a pre-company, acquired limited legal capacity before final registration and, in this case, the duly signed articles of association and the request for registration were submitted to the competent German authority; hence, the business entity was to be regarded as a pre-company at the time the Hungarian company's articles of association were signed.

In Case *Gf.1.30.059/2000/5*, the Supreme Court held that it was the plaintiff's duty and burden to prove that it had legal capacity under its personal law (in

11 Section 22 of the APIL.

this case: Russian law). This duty did not embrace the obligation to prove the content of the foreign law; the Court simply required the plaintiff to prove how (in what way) it acquired legal personality under its personal law. If this occurred through registration, an authentic copy of the entry in the company registry was required.

In Case *BH2001.537*, the choice-of-law question was the applicability of the then-effective rule of Hungarian company law that a one-person company, i.e., a company having only one shareholder or member, cannot be the only member of another one-person company. The court held that this provision is also applicable to foreign one-man companies when they want to establish a one-person company in Hungary. Accordingly, the court held that this prohibition was not part of the founder's personal law but was a question coming under the *lex personae* of the Hungarian company the founder aimed to establish.

2.4 *Personality Rights*

Article 1(2)(g) of the Rome II Regulation excludes from its scope non-contractual obligations arising out of violations of privacy and rights relating to personality, including defamation.[12] This raises questions of interpretation in the context of Hungarian law's wide definition of personality rights, which extends to all illicit acts concerning the personality, including personal injury.

In Case *Pfv.VIII.20.109/2019*,[13] the Supreme Court encountered this question of characterization. In this case, the parents claimed non-pecuniary damages because their child was killed in a traffic accident, as this interfered with their personality right to the protection of private and family life.[14] Under Hungarian law the legal basis of the claim for damages was the violation of a personality right. Nonetheless, the Supreme Court held that the terms used in Article 1(2)(g) of the Rome II Regulation had to be given an autonomous meaning and the term 'personality rights' had a narrower import under the Regulation than under Hungarian law. The Supreme Court established that a closer look to the legislative history demonstrated that Article 1(2)(g) of the Rome II Regulation was destined to address violations of personality rights committed via the media and the EU legislator aimed to create a uniform regime for delictual

---

12 See Cs.I. Nagy & S. Szabó, "A way ahead toward a deeper integration of EU PIL: the unification of the rules on violation of privacy and rights relating to personality," in R. Somssich & T. Szabados, *Central and Eastern European Countries After and Before the Accession, vol 1.* (ELTE – Jean Monnet Center of Excellence, Budapest, 2011), 191–211, at 206–209.

13 Reported as BH 2020.8.242, appealed from Case Pf.633945/2018/6 (Budapest-Capital Regional Court), appealed from Case P.89585/2015/55 (Central District Court of Pest).

14 Para. 22.

claims emerging from traffic accidents both as to personal injuries and pecuniary damages. This is reflected also in various parts of the preamble to and the provisions of the Regulation, such as recitals (17) and (33) and Articles 2(1) and 4(1).[15] This was confirmed also in Case C-350/14 *Florin Lazar v Allianz SpA*.[16] As a corollary, the Supreme Court applied English law.[17]

Outside the scope of the Rome II Regulation, the law applicable to personality rights is determined by Section 23 of the APIL. The APIL here has a two-fold approach. The existence of individual personality rights comes under the purview of personal law, while their violation and its legal consequences are subject to choice-of-law rules similar to those applicable to delictual liability.

According to Section 15(1) of the APIL, the personal law of humans embraces personality rights. Section 22(4)(d) of the APIL contains the same rule for legal persons.

Violation of personality rights and its legal consequences (as this is a question having delictual features) are governed by the law of the injured party's habitual residence (the registered seat in the case of legal persons). The party has, however, the right unilaterally to choose the law of his center of interests, the law of the wrongdoer's habitual residence (the registered seat in the case of legal persons) or Hungarian law.[18]

3 Contractual Obligations

The law applicable to contracts is predominantly regulated by the Rome I Regulation, and Hungarian courts have produced a significant amount of case law on the Regulation's application. The APIL applies only in matters falling outside the scope of the Regulation and it is of highly limited practical relevance. Notable matters not covered by the Rome I Regulation include negotiable instruments, arbitration, and choice-of-court agreements, the question of representation (power of attorney), trusts, and certain insurance contracts.

In Case *G.20348/2013/83*, the Rome I Regulation was not applicable *ratione temporis*. However, the Győr Regional Court, as *obiter dictum*, indicated that the Rome I Regulation would not apply anyway; one of the contracting parties was Austrian but the other one was from the Cayman Islands. It seems that the court conceived the scope of the Rome I Regulation as applying only to EU

15 Para. 24.
16 EU:C:2015:802, paras 25–26.
17 Para. 27.
18 Section 23 of the APIL.

matters. This view is flawed, since the Rome I Regulation has universal application and is applicable irrespective of whether the case has an EU element or not (Article 2 of the Rome I Regulation).

3.1 *Hungarian Choice-of-Law Rules*

Sections 50–51 of the APIL establish the general rules applicable to contracts falling outside the scope of the Rome I Regulation. The parties have the right to choose the applicable law. In the absence of a choice, the most closely connected law has to be applied. Section 52 of the APIL contains special choice-of-law rules for arbitration agreements. Unilateral declarations are governed by the same choice-of-law rules as contracts unless the APIL provides otherwise.

The scope of the *lex contractus* covers the conclusion, existence, validity, interpretation, performance, and breach of the contract, including contractual damages, as well as its cancellation, rescission, and termination.

The existence and validity of the contract come under the *lex contractus* (Section 53 of the APIL), which is, as noted above, the most closely connected law (Section 51 of the APIL), provided the parties did not choose the law to be applicable. Nonetheless, the APIL also uses a set of alternative connecting factors driven by the motivation as far as possible to save the formal validity of the contract. According to Section 54 of the APIL, if the parties are present in the same country when concluding the contract, the latter is valid if it complies with either the *lex contractus* or the *lex loci actus*. If the parties are in different states, the contract is formally valid if it complies with the *lex contractus* or with the law of the state where either of the parties was or had his place of habitual residence at the time of its conclusion. Unilateral declarations made in the context of an existing or contemplated contract are formally valid if they comply with the *lex contractus*, the *lex loci actus,* or the law of the habitual residence. If, however, the contract concerns property rights in or the lease of immovable property, those mandatory rules of the *situs* that apply irrespective of the place of the contract's conclusion and the *lex contractus* shall apply.

Representation is one of the very few contractual issues that are excluded from the scope of the Rome I Regulation and are regulated by the APIL. Agency gives rise to two legal relationships. The internal relationship between the principal and the agent is governed by the Rome I Regulation. It qualifies as a contract for the provision of services under Article 4(1)(b) and is governed by the law of the country where the service provider has his habitual residence. The external relationship based on the authority of the agent is excluded from the scope of the Rome I Regulation pursuant to its Article 1(2)(g). The law applicable to the external dimension of agency (representation) is determined by Section 53 of the APIL, which provides that the existence and validity of a contract or a contractual term are governed by the law which would be applicable based on this Act if the contract or the contractual term were valid. This implies that the question whether the agent's action binds the principal comes under the *lex contractus*, which is the most closely connected law (Section 51 of the APIL), provided the parties did not choose the applicable law.

In Case *Gf.40063/2017/13*,[19] the contractual dispute centered around the right of representation. The parties concluded a guarantee agreement. However, the signatory on behalf of the guarantor had no right of representation. The employee who signed the contract (Mr. B. R.) was not a statutory representative of the guarantor and had no power of attorney. The question was whether Mr. B. R.'s action bound the defendant on account of implicit approval. This question appears to fall outside the scope of the Rome I Regulation: Article 1(2)(f) excludes from the scope of the Regulation 'questions governed by the law of companies', while Article 1(2)(g) excludes 'the question whether an agent is able to bind a principal, or an organ to bind a company or other body corporate or unincorporated, in relation to a third party'. Nonetheless, the High Court of Appeal of Budapest affirmed the Budapest-Capital Regional Court's judgment which extended the *lex contractus* established under the Rome I Regulation (Hungarian law) to the question of representation. Under Hungarian law, the above issue qualifies as a contractual question,[20] and so may come under the *lex contractus*. Nonetheless, the rules limiting the scope of the Rome I Regulation, that is, the exclusions listed in Article 1(2), should have an autonomous EU law meaning, and the reference to 'the question whether an agent is able to bind a principal' seems to embrace the issue of implicit approval of the actions of a non-representative.

It has to be noted that the above error concerned the reasoning of the judgment alone and had no bearing on the substantive outcome. If the question of implicit approval is not covered by the Rome I Regulation, the applicable law has to be established on the basis of national choice-of-law rules, which also pointed to Hungarian law as the *lex contractus*. The court considered that the parties had chosen Hungarian law to govern their contractual relationship, and this choice was valid also under Hungarian PIL.[21] The question of

19 Appealed from Case G.42206/2012/102 (Budapest-Capital Regional Court).

20 Under Hungarian law, the actions of a person may bind the principal even if the former has no right of representation if the principal approves them either explicitly, or implicitly (that is, by indicative behavior). See Section 221(1) of the old Civil Code, which was applied in this case, and Section 6:14 of the Civil Code, the currently effective provision.

21 Section 25 of the APIL, the applicable provision during the relevant time, and Section 50 of the APIL, the currently effective provision.

characterization under the APIL is governed, in principle, by Hungarian law,[22] and, in Hungarian law, the question of implicit approval qualifies as a contractual issue.[23] Accordingly, that question would have come under Hungarian law even if the court had found that the Rome I Regulation did not apply and established the applicable law on the basis of Hungarian choice-of-law rules.

Negotiable instruments, such as bills of exchange (drafts), checks, promissory notes, and letters of credit, are excluded from the scope of the Rome I and Rome II Regulations.[24] Thus, they come under the scope of the APIL.

According to Section 57 of the APIL, the formalities and nature of negotiable instruments, including the question whether they are payable to bearer or to order, are governed by the law that applies to the incorporated right. If the security incorporates an *in rem* right, the rules on property rights, including the principle of *lex rei sitae,* apply.

The *ad rem* right incorporated in the negotiable instruments is governed by the law chosen by the parties or, absent this, the law of the place where the security was issued, or, if this cannot be ascertained, the personal law of the issuer shall apply. The membership rights incorporated in instruments such as shares are governed by the personal law of the issuer. The *in rem* rights incorporated in a security (such as a bill of lading) are governed by the law of the state where the security was issued. If the instrument incorporates more than one right, the parties may choose the applicable law; absent this, the law governing the right that constitutes the central element of the instrument shall apply.[25]

The law applicable to insurance contracts is partially regulated by the Rome I Regulation. Article 1(2)(j) of the Regulation excludes certain insurance contracts from its scope, and these, hence, are governed by national choice-of-law rules. The APIL contains no specific provisions on insurance contracts. Accordingly, insurance contracts not covered by the Rome I Regulation are governed by the APIL's general contractual choice-of-law rules included in Sections 50–51, that is, the *lex pro voluntate* and, in the absence of a choice by the parties, the most closely connected law.

---

22 Section 3 of the old APIL, the applicable provision during the relevant time, and Section 4 of the APIL, the currently effective provision.

23 On the one hand, this question is regulated among the rules on contracts. See Section 221(1) of the old Civil Code, and Section 6:14 of the current Civil Code. On the other hand, Hungarian choice-of-law rules concern solely statutory representation (but not contract-based power of attorney) as a question coming under personal law. See Section 18(1) of the old APIL and Section 22(4)(c) of the APIL.

24 Article 1(2)(d) of the Rome I Regulation; Article 1(2)(c) of the Rome II Regulation.

25 Section 58 of the APIL.

Section 52 of the APIL contains special rules on the law applicable to arbitration agreement. In accordance with the general rules on contract, the parties have the right to choose the applicable law. If they fail to choose, the law governing the underlying legal relationship shall also apply to the arbitration agreement. If the parties designated the place of the arbitration, the law of that place shall apply, provided that this law is more closely connected to the agreement than the law governing the underlying legal relationship. Section 52(4) of the APIL contains a set of alternative connecting factors aimed to preserve the fomal validity of the arbitration agreement. Accordingly, the agreement is formally valid if it complies with the formal requirements of any of the above laws or the *lex fori.*

3.2 *The Rome I Regulation in the Practice of Hungarian Courts*

The Rome I Regulation comprehensively (almost exhaustively) regulates the choice-of-law questions of contracts and leaves only a very limited residual role to national regimes.[26] It has universal application; that is, it applies irrespective of whether or not the case contains an EU element and whether the law specified by the Regulation is the law of a Member State.[27]

3.2.1 Party Autonomy

The parties have the right to choose the applicable law under Article 3 of the Rome I Regulation. They may choose a law for the whole contract, or to apply to one or some of its parts, and they may choose different laws for different parts of the contract. They may also agree to change the applicable law, but this cannot prejudice the contract's formal validity and cannot adversely affect the rights of third parties.

Article 3(3)-(4) of the Rome I Regulation deals with the parties' choice of law in domestic contracts. Article 3(3) provides that the parties are free to choose the applicable law also in contracts that have no international element, but in this case the choice is only a 'choice in a substantive sense'. The mandatory rules of the law applicable in the absence of a choice cannot be derogated from, and if there is a conflict between the chosen law and the mandatory rules of the law applicable in the absence of a choice the latter prevails. Interestingly, the Regulation implicitly introduces the notion of purely EU matters (contracts)

26 Article 1 of the Rome I Regulation. For an overview of the Hungarian case-law on the Rome I Regulation, *see* Cs.I. Nagy, "Application of EU Private International Law in Hungary," in Cs.I. Nagy (ed.), *Cross-border litigation in Central-Europe: EU private international law before national courts* (Kluwer Law International, The Hague, 2022), 125–133.

27 Article 2 of the Rome I Regulation.

in Article 3(4), providing that if the contract has no connection to any country outside the EU, the parties' choice of the law of a non-EU country can 'not prejudice the application of provisions of' mandatory EU law.

Hungarian courts have applied the above provisions of the Rome I Regulation in numerous cases and have developed a case law concerning questions like implied choice, the timeframe of the parties' choice, and the effect on third parties.

In *Case Gf.40321/2014/9*,[28] the parties stipulated the application of the Hungarian Civil Code. The High Court of Appeal of Budapest considered this to be an implicit choice of Hungarian law under the Rome I Regulation.

On the other hand, in Case *Gf.40051/2014/8*,[29] the High Court of Appeal of Pécs, when examining whether the parties chose German law, found the references to the German Civil Code (BGB) insufficient because the contract also referred to the Hungarian Civil Code.

The parties were Hungarian companies (seated and registered in Hungary) and entered into a construction contract which used the '*Vergabe-und Vertragsordnung für Bauleistungen*'(VOB), a German standard contract worked out for construction projects. The VOB contains references to German law. The High Court of Appeal of Pécs held that the references by the VOB to the provisions of the German Civil Code (BGB) were not sufficient to establish the choice of German law, as the contract also contained references to certain sources of Hungarian law.

In Case *Pf.20370/2013/6*, the High Court of Appeal of Pécs apparently misconceived party autonomy and ignored the parties' choice of law without any detailed analysis. It found that the contract was invalid because the choice of Austrian law ran counter to the Rome I Regulation and the general principle of law that the law that must be applied is that of the country to which the case is most closely connected.

In Case *Pf.20024/2016/3*, the parties chose Austrian law in the contract but, during the civil proceedings, jointly asked the court to apply Hungarian law to the question of validity. The High Court of Appeal of Pécs, applying the Rome I Regulation, confirmed that the parties were free to choose different laws for different parts of the contract or different contractual questions: they had the right to choose Hungarian law to govern the existence and validity of the contract without impairing the applicability of Austrian law to the rest of the contractual issues.

28 Appealed from Case *G.40368/2012/52* (Budapest-Capital Regional Court).

29 Appealed from Case *G.40161/2013/47* (Zalaegerszeg Regional Court).

In Case *Gf.40063/2017/13*,[30] the High Court of Appeal of Budapest encountered the situation where the parties had failed explicitly to choose the applicable law and examined whether such a choice might be inferred from the circumstances. The dispute emerged in the context of a distribution contract concluded between an Austrian producer's subsidiary in Hungary and a Polish distributor. The defendant, as the distributor's parent company (owning 50 percent of the shares), provided a guarantee (suretyship) to the supplier concerning the supplier's unpaid invoices. The guarantee agreement was separate from the distribution contract, although it explicitly confirmed that the parties were familiar with the terms of the latter, and the distribution contract was also attached to the agreement. In the distribution agreement the parties chose Austrian courts and Austrian law. The guarantee agreement was, however, less explicit. While here the parties stipulated the exclusive jurisdiction of the Hungarian courts, as to the applicable law, they simply referred to the 'Act on the Civil Code'. Since the guarantee agreement was in English, it could not be argued that this reference implied the choice of Hungarian law, as – at least theoretically – this expression could refer to any civil code.

The Budapest-Capital Regional Court, upheld by the High Court of Appeal of Budapest, found that, taking into account the circumstances of the case, the above clause embedded an implicit choice of Hungarian law. First, the choice-of-law clause in the distribution contract did not extend to the guarantee agreement, because the parties to the latter specifically addressed the issues of jurisdiction and applicable law. Second, given that the parties chose Hungarian courts and one of them, the party seeking a security, was Hungarian, it could reasonably be inferred that the term 'Act on the Civil Code' referred to the Hungarian Civil Code and, in turn, the parties had implicitly chosen Hungarian law.

In Case *P.25471/2015/47*, the Budapest-Capital Regional Court dealt with the effects of choice-of-law and choice-of-court agreements on third parties under the Rome I Regulation. It held that while forum-selection clauses may not bind non-parties, the law chosen by the parties does. Choice-of-court agreements involve derogation of jurisdiction, which, as a waiver of a right, cannot bind non-parties. On the other hand, in choice of law, the parties' agreement cannot be conceived as a mutual waiver of a right and it qualifies as a connecting factor and, as such, determines the applicable law *erga omnes*.

30 Appealed from Case G.42206/2012/102 (Budapest-Capital Regional Court).

In Case *Pfv. V. 20.067/2019*,[31] the Supreme Court established that the Rome I Regulation does not time-bar the parties' freedom to choose the applicable law and they may make use of this freedom after the conclusion of the contract, even after the emergence of the legal dispute, during the court or arbitral proceedings. The choice of the applicable law may also be tacit. In this case, it was a requirement that it be clearly demonstrated by the terms of the contract or the circumstances of the case and that the parties' will could be established without doubt. At the same time, the choice of the court, in itself, does not imply a tacit choice of law. In this case, the plaintiff in his statement of claim relied on Hungarian law (expressly referring to the provisions of the then-effective Hungarian Civil Code) and the defendant responded to this in a detailed and substantive manner in his submission and presented his defense with reference to the provisions of Hungarian law. The Supreme Court considered this to be a choice of Hungarian law by indicative behavior. The Court stressed that the application of Hungarian law was not based on the parties' hypothetical will but on their clear and specific concurrence of wills.

In Case *Pfv.I.21.730/2019*,[32] the Supreme Court held that an implicit choice of law can be established under the Rome I Regulation if the parties made a choice in an earlier contract and it cannot be inferred from the circumstances that their intentions have changed, or if, in the context of the contractual rights and obligations, the parties refer to a law or other piece of legislation of a given country or if they refer to concepts of substantive law that exist only in a given country.[33] The parties' choice-of-court agreement can also indicate that they envisioned the law of the chosen court. However, forum selection in itself cannot be considered to imply the choice of the *lex fori*.[34]

3.2.2 Objective Connecting Factors

The Rome I Regulation establishes a clear but still flexible architecture for determining the *lex contractus* and a set of connecting factors relating to different specific contractual issues (see below). Where the parties do not choose the applicable law, the law generally applicable to the contract is determined by a three-layer system.

---

31 BH 2020.3.72. Appealed from Case Gf.40107/2018/8 (High Court of Appeal of Budapest), appealed from Case G.40375/2016/32 (Budapest-Capital Regional Court).

32 Reported as BH 2020.9.267. Appealed from Case Pf.20753/2019/4 (High Court of Appeal of Budapest), appealed from Case P.22918/2018/45 (Budapest-Capital Regional Court).

33 Para. 61.

34 Paras 62 and 64–66.

First, Article 4(1) of the Rome I Regulation attaches presumed connecting factors to a set of specific types of contract. As to the majority of these, the connecting factor is the habitual residence of one of the parties (the one that may be regarded as providing the contract's characteristic performance). In the case of a contract for the sale of goods this is the seller; in the case of a contract for the provision of services it is the service provider; in the case of a franchise contract, it is the franchisee; in the case of a distribution contract it is the distributor.[35] In the rest of the contracts, the applicable law is determined by the *locus*. In the case of a contract relating to a right *in rem* in or a tenancy of immovable property, the connecting factor is the location of the real estate, with the exception of tenancies for a period of no more than six consecutive months where the tenant is a natural person and the landlord and the tenant have their habitual residence in the same country. In that case, the law of this common habitual residence applies.[36] In the case of a contract for the sale of goods by auction, the connecting factor is the place where the auction is held.[37] Contracts concluded within multilateral financial trading systems are governed by the law that governs the systems in the frame of which the contract was concluded.[38]

Second, if the agreement does not come under any of the contracts listed above or combines the elements of two or more nominated contracts, the presumably applicable law is to be determined by means of the principle of characteristic performance (Article 4(2) Rome I Regulation).

Third, if the characteristic performance cannot be identified, the law that has to be applied is that of the country that has the closest connection with the contract (Article 4(3) of the Rome I Regulation).

The above connecting factors, however, entail merely rebuttable presumptions. The principle of closest connection is not only a subsidiary principle, which comes into play if the contract is not nominated and the characteristic performance cannot be determined, but may be used to depart from the above connecting factors and apply a law different from the one indicated above. Hence, the connecting factors determined for the nominated contracts and the concept of characteristic performance create only rebuttable presumptions. According to Article 4(4) of the Rome I Regulation, if the court finds that the contract is more closely connected to a different legal system, it has to

35 Article 4(1)(a)-(b) and (e)-(f) of the Rome I Regulation.
36 Article 4(1)(c)-(d) of the Rome I Regulation.
37 Article 4(1)(g) of the Rome I Regulation.
38 Article 4(1)(h) of the Rome I Regulation.

apply that law instead of the law indicated by the presumptions of Article 4(1) and (2) of the Regulation.

The above architecture is supplemented by a set of special rules governing different types of contracts. Contracts of carriage are regulated in Article 5 of the Regulation. The Rome I Regulation establishes special rules in respect of three types of contract involving a weaker party: consumer contracts (Article 6), insurance contracts (Article 7), and individual employment contracts (Article 8).

Hungarian courts have developed a significant amount of case law concerning sales contracts and contracts for the provision of services.

In Case *Pfv.I.21.730/2019*,[39] the parties, as part of an English-language settlement concluded in London, agreed that the defendants, as a form of indemnification, would for a certain price and within a certain time-limit purchase real estate located in Hungary and confer on the plaintiffs title to the real estate chosen by the latter. Nonetheless, the parties did not agree to transfer the ownership of specific estates. The Supreme Court applied the Rome I Regulation and found that this agreement came under none of the points of Article 4(1). Because it did not involve the transfer of ownership of specific properties, it did not come under Article 4(1)(c) ('contract relating to a right *in rem* in immovable property [...] shall be governed by the law of the country where the property is situated'). Instead, the court applied Article 4(2) of the Rome I Regulation (principle of characteristic performance) and concluded that, as the habitual residence of the obligor (the defendant), who promised to transfer the ownership of immovable assets, was in Hungary, Hungarian law applied. The Court noted that Article 4(3) of the Rome I Regulation also pointed to Hungarian law (most closely connected law).

In Case *43.Pf.632341/2019/4*,[40] the Budapest-Capital Regional Court held that a loan contract does not qualify as a contract for the provision of services under Article 4(1)(b) of the Rome I Regulation (which provides for the application of 'the law of the country where the service provider has his habitual residence'), but comes under Article 4(2), which provides for the application of the 'law of the country where the party required to effect the characteristic performance of the contract has his habitual residence'. The court held that the characteristic performance is effected by the creditor; hence, the two provisions pointed to the application of the same law.

39 Reported as BH 2020.9.267. Appealed from Case Pf.20753/2019/4 (High Court of Appeal of Budapest), appealed from Case P.22918/2018/45 (Budapest-Capital Regional Court).

40 Appealed from Case P.21637/2016/78 (Budapest District Court for the XX, XXI and XXIII Districts) and affirmed by Case Pfv.20211/2020/3 (Supreme Court).

In Case *Gf.20100/2017/5*,[41] the defendant, a Hungarian company, was a contractor of a construction project in Romania and hired the plaintiff, a German company, as sub-contractor. The works contract between the contractor and the Romanian customer stipulated Romanian law; however, the contract between the contractor and the sub-contractor contained no choice-of-law clause.

The High Court of Appeal of Győr, applying the Rome I Regulation, held that the works contract between the Hungarian contractor and the German sub-contractor was governed by German law, as this was the law of the party providing the characteristic performance. It found that the circumstances that the contract was concluded in Hungary, the construction was coordinated by the Hungarian company and that the contract was related, in economic terms, to another construction contract were irrelevant. Interestingly, although, as a contract for the provision of services, the works contract arguably came under Article 4(1)(b) of the Rome I Regulation, the court based its conclusion on Article 4(2), which provides that 'the contract shall be governed by the law of the country where the party required to effect the characteristic performance of the contract has his habitual residence'.

In Case *Pfv.V.20.594/2017/6*,[42] the plaintiff, a German national, and a Hungarian company concluded a contract whereby the plaintiff promised to establish a company in Russia and become the managing director of that company (including by acquiring a work permit). The plaintiff's place of living could not be ascertained; it was either Germany or Russia. The parties did not choose the applicable law. The plaintiff sued for his fee, while the defendant refused to pay, arguing that although the company was registered, the plaintiff did not acquire a work permit and, thus, could not become the company's managing director.

The Budapest-Capital Regional Court[43] affirmed the first instance court's decision[44] to apply Hungarian law. The Supreme Court upheld that judgment. Article 4(1)(b) of the Rome I Regulation provides that 'a contract for the provision of services shall be governed by the law of the country where the service provider has his habitual residence'. Article 19(1) of the Rome I Regulation defines '[t]he habitual residence of a natural person acting in the course of his business activity' as 'his principal place of business'. On the basis of this, either Russian or German law should have been applied. Nonetheless, the plaintiff's

41 Appealed from Case G.20969/2014/61 (Győr Regional Court).

42 Reported as BH 2018.9.250.

43 Case Pf.638807/2016/4 (Budapest-Capital Regional Court).

44 Case P.22689/2012/57 (Central District Court of Buda).

place of business could not be clearly ascertained. On the one hand, in the contract the plaintiff gave an address in Moscow as his place of living and his duties were to be carried out in Russia. On the other hand, had his place of living been in Russia, the plaintiff would not have needed a work permit there. Nonetheless, this question was avoided as all courts found that 'the contract [was] manifestly more closely connected with' Hungary and, hence, due to Article 4(3) of the Rome I Regulation, Hungarian law applied.

The Supreme Court, in line with the Budapest-Capital Regional Court, reasoned that the contract had no connection to either German or Russian law. The parties had envisioned entering into an employment contract under Russian law once the plaintiff had acquired the necessary work permit and concluded the service contract for the interim period. When concluding the contract, the parties were aware of the opportunity to choose the applicable law. They agreed that the the employment contract, which was to be concluded after the acquisition of the work permit, should be governed by Russian law, but did not choose the law applicable to the provisional service agreement. In fact, the purpose of the latter was to avoid breaching the Russian rules on employment (the contract was concluded between the plaintiff and the defendant and not the plaintiff and the Russian company that was supposed to be his later employer). The Supreme Court established that the parties wanted to make use of the possibilities offered by the internal market and, at the time the contract was concluded, none of them wished to have Russian law applied. The Court inferred that the reason why the parties did not choose the law applicable to the service contract was that they considered it to be truly provisional and the choice of the applicable law not to be relevant. The Supreme Court noted that this also underpinned the conclusion that the business relationship between the parties, as well as the contractual construction was more closely connected to the defendant's personal law, that is, Hungarian law.[45]

In Case *Gf.20090/2020/5*, the parties concluded a service contract. The High Court of Appeal of Győr established that, due to Articles 4(1)(b) and 19 of the Rome I Regulation, Hungarian law applied, because the service provider's principal place of business was in Hungary. The Court stressed that the fact that the service was provided in Austria (place of performance) could, in itself, not give rise to the application of the escape clause contained in Article 4(3) of the Regulation.

45 Para. 52.

3.2.3 Special Contractual Issues

In Articles 10–18 the Rome I Regulation sets out special rules (connecting factors) for specific contractual issues.

Article 10(1) of the Regulation provides that consent and material validity are governed by the law that would otherwise govern the contract if the contract were to come into existence and were valid. Article 10(2) adds, however, that 'a party, in order to establish that he or she did not consent, may rely upon the law of the country in which he or she has his habitual residence if it appears from the circumstances that it would not be reasonable to determine the effect of his conduct in accordance with the law' that governs the contract.

A good example of the potential application of Article 10(2) of the Regulation is the German legal institution of 'confirmation letter' ('*kaufmännisches Beschtätigungsschreiben*'). The confirmation letter is sent after the conclusion of the agreement (which may occur orally or by telephone or telex). The fundamental rule is that if the receiver of the letter remains silent, the content of the contract is determined by the confirmation letter unless the sender did not observe the requirement of good faith or the difference between the initial agreement and the confirmation letter is so great that the sender could not reasonably have expected the receiver to approve it. The confirmation letter works also in cases where the parties 'almost' concluded the initial agreement ('*abschlussreif*'). In this case the letter not only confirms or changes but creates the contract. The receiver is expected to object immediately; otherwise, the letter determines the content of the agreement. The notion of the confirmation letter is a commercial law concept; nevertheless, only the receiver needs to be a merchant.

Although confirmation letters may have evidentiary value in different legal systems, their decisive impact on the content of contractual relationships is peculiar to German law.[46] In Hungarian law, silence, in itself, infers no agreement. The parties' concurrence of wills is based on an offer and an acceptance, and the same rule applies to amendment of the contract. Hence, the silence of the recipient of a confirmation letter, in itself, does not infer agreement.

Assume that a German and a Hungarian enterprise, after several long weeks of negotiation, reach a compromise whereby the Hungarian firm becomes the distributor of the German supplier's products. The parties conclude no written agreement, but their email conversation and the minutes of the meetings reveal a consensus on the substantial issues, including the choice of German

---

46 M. Esser, Commercial Letters of Confirmation in International Trade: Austrian, French, German and Swiss Law and Uniform Law Under the 1980 Sales Convention, available at http://www.cisg.law.pace.edu/cisg/biblio/esser.html#me*.

law. Nonetheless, the concurrence of wills does not extend to several details, such as the interest rate for late payment. After the conclusion of the verbal agreement, the German party sends a long and elaborate confirmation letter. The Hungarian party does not react to this but starts reselling the products. Based on German law, the German firm's confirmation letter determines the substance of the contract, and the Hungarian firm would be obliged to pay very high interest for late payments. Nonethless, the Hungarian reseller may argue that although the effects of the confirmation letter are, in principle, to be determined on the basis of the law that would apply to the contract, it would not be reasonable to determine the effect of his conduct in accordance with German law, given that in Hungarian law confirmation letters lack legal force. At the same time, the German party may argue that, even if the confirmation letter cannot have substantive-law effects, it may have evidentiary effects. In other words, an unresponded and unobjected to confirmation letter shifts to the addressee the burden of proof that the initial agreement differed from the subsequent confirmation letter. Article 18(1) of the Regulation provides that '[t]he law governing a contractual obligation under this Regulation shall apply to the extent that, in matters of contractual obligations, it contains rules which raise presumptions of law or determine the burden of proof'.

Article 11 of the Rome I Regulation sets out alternative connecting factors for formal validity to save the contract if it is formally invalid under the *lex contractus*. This provision does not apply to consumer contracts, since here the formal requirement serves the purpose of protecting the consumer as the weaker party.

If the contract is concluded between persons present in the same country, the law of the country where the contract was concluded can save it (*locus regit actum*) if it is eventually formally invalid under the *lex contractus*. If the contract is concluded between persons present in different countries, the contract is valid if it satisfies the formal requirements of the *lex contractus*, the law of the place where any of the parties was present when concluding the contract or the law of the habitual residence of any of the parties.

Article 11(3) of the Rome I Regulation deals with unilateral acts done in the context of an existing or contemplated contract, for instance, declarations and notices of termination, rescission, cancellation, the exercise of other rights for breach of contract (e.g., price reduction, determination of a grace period) and the exercise of an option). They are formally valid if they comply with the *lex contractus*, the *lex loci actus,* or the law of the habitual residence of the person who carries out the act.

Article 11(5) of the Rome I Regulation subjects contracts concerning *in rem* rights in or tenancies of real estate to the unconditionally applicable formal requirements of the *situs* (which are imposed irrespective of where the contract is concluded and which law governs the contract, and cannot be derogated from by agreement). This provision has practical relevance only if the parties do not change the applicable law. According to Article 4(1)(c) of the Rome I Regulation, these contracts anyway come under the *lex rei sitae*, which is the law Article 11(5) points to.

The above provision raises an interesting question of interpretation under Hungarian law. On the one hand, simple written form is sufficient for the formal validity of contracts concerning *in rem* rights in immovable property.[47] On the other hand, simple written contracts cannot serve as the basis of an entry into the land registry. Entries may be made only on the basis of deeds that meet extra formal requirements, such as deeds countersigned by an attorney and notarial deeds. This creates a divergence between the fomal validity of the contract and its registrability in the land registry. It is notworthy that, according to Hungarian property law, registration is constitutive: albeit that, in certain exceptional cases, legal title to real estate can be acquired without registration (for instance, in cases of adverse possession and matrimonial common property), the acquisition of *in rem* rights, in principle, requires registration. If a written contract does not meet the formal requirements established by the land registry, the contract may still be valid, but not registrable. In this case, the party may seek a declaratory judgment which, in turn, can serve as the basis of registration. This means that the formal requirements governing registrability in the land registry are not covered by Article 11(5) of the Rome I Regulation, as they are not mandatory and do not affect the validity of the contract.

Article 12(2) of the Rome I Regulation provides that '[i]In relation to the manner of performance and the steps to be taken in the event of defective performance, regard shall be had to the law of the country in which performance takes place'. This provision does not prescribe the application of the *lex loci solutionis* but provides for its consideration. The *lex contractus* remains applicable to the question of performance and the steps to be taken in the event of defective performance, but the law of the place of performance must be taken into account to avoid unforseen effects.

Article 13 of the Rome I Regulation aims to obviate unforseen effects concerning incapacity, which is otherwise a question of personal law. A party may have no or scant information about the position of the other party's personal law on capacity and, hence, may, without knowing, conclude a contract with a

47 See Civil Law Doctrinal Decision XXV on the validity of contracts for transfers of real estate.

person who has no contractual capacity. According to Article 13, where a contract is concluded *inter praesentes* and the natural person has capacity under the *lex loci actus*, that person 'may invoke his incapacity resulting from the law of another country, only if the other party to the contract was aware of that incapacity at the time of the conclusion of the contract or was not aware thereof as a result of negligence'.

Article 14 of the Rome I Regulation deals with the issues of assignment and contractual subrogation. Here two legal relationships are to be distinguished. The first is the relationship between the assignor and the assignee, which is an independent 'sale of claim' agreement. This relationship is characterized by the privity of the assignor and the assignee, which has, in principle, nothing to do with the claim sold. Accordingly, '[t]he relationship between assignor and assignee under a voluntary assignment or contractual subrogation of a claim against another person (the debtor) shall be governed by the law that applies to the contract between the assignor and assignee under this Regulation'.[48] Nevertheless, this principle is not applicable to the questions attached to the 'act of assignment', like the assigned or subrogated claim's 'assignability, the relationship between the assignee and the debtor, the conditions under which the assignment or subrogation can be invoked against the debtor and whether the debtor's obligations have been discharged'. For instance, different laws may regulate differently whether the claim can be assigned at all, whether and when the debtor is to be notified about the assignment, whether the debtor can object to the assignment or set off against the assignee claims he or she has against the assignor (the original creditor). These questions cannot be separated from the law governing the contractual claim 'to be sold', and, hence, are subjected to '[t]he law governing the assigned or subrogated claim'.[49] Under Article 14, '[t]he concept of assignment in this Article includes outright transfers of claims, transfers of claims by way of security and pledges or other security rights over claims'.[50]

Legal subrogation raises an additional question: which law governs the question whether the claim is transferred by law? Article 15 provides that this question is governed by the law that obliges the third person to pay instead of the debtor. Assume that a French insurer concludes an insurance contract with an English company, subjecting their agreement to English law. Subsequently, a Hungarian firm causes damage to the English company in Hungary, and it, in turn, submits a claim to the French insurer. Assume that the English company's

48 Article 14(1).
49 Article 14(2).
50 Article 14(3).

claim for damages against the Hungarian firm is governed by Hungarian law, as this is the place where the damage occurred,[51] and the insurance contract is governed by French law by reason of the parties' choice of law. As French law is applicable to the French insurer's duty to satisfy the English company, this law will determine whether and to what extent the insurer has stepped into the shoes of the English company to enforce the claim against the Hungarian tortfeaser. Obviously, the question whether the English company has a valid claim at all remains governed by Hungarian law.[52]

Unfortunately, Article 15 of the Rome I Regulation is silent as to some important questions. First, it does not tell us which law governs the legal subrogation if the third party satisfies the creditor without being obliged to do so. For instance, the buyer realizes that the real estate purchased serves as a collateral and decides to pay the full amount of the loan to the bank in order to avoid the auctioning of the property. This situation may give rise to legal subrogation, though the third party had no duty to satisfy the bank. Article 15 reckons with this situation ('or has in fact satisfied the creditor in discharge of that duty') but still determines the applicable law with reference to the law governing the third person's duty to satisfy the creditor. Second, Article 15 is at fault for determining the law that governs the defenses (objections, set-off) of the debtor.

Article 16 of the Rome I Regulation determines the law applicable to contribution among debtors having multiple (joint and several) liability. This states that 'the law governing the debtor's obligation towards the creditor also governs the debtor's right to claim recourse from the other debtors. The other debtors may rely on the defences they had against the creditor to the extent allowed by the law governing their obligations towards the creditor'.

Set-off is 'governed by the law applicable to the claim against which the right to set-off is asserted'.[53]

According to the generally accepted principle, procedure is governed by the *lex fori*. Article 1(3) of the Rome I Regulation excludes evidence and procedure from the Regulation's scope. Nonetheless, the distinction between substantive and procedural questions may raise questions of characterization. Article 18 of the Rome I Regulation addresses an important set of these delimitation issues: the burden of proof and legal presumptions. Although predominantly a procedural question, substantive law may establish rules on the burden of

51 See Article 4(1) of the Rome II Regulation.

52 An interesting question of interpretation arises if the surrogation is based on both law and contract.

53 Article 17 of the Rome I Regulation.

proof in certain cases. For instance, under Hungarian tort law a person who caused damage can exonerate himself by proving that he or she was not at fault.[54] This burden of proof is allocated by Section 6:519 of the Civil Code, that is, by substantive law. Article 18(1) of the Rome I Regulation provides that the *lex contractus* also applies to the burden of proof and legal presumptions, as long as these issues are regulated by the substantive law of the legal system invoked. Furthermore, Article 18(2) of the Rome I Regulation provides that a 'contract or an act intended to have legal effect may be proved by any mode of proof recognised by the law of the forum or by any of the laws referred to in Article 11 under which that contract or act is formally valid, provided that such mode of proof can be administered by the forum'. The language of the provision suggests that this term embraces only the methods of proof (written evidence, parole evidence, digital evidence, etc.) and not the presumptions and evidentiary values attached to the different types of deeds (deed signed by two witnesses, deed counter-signed by an attorney, notarial deeds, etc.).

4 Non-contractual Obligations

EU legislation almost entirely took over national rules on non-contractual obligations. The Rome II Regulation comprehensively (almost exhaustively) regulates the choice-of-law questions of non-contractual obligations and leaves only a very limited residual role to national regimes. The Regulation has universal application, that is, it applies irrespective of whether the case contains an EU element and whether or not the law specified by the Regulation is the law of a Member State.[55] Notable matters not covered by the Rome II Regulation include non-contractual obligations arising out of company law including the personal liability of officers and members for the obligations of the company and the personal liability of auditors to the company or its members in the statutory audits of accounting documents, nuclear damage, and violations of privacy and rights relating to personality, including defamation.[56]

4.1 *Hungarian Choice-of-Law Rules*

Sections 60–63 of the APIL set out the choice-of-law rules on non-contractual obligations. These rules are of limited relevance, given the Rome II Regulation's

54 Section 6:519 of the Civil Code.
55 Article 2 of the Rome I Regulation.
56 Article 1(2) of the Rome II Regulation.

wide scope and the fact that the APIL's rules are generally modeled on the Rome II Regulation.

As regards party autonomy, there is an important difference between the APIL and the Rome II Regulation. The APIL allows the choice of the applicable law only after the event has occured (the legal relationship has come into existence). Under the Rome II Regulation, economic entitites may make a choice at any time (before or after the event occurrs) and the *ex post facto* limitation applies only to cases where not all the parties are pursuing an economic activity. According to Section 63 of the APIL, the parties have the right to choose, explicitly or implicitly, the applicable law but only after the legal relationship has emerged. On the other hand, Article 14 of the Rome II Regulation also enables the parties to choose the applicable law beforehand, provided 'all the parties are pursuing a commercial activity'.

The rules on the law applicable to non-contractual obligations absent party choice are set out in Sections 60–62 of the APIL, which mirror Article 4 of the Rome II Regulation. If the parties do not choose the applicable law the principle of *lex loci damni* applies. If the habitual residence of the parties is in the same state, the law of that state shall apply. If the non-contractual legal relationship is closely connected to a pre-existing legal relationship, the law governing the latter shall apply to this legal relationship too.

The old APIL, in Sections 32–35, followed the principle of *lex loci delicti commissi* (*delictum* implied both conduct and omission), which was supplemented by the ubiquity principle (the law of the country where the damage occurred, i.e. the *lex loci damni*, was to be applied if it was more favorable to the injured person), the notion of common domicile (common place of living), and the application of the *lex bandi* in the case of registered watercraft and aircraft. Special connecting factors were applied to the question whether a person was capable of being liable for the loss and to traffic regulations. The currently effective APIL discarded this principle and switched to the *lex loci damni*. The legislative choice to adopt the approach of the Rome II Regulation and, thus, to create harmony between the EU and national choice-of-law rules was justified by the fact that the overwhelming majority of tort matters come under the Rome II Regulation and the APIL's rules play a very marginal role in this field.

4.2 *The Rome II Regulation in the Practice of Hungarian Courts*

The Rome II Regulation regulates non-contractual obligations in a rather exhaustive manner. Besides delictual liability (torts), it also covers unjust enrichment, *negotiorum gestio,* and *culpa in contrahendo*. Furthermore, the regulation covers not only claims for damages but also claims emerging from events that are likely to cause damage.[57] The rules of the Rome II Regulation have universal application, i.e., they are to be applied irrespective of whether or not they lead to the application of the law of an EU Member State.[58]

Hungarian courts have produced a significant amount of case law concerning the Rome II Regulation. This has extended, among others, to questions like the difference between contractual and non-contractual matters, the Regulations's exclusion of violations of personality rights, party autonomy, and the determination of the place where the damage occurred.[59]

4.2.1 Scope of Application; Delimitation of Contractual and Delictual Matters

The distinction between contractual and delictual matters may raise questions of interpretation under the Rome II Regulation in matters where the plaintiff's claim may be considered both contractual and delictual.

If the injured person has insurance cover for the risk (damaging event), the law applicable to the delictual matter is to be separated from the legal relationship between the insurer and the insured, as well as from the subrogation of the insured person's claim to the insurer. In Case *Pf.VIII.22.740/1997/3.*, the Austrian shipper contracted with an Austrian forwarding company for transporting certain goods from Vienna to St. Petersburg; the latter contracted with a Hungarian company for the carriage of the goods. At the same time, the shipper concluded an insurance contract with an Austrian insurer, which covered the loss of the consignment. As the goods did not arrive at the place of destination, the Austrian insurer compensated the Austrian shipper for the loss and, afterwards, it sued the carrier directly. Since the plaintiff did not sue the forwarding company, the shipper had a direct contractual relationship with, the Supreme Court considered it to be non-contractual and applied the corresponding choice-of-law rules, applying Hungarian law to this issue. In respect of the question whether the insurer acquired the Austrian shipper's claim due to subrogation, the Supreme Court applied Austrian law and established the statutory subrogation of the claim.

In Case *P.24487/2012/47*, the Hungarian plaintiff sued a Greek hospital for medical malpractice that occurred in Greece. The plaintiff was spending his

57 Article 2 of the Rome II Regulation.

58 Article 3.

59 For an overview of the Hungarian case-law on the Rome II Regulation, *see* Cs.I. Nagy, "Application of EU Private International Law in Hungary," in Cs.I. Nagy (ed.), *Cross-border litigation in Central-Europe: EU private international law before national courts* (*Kluwer Law International*, The Hague, 2022), 134–137.

vacation in Greece and suffered serious injuries in a traffic accident. In the hospital he was mistreated, which resulted in his permanent bodily injury. The case could have given rise to both contractual and delictual claims against the hospital. The Budapest-Capital Regional Court avoided deciding the issue whether the claim was contractual or delictual in nature (or both). It identified the applicable law under both the Rome II Regulation and the choice-of-law rules of contracts (the case occurred before the Rome I Regulation's entry into force) and concluded that both led to the same law (Greek law).

Issues of characterization and scope emerged in cases involving traffic accidents. Courts have considered the law applicable to delictual liability to extend to the rules on compulsory motor vehicle liability insurance. While in the cases encountered by the courts this entailed no practical problems (because the *lex contractus* as to the insurance contract and the law applicable to the tort were the same), this summary approach will have to be rectified in cases where the wrongdoer's insurance contract is governed by a law different from that of the tort.

In Case *Pfv.20852/2014/6*,[60] although both the tortfeasor and the victim were Hungarian citizens and the accident happened in Hungary, the Supreme Court examined the question of applicable law, as the car owned by the plaintiff was registered in Germany. The Supreme Court held that Hungarian law was applicable to the claim and, as part of that, also applied Act LXII of 2009 on mandatory motor vehicle liability insurance. Interestingly, Act LXII of 2009 addresses various issues related to the motor vehicle liability insurance contract: the duty to have insurance coverage, the conclusion and termination of the insurance contract, the insurance company's payment obligation and extent, the geographical and temporal scope of the insurance contract, the payment of the insurance fee, the insurance company's right of subrogation, etc.

Although in the case concerned this made no substantive difference, it has to be noted that the Court's reference appears to have been excessive and treating the rules on mandatory motor vehicle insurance as delictual in nature may be regarded as an error of characterization. The Rome II Regulation determines the law applicable to non-contractual obligations (the relationship between the tortfeasor and the injured person) and does not apply to contractual obligations (the relationship between the tortfeasor and the insurance company it has a contract with). It may have made a difference (that may have made the Supreme Court engage in a more detailed characterization) if the wrongdoer's

60 Appealed from Case Pf.640701/2013/4 (Budapest-Capital Regional Court), appealed from Case P.87875/2012/31 (Pest Central District Court).

motor vehicle had been stationed in another Member State and he had had a contract with a foreign insurance company.

The same was established in Case *Pf.641647/2013/4*,[61] where the Budapest-Capital Regional Court applied Hungarian law (as that of the place of the accident) and the Hungarian rules on mandatory motor vehicle liability insurance.

In Case *Pfv.VIII.20.109/2019*,[62] the Supreme Court encountered an interesting question of characterization. Article 1(2)(g) excludes non-contractual obligations arising out of violations of privacy and rights relating to personality, including defamation, from the scope of the Rome II Regulation. In Hungarian law, personality rights have a wide meaning and extend to protection against various illicit acts entailing non-monetary damage (e.g., personal injury). In this case, the parents claimed non-monetary damage because their child was killed in a traffic accident, as this impaired their personality right to the protection of private and family life.[63] As a corollary, under Hungarian law the legal basis of the claim for damages was the violation of a personality right. Nonetheless, the Supreme Court held that the terms used in Article 1(2)(g) of the Rome II Regulation have to be given an autonomous meaning and the term 'personality rights' has a narrower import under the Regulation than under Hungarian law. The Supreme Court established that a closer look at the legislative history demonstrates that Article 1(2)(g) of the Rome II Regulation is destined to address violations of personality rights committed via the media and the EU legislator aimed to create a uniform regime for delictual claims emerging from traffic accidents as to both personal injuries and monetary damages. This finds reflection also in various parts of the preamble to and the provisions of the Regulation, such as recitals (17) and (33) and Articles 2(1) and 4(1).[64] This was confirmed also in Case C-350/14 *Florin Lazar v Allianz SpA*.[65] As a corollary, the Supreme Court applied English law.[66]

4.2.2 Party Autonomy

Article 14 of the Rome II Regulation gives the parties the freedom to choose the law applicable to the non-contractual relationship. This freedom applies

61 Appealed from Case P.101521/2011/42 (Pest Central District Court). Affirmed in Case Pfv.21135/2014/4 (Supreme Court).

62 Reported as BH 2020.8.242, appealed from Case Pf.633945/2018/6 (Budapest-Capital Regional Court), appealed from Case P.89585/2015/55 (Central District Court of Pest).

63 Para. 22.

64 Para. 24.

65 EU:C:2015:802, paras 25–26.

66 Para. 27.

to non-contracutal obligations in general and not just to delictual matters, with the exeptions related to matters concerning unfair competition and acts restricting free competition,[67] and the infringement of intellectual property rights.[68] As to relations between enterprises, the applicable law can be chosen without time restriction, while in all other cases that can be done only after the emergence of the non-contractual relationship. Accordingly, choice of law is generally allowed in the case of business-to-business transactions, while in that of business-to-consumer and consumer-to-consumer transactions this can take place only after the event has occurred.[69] Article 14(2) and (3) of the Rome II Regulation provides that choice of law in purely domestic and purely EU matters has to be conceived as 'choice in a substantive sense'.

Hungarian courts have been very permissive as to party autonomy.

In Case *P.21013/2011/49*, the parties requested the court to apply Hungarian law. The Győr Regional Court treated this as a choice-of-law agreement under Article 14(1) of the Rome II Regulation.

In Case *Pf.631007/2014/3*,[70] the parties chose Hungarian law in the appeal proceedings and the Budapest-Capital Regional Court considered this a valid choice. It must be noted that the first instance court applied Hungarian law, as the law applicable absent the parties' choice; the appeal court disagreed with the first instance court on this but accepted the parties' agreement on the application of Hungarian law. The sanctioning of this belated party choice goes against scholarship's majority opinion that the applicable law can be chosen at any time until the first instance judgment is entered.[71] Furthermore, the 2017 APIL, adopted since then, specifically limits the choice of the applicable law to the preliminary stage of the first instance proceedings.[72]

4.2.3 Objective Connecting Factors for Delictual Liability

The Regulation establishes an elaborate scheme for delictual liability, which consists of a general rule (Article 4) and several special rules tailored to the particulars of delictual matters: product liability (Article 5), unfair competition and acts restricting free competition (Article 6), environmental damage

67 Article 6(4) of the Rome II Regulation.
68 Article 8(4) of the Rome II Regulation.
69 Article 14 of the Rome II Regulation.
70 Appealed from Case P.8921013/2012/31 (Central District Court of Pest).
71 Cs.I. Nagy, *Private International Law in Hungary* (Kluwer, 2012). 76–77, para 158.
72 Section 50(2) of the 2017 APIL.

(Article 7), infringement of intellectual property rights (Article 8),[73] and industrial action (Article 9).

The Rome II Regulation's general rule on delictual liability (torts) consists of three layers: the law of the country where the damage occurred (*lex loci damni*), the law of the common habitual residence,[74] and an escape clause based on the principle of closest connection.

According to the general rule, the law applicable to a non-contractual obligation arising out of a tort/delict shall be the law of the country in which the damage occurs irrespective of the country in which the event giving rise to the damage occurred and irrespective of the country or countries in which the indirect consequences of that event occur.[75]

The Regulation discarded the principle of *lex loci delicti commissi* (the law of the place where the harmful action or omission occurred). At the same time, it must be noted that the *damnum* relevant from the point of view of determining the applicable law should not be confused with the *damnum* in relation to which the tortfeasor may be liable under substantive law. From the perspective of choice of law, not all detriments resulting from an injurious act or omission (delict, tort), but only direct ones, are to be taken into account.[76] The place of the *damnum* is to be established irrespective of the 'indirect consequences'. Obviously, the foregoing is far from implying that the indirect consequences would not be relevant from a substantive law point of view. Quite the contrary: Article 4(1) of the Rome II Regulation deals exclusively with the choice-of-law relevance of indirect damage. Recital 17 of the Regulation provides clear guidance in this regard: in cases of personal injury or damage to property, the country in which the damage occurs should be the country where the injury was sustained or the property was damaged. Accordingly, the *lex loci damni* approach leads to the application of a law different from the law of the place

73 Article 8 applies to non-contractual obligations arising from an infringement of an intellectual property right also where the infringement is not delictual but arises from unjust enrichment, *negotiorum gestio*, or *culpa in contrahendo*. Article 13 of the Rome II Regulation.

74 The Rome II Regulation does not define the term 'habitual residence' for natural persons acting outside their business, see Art. 23. See also T.C. Hartley, "Choice of Law for non-contractual liability: selected problems under the Rome II Regulation," 57 *International and Comparative Law Quarterly* (2008) 899–908, at 902. The terms may have been borrowed from the Hague conventions which, nevertheless, consitently refrain from defining this concept.

75 Article 4(1) of the Rome II Regulation.

76 See Cs.I. Nagy, "A jogellenes károkozás kollíziós szabályai a Róma II Rendeletben," 55 *Magyar Jog* (2008), 542–549, at 543–544.

of the *delictum* mainly in the case of distance delicts, where the conduct (or omission) and the loss caused occur in different countries.

The principle of common domicile became, in effect, a standard principle in the field of delictual liability.[77] The Rome II Regulation provides that if the habitual residence of the parties is in the same country, it is not the *lex loci damni* but the common habitual residence that determines the applicable law. According to Article 4(2) of the Rome II Regulation: where the person claimed to be liable and the person sustaining damage both have their habitual residence in the same country at the time when the damage occurs, the law of that country shall apply.

Finally, the third step of the Rome II Regulation contains an escape clause,[78] which authorizes the court to apply the law of another country if it is clear from all the circumstances of the case that the tort/delict is manifestly more closely connected with that country. A manifestly closer connection with another country might be based in particular on a pre-existing relationship between the parties, such as a contract, that is closely connected with the tort/delict in question.[79]

Hungarian courts have developed an extensive case law in the application of the Regulation.

In Case *P.24487/2012/47,* when it came to the application of the principle of *lex loci damni*, the Budapest-Capital Regional Court, in line with preamble (17) to the Rome II Regulation, took into account the direct damage alone (personal injury in Greece) and considered the indirect (consequential) damage occurring in Hungary to be irrelevant in the context of determining the applicable law. This is noteworthy in the light of the circumstance that, concerning jurisdiction, the Court found that the indirect damage sustained in Hungary gave rise to Hungarian jurisdiction under the Brussels I Regulation and otherwise established the liability of the Greek defendant for that indirect damage based on Greek substantive law.

On the other hand, in Case *P.24479/2015/96*,[80] the Budapest District Court for the II and III Districts erroneously construed the principle of *lex loci damni*.

---

77 The principle's roots are to be found in the German *Rechtsanwendungsverordnung* of December 7, 1942 (RGBl. I 706), see J. Kropholler, *Internationales Privatrecht* (Mohr Siebeck, Tübingen, 2004), 516–518, in the US judgment in *Babcock v Jackson*, 12 N.Y. 2d 473 (1963), and in the House of Lords judgment in *Boys v Chaplin* [1969] 2 All ER 1085.

78 See recital 14 of the Rome II Regulation.

79 Article 4(3) of the Rome II Regulation.

80 The judgment was appealed but the question of the law applicable was not revisited. Case Pf.632162/2019/4 (Budapest-Capital Regional Court).

The Hungarian plaintiff suffered serious injuries in a traffic accident abroad. The Court applied Hungarian law because the plaintiff's place of living was in Hungary; thus, the bulk of the damage emerged in Hungary (permanent bodily injury, medical treatment, loss of earnings). This goes against recital (17) to the Rome II Regulation, which provides that, when determining the place of loss with the purpose of determining the applicable law, direct damage alone is to be taken into account.

In Case *Pfv.V.20.490/2018/10*,[81] the Supreme Court held, in the context of a traffic accident which occurred in Germany, that the existence and extent of delictual liability is governed by the Rome II Regulation and, hence, German law applies irrespective of whether the injured person sues the tortfeasor or the insurer directly.

As to the purview of the law applicable under the Rome II Regulation, the Supreme Court interpreted Article 15 of the Regulation. It held that the notions contained in this provision had an autonomous EU-law meaning. As regards Article 15(c), which provides that the law to be applied under the Rome II Regulation extends to 'the existence, the nature and the assessment of damage or the remedy claimed', the Supreme Court established that this provision embraces the question whether in-kind or pecuniary compensation must be awarded and, in the latter case, which rules apply in the event that there is a delay in payment. As a corollary, the Court concluded that default interests come under Article 15(c) of the Rome II Regulation and, hence, in this case they were governed by German law.

4.2.4 Objective Connecting Factors for Unjust Enrichment, *Negotiorum Gestio,* and *Culpa in Contrahendo*

Article 10 of the Rome II Regulation sets out four subsidiary connecting factors to determine the law applicable to unjust enrichment. First, if the unjust enrichment occurs in the context of a pre-existing legal relationship, the law governing this legal relationship is to be applied to the question of unjust enrichment. Second, in the absence of such a pre-existing legal relationship, if the parties have their habitual residence in the same country, the law of that country is applicable.[82] Third, if the law cannot be determined on the basis of the foregoing rules, the law that has to be applied is that of the country in which the unjust enrichment took place. Finally, Article 10 contains an escape

81 Reported as BH 2019.10.270.

82 Cf. the application of the law of common domicile in the case of delicts.

clause: if the matter is more closely connected to another country, the law of that country shall be applied.

Article 11 of the Rome II Regulation uses essentially the same model to determine the law applicable to *negotiorum gestio*, with the difference that in the third step – in the absence of a pre-existing legal relationship and common habitual residence – the *lex loci actus* (law of the country 'in which the act was performed') has to be applied. The concept of 'manifestly closest connection' applies as an escape clause in the fourth step.

The classification of the *culpa in contrahendo* as contractual or non-contractual is diverse in the various legal systems. The Rome II Regulation treats it as a non-contractual obligation, but when it comes to the connecting factor, it subjects the question, in principle, to the *lex contractus*. According to Article 12(1) of the Rome II Regulation, '[t]he law applicable to a non-contractual obligation arising out of dealings prior to the conclusion of a contract, regardless of whether the contract was actually concluded or not, shall be the law that applies to the contract or that would have been applicable to it had it been entered into'. If the applicable law cannot be identified on the basis of the foregoing provision, the connecting factors of delictual liability (Article 4 of the Rome II Regulation) apply: these are the *lex loci damni*, the law of the parties' common habitual residence, and the principle of closest connection.[83]

5 Property Law

5.1 *The General Principle of Lex Rei Sitae*

In principle, *in rem* rights (ownership, usufruct, right to use, mortgage, pledge, possession, easements, etc.) are governed by the law of the country where the property is located (*lex rei sitae*).[84] This applies to both movable and immovable property. As set out below, the APIL establishes quite a few exceptions to the *lex rei sitae* principle as to movables but not as to immovables, which are always subject to the *lex rei sitae*.

The APIL contains no specific rules on pollution. It can be established that the property law aspects of pollution are governed by the *lex rei sitae*, and the delictual aspects by the law applicable to torts (which is determined, predominantly, by the Rome II Regulation). The distinction between the two legal categories may raise questions of characterization, which, pursuant to Section 4 of

83 Article 12(1) of the Rome II Regulation.

84 Section 39 of the APIL.

the APIL, has to be carried out, at least in principle, according to Hungarian law, while the terms of the Rome II Regualtion have to be construed autonomously.

The APIL contains no specific rules on expropriation. The act of expropriation is generally viewed as having a public law nature and, as such, falls outside the scope of the APIL. On the other hand, the property consequences of expropriation (such as acquisition of title, the character of the mode of acquisition) are property-law questions and governed by the *lex rei sitae*.

The law applicable to the main thing also extends to its components and accessories. Other connections between and the aggregate of things are governed by the most closely connected law.[85]

The relevant moment from the point of view of the *situs* is the moment when the fact triggering the legal effect comes into existence. In the case of adverse possession, this is the time when the term of acquisitive prescription ends. The adverse possession of movables is governed by the law of the state where the property is situated when the prescriptive deadline expires. The mere fact that the location of the property changes does not interrupt the flow of prescription.[86]

An example could clarify the above rules. The deadline of prescription under Hungarian law is ten years for movables and 15 years for immovables.[87] Under Austrian law the deadline of prescription is basically 30 years.[88] If someone in Vienna possesses an artwork for 15 years and takes it to Szeged (Hungary) to an exhibition and then brings it back to the Austrian capital, he or she acquires legal title over it, since at the end of the deadline the property is located in Hungary. However, in such a case, the court may apply Austrian law on the basis of the general excape clause embedded in Section 10 of the APIL on the ground that, although the specific choice-of-law rule points to Hungarian law, the matter is more closely connected with Austrian law.

Section 41(1)-(2) of the APIL deals with the change of the *situs*. In this case, 'the rights acquired previously may be recognised in accordance with the law of the new place of location of the thing. If the legal effect of the acquisition of a right in rem did not take place at the previous place of location and the movable thing is relocated to the territory of another state permanently, the law of this latter state shall apply to the acquisition of rights'.

85 Section 39(3) of the APIL.
86 Section 41(3)-(4) of the APIL.
87 Section 5:44(1) of the Civil Code.
88 Section 1468 of the Austrian Civil Code (ABGB).

5.2 *Exceptions to the Lex Rei Sitae*

The APIL establishes several exceptions to the general principle of *lex rei sitae*. First, Sections 42–44 of the APIL set out objective different connecting factors in respect of movable property. Second, Sections 44(3) and (5), 45 and 47 provide for party autonomy in certain cases and allow the choice of particular laws. Third, Section 46 establishes special rules for cultural goods.

5.2.1 Special Objective Connecting Factors

Registered vessels and aircraft are governed by the *lex bandi* (flag, emblem), railways by the law of the state where they were put into operation.[89] Goods in transit (*res in transitu*) come under the law of the state of destination; however, the *lex rei sitae* applies to their eventual forced sale, storage, and pledging. The passenger's personal law governs his personal items.[90]

The *lex rei sitae* also applies to security rights of an *in rem* character, including mortgage.[91] Nonetheless, Section 44 of the APIL contains special rules for *in rem* security rights. Such rights created (coming into existence) by registration are governed by the law of the state where the register is kept. This rule does not apply to registered *in rem* security rights, but only to those which are subject to constitutive registration, that is, that are created by the registration itself. If the coming into existence of the *in rem* security right does not require registration or the place of the register cannot be established, the applicable law will be the security debtor's personal law.[92] Security rights concerning payment accounts, bank deposits, or dematerialized negotiable instruments are governed by the law of the country where the register or account is kept or the central depository system operates.[93] Security rights over claims are governed by the law chosen by the parties or, if they make no choice, by the *locus* of the register, and, in the absence of registration, by the security debtor's personal law.[94]

5.2.2 Party Autonomy

In certain cases, the APIL authorizes the parties to choose the law applicable to *in rem* rights. A common feature of these rules is that they apply in specific cases and limit the choice to the law or laws offered by the APIL. In a case of

89 Section 42 of the APIL.
90 Section 43 of the APIL.
91 Cs.I. Nagy, *Nemzetközi magánjog* (HVG-Orac, Budapest, 2017) 115.
92 Section 44(1)-(2) of the APIL.
93 Section 44(4) of the APIL.
94 Section 44(5) of the APIL.

reservation of title, the parties may choose the law of the place of destination instead of the *lex rei sitae*, which would apply otherwise.[95] The parties may choose the law as to security rights over a claim; as an exception to other cases of property law party autonomy, here, the APIL establishes no restriction as to which law they may choose.[96] In the case of transfer of ownership over a movable, the parties may choose, instead of the *lex rei sitae*, the law of the state of destination.[97] If an undertaking (the assets of an undertaking) is transferred as a whole, the parties may choose the personal law of the legal predecessor. This choice, however, does not affect immovable property, which remains under the scope of the *lex rei sitae*.[98] The statutory text does not mention it, but the APIL's explanatory memorandum notes that the parties may choose the law in relation to the transfer of a business only if its assets are situated in different states. In the case of claims of ownership, the original owner may choose the *lex rei sitae* according to two time dimensions. It may choose the law where the thing was located at the time he or she illegally lost possession over it, or the law where the thing is located at the time of vindication. Nonetheless, if the former does not provide protection for a *bona fide* possessor, that person may claim protection in accordance with the latter.[99]

The general rule embedded in Section 9 of the APIL applies to party autonomy in property matters. The choice of the applicable law can be made only expressly; the parties cannot make a choice implicitly. The APIL's explanatory memorandum notes that the parties' choice of law binds only the parties, so it does not prejudice the rights of third parties acquired beforehand.

5.2.3 Cultural Property

Section 46 of the APIL deals with the property law questions of unlawfully taken cultural property. Section 47 has general application, so it not only applies to cultural property, but has important implications for illegally transferred cultural property. Directive 2014/60/EU[100] establishes rules and a mechanism for the return of cultural objects unlawfully removed from the territory of a Member State. It contains no choice-of-law rules.

95 Section 44(3) of the APIL.
96 Section 44(5) of the APIL.
97 Section 45(1) of the APIL.
98 Section 45(2) of the APIL.
99 Section 47 of the APIL.
100 Directive 2014/60/EU of the European Parliament and of the Council of 15 May 2014 on the return of cultural objects unlawfully removed from the territory of a Member State and amending Regulation (EU) No 1024/2012 (Recast), [2014] OJ L 159/1.

Illicit trafficking in cultural property can, in essence, take two forms. In the first case, the owner of the property violates a country's export restrictions and sells the cultural property to a foreign buyer. In the second case, the thing is stolen or otherwise unlawfully taken from the original owner and the person who unlawfully acquired it, or a subsequent possessor, takes it to another state. In both cases, the cultural property may end up in the hands of a purchaser who acquired it in good faith. The property may knowingly be transferred to a state that protects *bona fide* purchasers more generously. Accordingly, there may be a conflict between the law of the country of origin, in particular its export restrictions, and the *lex rei sitae*.

In the case of illegally removed cultural goods, the state may base its claim of revindication, at its choice, on either its own law or the *lex rei sitae*. According to Section 46 of the APIL, if cultural property is illegally transferred to another country, the country of origin may base its claim of revindication either on its own law or on the law of the state the thing was moved to (*lex rei sitae*). If, however, the law of the country of origin does not provide protection for a *bona fide* possessor, the possessor may claim such protection under the *lex rei sitae*. Section 47 of the APIL extends this principle to claims of ownership in general.

6 Intellectual Property Rights

Hungarian private international law and the Rome II Regulation unequivocally follow the principle of territoriality as regards intellectual property rights, i.e., the territorially competent state's law governs intellectual property issues. Nevertheless, since intellectual property law has been largely unified through international treaties, especially the 1883 Paris Convention for the Protection of Industrial Property and the 1886 Berne Convention for the Protection of Literary and Artistic Works, the perspective of a substantive conflict between the legal systems is often restricted.[101] At the same moment, there are several points of potential divergence: e.g. the existence of moral rights, and the royalty to be paid to visual artists on the resale of artworks ('*droit de suit*', '*Folgerecht*').

The law applicable to non-contractual obligations, including non-contractual obligations arising from the infringement of intellectual property rights, is regulated by the Rome II Regulation. Article 8 of the Regulation deals

101 Note that Hungary is party to both treaties.

specifically with the infringement of intellectual property rights, applying the principle of territoriality.

Essentially, the same principle governs non-contractual obligations arising from unitary EU intellectual property rights, e.g., the Community Trade Mark (CTM); here, the connecting factor is the place of infringement. Article 8(2) of the Rome II regulation provides that '[i]n the case of a non-contractual obligation arising from an infringement of a unitary Community intellectual property right, the law applicable shall, for any question that is not governed by the relevant Community instrument, be the law of the country in which the act of infringement was committed'.

Although Article 14 of the Regulation, under certain conditions, gives the parties the right to choose the law applicable to the non-contractual obligation, Article 8(3) excludes this possibility in respect of non-contractual obligations arising from the infringement of intellectual property rights.

Due to the adoption of the principle of territoriality and the exclusion of party choice, the provisions of the Rome II Regulation are essentially in line with those of the APIL.

Hungarian private international law follows the principle of *lex loci protectionis* as to intellectual property rights, including authors' rights and industrial property.

6.1 *Authors' Rights*

Section 48 of the APIL determines the law applicable to authors' rights (existence, content, termination, and enforcement) as the law of the state 'for whose territory the protection is claimed'. The questions whether a copyright was infringed and what legal consequences the infringement triggers are governed by the *lex loci protectionis*. Accordingly, as to authors' rights, the connecting factor is the territory over which the protection is requested. For example, if Hungarian courts encounter an allegation that an author's rights were violated in Austria, it is Austrian law that is applicable to the question of 'authors' rights', as it is the territory of Austria over which the protection is requested.

The interpretation of the term 'authors' rights' is central to the application of the above provision. This much is certain that characterization under the APIL is to be accomplished according to Hungarian law; hence, one must proceed from the Hungarian Act on Authors' Rights.

The ownership and transfer of copyright (including its transferability or lack of transferability) are governed by the *lex loci protectionis;* however, the contractual aspects of the transfer come under the *lex contractus*.

In Case *Albert Wass de Czege*[102] the Supreme Court faced a very exciting problem of characterization concerning the transfer (transferability) of copyright. Albert Wass de Czege (1908–1998) was a Hungarian nobleman, writer, and forest engineer from Transylvania (now part of Romania), who emigrated to the US after the Second World War. He gained recognition for his literary works in the 1990s and became one of the most popular Hungarian authors (his works were completely unknown in Hungary before the collapse of the communist regime in 1989). In 1989, with the view of getting his works in the public domain, he transferred his copyrights to an American-Hungarian citizen (the plaintiff). The contract provided that the author transferred the copyright in all his published and unpublished works to the plaintiff. Afterwards, between 1992 and 1997, the author granted licenses for the publication of some of his individual pieces. In 1997, he transferred the copyright in all his works exclusively to the defendant. In 2001, the legal successors terminated the contract with the plaintiff due to breach of contract. The plaintiff, in his statement of claims, requested the court to declare that the defendants had violated the law and to apply the corresponding legal consequences. In their counterclaim, the defendants, in turn, requested the court to establish that the plaintiff had violated the law when he had kept publishing the author's titles after termination.

The legal question to be answered by the Supreme Court was whether the author's rights over the works could be transferred to the plaintiff (i.e., whether the plaintiff was the owner or only a licensee of these rights). The Court distinguished 'authors' rights' questions from contractual issues and took the position that the question whether the 'authors' rights' are transferable (and what restrictions are applicable to this transfer) comes under the concept of 'authors' rights', demarcating it from the contractual features of the agreement (validity, performance, breach of contract, etc.). Since the plaintiff requested legal protection over the territory of Hungary, Hungarian law was the *lex loci protectionis*. As under Hungarian law authors' rights cannot be transferred and only licenses can be granted, the parties' agreement had to be re-characterized under the terms of Hungarian intellectual property law. Accordingly, the Supreme Court held that the parties' contract for the transfer of copyright qualified as a non-exclusive license agreement under Hungarian law. Hence, since the plaintiff had no exclusive license, the author did not interfere with his rights when he granted an exclusive license to the defendant and the latter's right could not impair the plaintiff's license.

102 Case Pfv. X. 21.909/2004. (Supreme Court), published under number BH 2006.114.

6.2 *Industrial Property*

The APIL follows the principle of territoriality (*lex loci protectionis*) as regards industrial property, such as patents, industrial designs, and trademarks. The scope of the *lex loci protectionis* extends to the creation, protection, and infringement of these rights. According to Section 49 of the APIL, the existence, content, termination, and enforcement of industrial property rights are governed by the law of the state where the protection was granted or the application was made. Accordingly, the ownership and transfer of patents are governed by the *lex loci protectionis*; however, the contractual aspects of the transfer come under the *lex contractus*.

For instance, the questions whether a patent was infringed and what legal consequences the infringement triggers are governed by the *lex loci protectionis*. In a legal dispute between an Austrian plaintiff and a Polish defendant the Supreme Court established that the question whether a patent infringement was committed in Hungary was governed by Hungarian law.[103]

7 Family Law

7.1 *Marriage*

7.1.1 Existence, Validity, and Annulment

In Hungarian private international law, the connecting factors regarding the preconditions of marriage (validity, existence, non-existence) are twofold. The formal requirements, i.e., the technicalities of the conclusion of the marriage, are subject to the *lex loci celebrationis*, the substantive requirements, including marriage impediments, are subject to the personal laws of both spouses (cumulatively).

The interpretation of the terms 'formal requirements of validity' and 'substantive law preconditions' are pivotal to the interpretation of the above provision. As noted above, Hungarian choice of law follows the *lex fori* approach in respect of characterization; thus, the foregoing concepts are to be defined according to Hungarian substantive law.

The substantive law preconditions (age, prohibition of bigamy, interdiction of marriage between relatives) are based on the parties' personal law. In order to avoid limping marriages, which are recognized in one country but not in another, the APIL uses cumulative connecting factors: the parties can marry only if the personal law of neither of them precludes this; that is, the

103 Case IV. 20 221/1983 (Supreme Court), published under number BH 1984.151.

substantive law preconditions are to be examined under the personal laws of both parties. The APIL also contains an important imperative rule: irrespective of the applicable law, the marriage cannot be contracted in Hungary if the contraction has an unavoidable impediment according to Hungarian law. It amounts to an unavoidable impediment if one of the parties is married, the parties are close relatives, or they are of the same sex.[104]

7.1.2 Personal and Property Effects

The APIL addresses the personal and property effects of the marriage jointly. Hungary does not take part in the enhanced cooperation concerning the Matrimonial Property Regulation; hence, the PIL aspects of matrimonial property are regulated by the APIL.

The property relations between the spouses, where they did not make use of the ability to choose the applicable law, and their personal relations, as to which there is no opportunity to choose the applicable law, are, according to Section 27 of the APIL, governed by the law of the spouses' joint citizenship or, failing this, by the law of their common habitual residence or last common habitual residence (if they no longer have such a residence) or, failing this, by Hungarian law. Section 29 of the APIL establishes an alternative connecting factor for marriage contracts: they are fomally valid also if they comply with the *lex loci contractus*.

The parties may choose the law applicable to the property law relationships (but not the personal relationships). Three limitations apply to this choice. First, the parties have no unlimited right to choose any law they wish, but can choose from only the laws set out in Section 28 of the APIL. Second, the parties must choose the applicable law expressly; implied choice of law is not recognized here. Third, the choice of the law applicable to the property relations between the spouses cannot impair the rights of third parties.[105]

The term 'personal and property relations' has a wide meaning and covers all aspects of the family law relationships between the spouses, except for maintenance, as that comes under the scope of the Maintenance Regulation.

Questions of characterization emerging from the delimitation between matrimonial and succession law issues are subject to the general rules of characterization embedded in Section 4 of the APIL.

---

104 Section 26 of the APIL.

105 Section 9 of the APIL.

7.1.3 Divorce

Hungary takes part in the enhanced cooperation concerning the Rome III Regulation. Hence, the law applicable to divorce is determined by this legal instrument.[106]

The Rome III Regulation's application is strictly limited to the question of divorce and legal separation, with the exclusion of all the ancillary issues. The term 'divorce' is defined narrowly, and it does not embrace marriage annulment and the existence (or non-existence) of the marriage.[107]

The Regulation is widely based on party autonomy, albeit – contrary to contractual matters – that this is restricted to a set of laws determined by the Regulation. The spouses may designate one of the following laws: the law of common habitual residence, the law of the last common habitual residence, provided one of the spouses still resides there, the law of the state any of the spouses is a national of, and the *lex fori*.[108]

Section 30 of the APIL provides that '[t]he spouses may choose the applicable law in accordance with Articles 5–7 of Council Regulation (EU) No 1259/2010 at the latest within the deadline set by the court in the pleading phase'.

Articles 6 and 7 of the Regulation deal with consent, as well as formal and material validity. The existence and material validity of the spouses' choice is governed by the chosen law ('the law which would govern it under this Regulation if the agreement or term were valid'). Article 7 establishes minimum formal requirements: the agreement shall be reduced to writing (electronic communication providing a durable record is deemed equivalent to writing), dated and signed by both spouses. In respect of additional formal requirements, the following scheme applies. The law of habitual residence is to be applied; however, habitual residence in non-participating Member States is disregarded. If the spouses have their habitual residence in the same participating Member State, the additional formal requirements of that country apply. If they have their habitual residences in different participating Member States, 'the agreement shall be formally valid if it satisfies the requirements of either of those laws'. If only one of the spouses resides habitually in a participating Member State, the law of that state applies.

---

106 As for the Hungarian case law on the Rome III Regulation see Case Pf.634936/2019/12 (Budapest-Capital Regional Court), appealed from Case P.101627/2017/112 (Central District Court of Pest); Case Pfv.21582/2019/4 (Supreme Court), appealed from Case Pf.21234/2018/20 (Szolnok Regional Court), appealed from Case P.20663/2017/5 (Jászberény Local Court).

107 Article 1 of the Rome III Regulation.

108 Article 5 of the Rome III Regulation.

Article 8 of the Rome III Regulation determines the law applicable in the absence of party choice and sets out the following subsidiary connecting factors: law of the spouses' habitual residence; law of last habitual residence, provided that the spouses' common place of habitual residence did not end more than one year before the court was seized and one of the spouses still resides there; common nationality; and *lex fori*.

The Rome III Regulation takes the sensitive nature and public policy character of divorce regulation into account. The rule that the marriage cannot be dissolved at all and the rule that it can be dissolved may equally raise public policy concerns. Hence, besides the public policy clause embedded in Article 12, Article 10 of the Regulation provides that if the applicable law 'makes no provision for divorce or does not grant one of the spouses equal access to divorce or legal separation on grounds of their sex, the law of the forum shall apply'. On the other hand, Article 13 provides that '[n]othing in this Regulation shall oblige the courts of a participating Member State whose law does not provide for divorce or does not deem the marriage in question valid for the purposes of divorce proceedings to pronounce a divorce by virtue of the application of this Regulation'.

7.2 *Same-Sex Registered Partnership*

Hungary does not take part in the enhanced cooperation concerning the Regulation on the Property Consequences of Registered Partnerships; hence, the choice-of-law aspects of registered partnerships are regulated by the APIL.

Same-sex marriage is unknown to both Hungarian substantive law and PIL. Article L of the Constitution defines marriage as being between a man and a woman. Nonetheless, same-sex civil unions (registered partnerships) are recognized and are subject to essentially the same rules in terms of both substantive law and choice of law. The major substantive difference is that the rules on married name do not apply to same-sex registered partnerships and the couple cannot adopt children jointly.[109]

The law applicable to registered partnerships of same-sex couples is determined by Section 37 of the APIL, which, in essence, reproduces the choice-of-law rules applicable to marriage. The formal requirements of the conclusion of a same-sex civil union (registered partnership) are governed by the *lex loci celebrationis*. The substantive requirements are subject to the personal laws of both spouses (cumulatively). The law governing the personal and property effects of same-sex registered partnerships is determined by the connecting

109 Act XXIX of 2009.

factors used in relation to marriage. These include the parties' right to choose the law that applies to their property relations. Section 38 of the APIL sets out provisions on the dissolution of registered partnerships. These provisions have no counterparts in the rules on marriage, given that divorce is not regulated by the APIL but by the Rome III Regulation.

It is worth noting that the registration of a same-sex civil union cannot be accomplished in Hungary if the partners have neither Hungarian citizenship, nor place of living in Hungary, and their personal laws recognize same-sex marriage. Such legal systems generally do not know the concept of same-sex civil union (as the latter is essentially the surrogate of same-sex marriage), hence, the condition embedded in the first sentence of Section 37(2) of the APIL is met: the personal law of the prospective partner in life does not recognize same-sex civil unions.

Section 37(2) of the APIL provides that

It is not an impediment to the conclusion of a registered partnership and the validity thereof is not affected if the personal law of the intended registered partner does not provide for the legal institution of registered partnership of same-sex couples, provided that

a) the intended registered partner not having Hungarian citizenship proves that there would be no impediment to the conclusion of marriage under his personal law, and

b) at least one of the intended registered partners is a Hungarian citizen or has his place of habitual residence in Hungary.

Accordingly, the same-sex civil union can be validly established if the conditions of Section 37(2)(a) and (b) are met. Section 37(2)(a) requires that under the personal law of the partner in life who has no Hungarian citizenship the conclusion of the same-sex marriage would have no obstacle. Section 37(2)(b) requires that at least one of the prospective partners in life be a Hungarian citizen or have his place of living on the territory of Hungary.

Accordingly, if two Dutch citizens who live in Austria decide to establish a same-sex civil union in Hungary (while not transferring their place of living to Hungary), their application would be refused by the Hungarian registry office. Albeit that the same-sex marriage has no bar under their common personal law (Dutch law), neither of them has Hungarian citizenship or a place of living in Hungary. Perversely, the lack of Hungarian citizenship and place of living is not a hurdle in the case where the relevant laws do not recognize the institution of same-sex marriage but are more conservative (and less tolerant towards same-sex cohabitation) and recognize merely same-sex civil unions. Accordingly, if two Italian women living in Austria envision establishing a same-sex civil union in Hungary, this is no problem since Italian law does not accept same-sex marriages but, instead, contents itself with the recognition of same-sex civil union.

7.3 *Cohabitation*

Section 35 of the APIL sets out subsidiary connecting factors for the existence, legal effects and dissolutation of cohabitation: the cohabitants' joint citizenship, joint habitual residence (last joint habitual residence), and the *lex fori*. Pursuant to Section 36 of the APIL, the parties have, however, the right to choose the law applicable to the property consequences of cohabitation under the same conditions as in respect to matrimonial property.

7.4 *Maintenance Law*

The choice of law for maintenance is comprehensively regulated by the Maintenance Regulation, which, in turn, in Article 15 refers to the 2007 Hague Protocol in respect of the determination of the applicable law. Pursuant to Articles 7–8 of the 2007 Hague Protocol, the parties may designate one of the laws listed here as applicable. In the absence of this, the applicable law is determined by Articles 3–6, which provide that, in principle, the law of the maintenance creditor's habitual residence shall be applied. Exceptions to this rule are included in Articles 4–6.

In Case *Pfv.22223/2017/4*,[110] the Supreme Court established that the 2007 Hague Protocol encapsulates a 'moving connecting factor'. Article 3 of the 2007 Hague Protocol subjects maintenance obligations to the law of the habitual residence of the creditor, which may change over time, leading to the application of another law 'from the moment when the change occurs'. In this case, the plaintiff, after the spouses separated, became habitually resident in Hungary; hence, Hungarian law applied to the claim for maintenance.

It is worth noting that Hungarian courts tend to take the foreign element into account also when Hungarian law is applicable to the matter and to interpret Hungarian substantive provisions accordingly. In Case *Pfv.II.21.906/1998/5.*, the German defendant was obliged to pay child maintenance, the amount of which was 7 percent of the father's income (per child). The children lived in Hungary. The Supreme Court affirmed the judgment, although according to Hungarian law the amount of the child maintenance was expected to range between 15 and 25 percent of the obligor's income. The Court justified this with

110 Appealed from Case Pf.630704/2017/12 (Budapest-Capital Regional Court), appealed from Case P.22943/2013/73 (Budapest District Court for the Districts of IV and XV).

the circumstance that earnings and expenses were higher in Germany than in Hungary, hence, the application of a lower ratio was appropriate in this case.

The Maintenance Regulation applies to 'maintenance obligations arising from a family relationship, parentage, marriage or affinity'. Accordingly, it regulates spousal maintenance and child maintenance but does not apply to the maintenance of cohabitants. At the same time, the maintenance of cohabitants is not dealt with by the APIL either. The reason is that this is a concept unknown to Hungarian law.

7.5 *Application of the Law More Favorable to the Child*

As a general choice-of-law rule, Section 25 of the APIL provides that in family matters Hungarian law shall be applied if that is more favourable to the child.

7.6 *Determination of Parenthood*

Section 31 of the APIL deals with family status and provides that the child's personal law at the time of birth shall apply to the establishment of fatherhood and motherhood, as well as the rebuttal of the presumption of fatherhood. In respect of the recognition of the child by the father, the child's personal law at the moment of recognition has to be applied. The recognition by the father of a conceived but unborn child is governed by the mother's personal law at the moment of recognition.

7.7 *Custody and Contact*

Hungary is party to the 1996 Hague Convention. Hence, the APIL applies only in matters that do not come under the Convention's scope. Section 34 of the APIL deals with the family law relationship between the parent and the child and guardianship over the child, and provides for the application of the *lex fori*. This provision does not apply to maintenance, as it comes under the scope of the Maintenance Regulation.

7.8 *Guardianship*

Section 34 of the APIL deals with guardianship over the child and provides for the application of the *lex fori*.

7.9 *Adoption*

Section 33 of the APIL sets out cumulative connecting factors in respect of the preconditions of adoption: the personal laws of the adopter and the person to be adopted are to be taken into account jointly. Contrary to the pre-conditions of adoption, its legal effects and termination are subject to the personal law of the adoptive person at the time of adoption and termination, respectively.

Special rules apply to joint adoption by married spouses. However, there are no special rules on joint adoption by non-married couples.

In Case *Pfv.II.20.996/2000/4*, the child was not adopted by both adopters at the same time: the defendant (a Hungarian citizen) adopted the child in 1990, while the plaintiff (a German citizen) adopted him some years later, after the parties had married. The Supreme Court established that this qualified as a joint adoption notwithstanding the fact that the parties had adopted the child separately at different times.

7.10 *Artificial Insemination, Surrogacy*

The APIL contains no specific rules on medically assisted procreation (e.g., test-tube baby, surrogacy). Questions related to family status emerging from medically assisted procreation are governed by the above general provisions. Lineage questions are, in principle, governed by the child's personal law. Unfortunately, there is no case law on this.[111]

In practice, the choice-of-law problems related to the determination of family status may be avoided due to Hungarian courts' generous recognition practice concerning foreign public deeds. This may be relevant especially in matters involving surrogacy. In Case *5.P.III.20.970/2011/2*, the Hungarian court recognized a Ukrainian birth certificate concerning a child who was born in the frame of a medically assisted procreation program.

7.11 *Child Abduction*

The APIL contains no specific rules on the law applicable to child abduction; however, Section 34 of the APIL establishes, as a general rule, that the legal relationship between the parent and the child is governed by the *lex fori*, but the court may take into account the law of another, closely connected state, if this is justified as being in the best interests of the child.

Hungary is a member to the 1980 Hague Convention. The Convention applies if the child has been wrongfully removed or retained abroad, and provides that the question of wrongfulness is governed by the law of the country the child was removed from. According to Article 3 of the Convention, the removal and the retention are wrongful if they violate a custody right (attributed to a person, an institution, or any other body) 'under the law of the state in which the child was habitually resident immediately before the removal or retention'

111 See Cs.I. Nagy, "Hungary," in K. Trimmings & P. Beaumont (eds.), *International Surrogacy Arrangements* (Hart Publishing, Oxford, 2013), 175–186.

and these rights were actually exercised at the time of removal or retention or 'would have been so exercised but for the removal or retention'.

Accordingly, one of the pre-conditions of the application of the Hague Convention is that the removal or retention is illegal under the law of the state where 'the child was habitually resident immediately before the removal or retention'. If the allegation is that the child was illegally abducted from Hungary, in principle, Hungarian law applies.

7.12 *Protection of Adults*

Hungary is not a member of the 2000 Hague Convention. Thus, the protection of adults, including guardianship over adults, is governed by national rules. Nonetheless, Hungary envisions joining the 2000 Hague Convention and, hence, the rules of the APIL were brought into conformity with the Convention's provisions.

Guardianship over adults and other protective measures that do not affect the person's capacity to act are not governed by the personal law but by the law of the habitual residence of the person concerned. However, if the interests of the adult concerned warrant it, the court may exceptionally apply or take into account the law of a state to which the case is more closely connected.[112]

The law of the habitual residence also applies to the legal declarations an adult makes where he or she would be placed under guardianship or protective measures which would be adopted to protect his interests; however, in his written declaration he or she may also choose the law of his citizenship, earlier habitual residence, or the *situs* of the assets.[113]

The law of the appointing court shall apply to the legal representation of a person restricted in managing his own affairs and to *ad hoc* guardianship over adults.[114]

8 Succession Law

The Succession Regulation sets out the choice-of-law rules concerning succession matters in a comprehensive manner and leaves very little room for national private international law norms. The APIL essentially regulates two aspects of international succession which fall outside of the scope of the Succession Regulation: verbal testaments and the status of unclaimed estate.

112 Section 18 of the APIL.
113 Section 19 of the APIL.
114 Section 20 of the APIL.

8.1 *Hungarian Choice-of-Law Rules*

The APIL does not provide for party autonomy as to the *lex successionis*.

According to Section 64 of the APIL, oral wills are formally valid if they comply with Hungarian law, the *lex loci actus*, the personal law or the law of the domicile or place of habitual residence of the deceased. Oral wills concerning immovable property are also valid if they are in conformity with the law of the *situs*.

According to Section 65 of the APIL, if an estate located in Hungary has no heir (unclaimed estate), Hungarian rules on succession by the Hungarian state shall apply.

The old APIL followed the 'unity of legacy' principle in the field of inheritance law. Accordingly, inheritance legal relationships were subject to a single law (personal law); contrary to the 'partition of legacy' principle, where movable and immovable property is subjected to different laws (personal law in respect of movables, and the law of the *situs* in respect of immovables).

8.2 *Scope and Application of the Succession Regulation*

Although the Succession Regulation has practically taken over the field, it has produced very scant case law consisting of a handful of reported court cases. It ought to be noted that international succession matters do emerge regularly; it is only the number of court cases that is low. In Hungary, succession matters are, in the first place, settled in a probate procedure carried out by a notary. This is not a court procedure, and the notary normally does not adjudicate on succession law disputes and his decisions are not published. This probate procedure filters the cases and apparently results in a situation where the parties rarely have recourse to the court.

In Case *Pfv.I.20.164/2019*,[115] the Succession Regulation was found to be inapplicable *ratione materiae*. Here, the plaintiff and the deceased (whose legal successor was the defendant, as the deceased's heir) had allegedly agreed that the plaintiff would provide care and support for the deceased and, in exchange for this service, the deceased would bequeath his entire property to the plaintiff. However, in his will, the deceased bequeathed all his property to the defendant. The plaintiff sued the defendant for compensation for the services provided and referred to the alleged oral agreement with the deceased. The Supreme Court established that this claim was contractual and not covered by succession law. Hence, it did not come under the Succession Regulation but under the Brussels I Regulation. The Supreme Court carried

115 Reported as BH 2020.3.78.

out an autonomous interpretation of the term 'succession' and, on the basis of the definition embedded in Article 3(1) of the Succession Regulation, stressed that it involves legal succession *mortis causa*. In this case, however, the plaintiff did not claim to be the deceased's legal successor but submitted a contractual claim as the deceased's creditor.

The Succession Regulation does not apply to legal capacity;[116] hence, this comes under the scope of the APIL, which treats it as part of personal law. Nonetheless, the Regulation's exclusion is not complete: Article 26(1)(a) of the Regulation provides that testamentary capacity (that is, 'the capacity of the person making the disposition of property upon death to make such a disposition') pertains to substantive validity, which is, in turn, governed by the *lex successionis* as established by the Regulation.

Compulsory portion (forced heirship) is governed by the *lex successionis* and comes under the scope of the Succession Regulation,[117] as does interpretation of the will.[118]

The will's formal validity is governed by the *lex successionis* and comes under the scope of the Succession Regulation, with the exception of the formal validity of oral wills, which are governed by the APIL. As noted above, according to Section 64 of the APIL, oral wills are formally valid if they comply with Hungarian law, the *lex loci actus*, the personal law or the law of the domicile or place of habitual residence of the deceased; oral wills concerning immovable property are also valid if they are in conformity with the law of the *situs*.

Legacies,[119] testamentary contracts,[120] and the liability for the debts under the succession[121] are governed by the *lex successionis* and come under the scope of the Succession Regulation.

9 The Law Applicable to Procedure

According to Section 66 of the APIL, the procedure of Hungarian courts is governed by the *lex fori* unless the APIL provides otherwise.

The distinction between substance and procedure may raise questions of characterization. In the application of the APIL, characterization has to be

116 Article 1(2)(b) of the Succession Regulation.
117 Article 23(2)(h) of the Succession Regulation.
118 Article 26(1)(d) of the Succession Regulation.
119 Article 23(2)(e) and Recital 47 of the Succession Regulation.
120 Article 3(1)(b) and (d) of the Succession Regulation.
121 Article 23(1)(g) and (d) of the Succession Regulation.

carried out, in principle, on the basis of Hungarian law. A borderline issue is, for instance, the burden of proof. In Hungarian law, the burden of proof is, in principle, a question of procedure; however, in some cases substantive law regulates the allocation of the burden of proof. For instance, in delictual liability cases, the allocation of the burden of proof as to fault is a question of substantive law. Section 6:519 of the Civil Code enables the tortfeasor to exonerate himself by proving lack of culpability and provides that, in this regard, the burden of proof is placed on the tortfeasor.

The EU choice-of-law instruments do not deal with the law applicable to procedure; however, they address certain borderline cases. The Rome I Regulation does not apply to evidence and procedure,[122] but provides that '[t]he law governing a contractual obligation under this Regulation shall apply to the extent that, in matters of contractual obligations, it contains rules which raise presumptions of law or determine the burden of proof'. Furthermore, a 'contract or an act intended to have legal effect may be proved by any mode of proof recognised by the law of the forum or by any of the laws referred to in Article 11 under which that contract or act is formally valid, provided that such mode of proof can be administered by the forum'.[123] The same approach is followed by the Rome II Regulation.[124]

122 Article 1(3) of the Rome I Regulation.
123 Article 18 of the Rome I Regulation.
124 Article 1(3) & 21–22 of the Rome I Regulation.

CHAPTER 4

International Civil Procedure

1 Sources of International Civil Procedure

International civil procedural law encompasses three fields: jurisdiction, recognition and enforcement, as well as judicial cooperation. In Hungary, these rules are included in the APIL. Nonetheless, as with choice of law, or even more so, EU law has largely superseded national provisions.

The most important EU law instrument is the Brussels I Regulation, which governs jurisdiction, as well as recognition and enforcement, in civil and commercial matters. The Brussels I Regulation's jurisdictional rules apply, with some exceptions, only when the defendant is domiciled in the EU. On the other hand, its rules on recognition and enforcement apply to the judicial decisions of sister member states, irrespective of the identity of the defendant. The Brussels II Regulation governs matters related to the dissolution of the marital bond and cases related to parental responsibility, as well as international child abduction. It is applicable in civil matters relating to divorce, legal separation, and marriage annulment, and the attribution, exercise, delegation, restriction, and termination of parental responsibility. The Insolvency Regulation, the Maintenance Regulation, and the Succession Regulation deal with both the choice-of-law and international civil procedural aspects of insolvency proceedings, maintenance matters, and succession, respectively.

2 State Immunity

The doctrine that PIL applies to private law matters raises questions in matters concerning states, which enjoy immunity under international law. The immunity of sovereign states is a classical question of PIL and may appear in all three areas (choice of law, jurisdiction, and recognition and enforcement). Nonetheless, the practical significance of the issue has been seriously reduced, as states usually do not directly engage in international business transactions, but hide behind legal entities, such as corporations and sovereign funds.

The starting point of state immunity in PIL is the principle of '*par in parem non habet jurisdictionem*': equals have no jurisdiction over each other. As states are equal under public international law, no state can exercise power

 | DOI:10.1163/9789004694569_005

(jurisdiction) over another. The consequence of this principle was that until the end of the nineteenth century courts could not adjudicate on claims against foreign states even in purely private law matters. This implies that a state could be sued only before its own courts. This absolute immunity was later qualified and turned into relative immunity. The latter distinguishes between acts *jure imperii* and *jure gestionis*. The theory of relative immunity implies that courts have no jurisdiction over foreign states' exercise of their public power, while their private law acts are treated in the same way as general private transactions. Accordingly, the doctrine of relative immunity is based on the notion that it is not all acts of the state that are immune to foreign jurisdiction, but only those that are closely connected with the exercise of public power. Conversely, in respect of private transactions, the state must be treated in the same way as any other trader.

The notion of state immunity emerges in the APIL in the fields of jurisdiction and recognition and enforcement. Sections 82–87 deal with the international civil procedural aspects of state immunity. These provisions were modeled after the United Nations Convention on Jurisdictional Immunities of States and Their Property signed on December 2, 2004 and are based on the principle of relative immunity. They cover the state, its public authorities, and persons acting on behalf of the state (Section 82).

As regards jurisdiction, the APIL provides that a state may be sued only before its own courts (Section 83) and sets out numerous exceptions to this principle (Section 84). A state has no immunity to foreign jurisdiction if it has expressly waived it and if the action was launched by it. This also extends to connected counterclaims. Furthermore, as a general principle, states have no immunity in private law matters, such as civil contracts, employment contracts, claims for damages, *in rem* rights in real estate, membership, shares and interests in a legal person, succession matters, intellectual property disputes, insolvency proceedings, and arbitration. Diplomatic representatives enjoy immunity unless the immunity was waived (Section 86).

The principle of relative immunity also applies to the enforcement of foreign judicial decisions. Enforcement against the property of a foreign state can be carried out only if the asset is used outside of the state's non-commercial activities or the state expressly consented to this or separated it for the satisfaction of the claim (Section 85(3) of the APIL). The non-commercial activities include assets by diplomatic missions, assets serving a military function, the property of central banks and other financial authorities, property that belongs to the cultural heritage or archives, and property displayed in a scientific, cultural, or historical exhibition (Section 85(4)).

3 International Jurisdiction: Hungarian Rules, EU Rules

The APIL's rules of jurisdiction apply only if the matter is not governed by an EU PIL instrument.

The jurisdictional rules of the Brussels I Regulation apply, apart from some exceptions,[1] solely relating to matters where the defendant is domiciled in the EU. According to Article 4(1) of the Brussels I Regulation, 'persons domiciled in a Member State shall, whatever their nationality, be sued in the courts of that Member State'. Article 5 provides that EU domiciliaries may be sued in a Member State different from that of their domiciles only on the basis of the rules set out in the Regulation. Article 5(2) explicitly stresses that national exorbitant rules of jurisdiction, as set out in Annex I to the Regulation, shall not be applied against EU domiciliaries.

The above rule is frequently criticized for being unfriendly towards non-EU defendants. In particular, the application of exorbitant jurisdictional rules, such as Section 97 of the APIL which confers jurisdiction on Hungarian courts in cases where the defendant has assets in Hungary, is excluded by the Regulation, but this applies, obviously, only as regards defendants coming under the scope of the Regulation *ratione personae*; as a consequence, national exorbitant rules on jurisdiction remain applicable to non-EU defendants, since the lawsuits against them remain governed by national jurisdictional rules.

What is more, Article 4(2) of the Brussels I Regulation provides that national exorbitant bases of jurisdiction should be made available also to those EU domiciliaries who are not nationals of the Member State concerned: '[p]ersons who are not nationals of the Member State in which they are domiciled shall be governed by the rules of jurisdiction applicable to nationals of that Member State'.

Finally, under the Brussels I Regulation, non-EU defendants are not merely denied the protection that is afforded to their EU fellow-sufferers, but they are even deprived of a shield that once protected them. The rules on recognition and enforcement, contrary to those on jurisdiction, apply irrespective of the identity of the defendant; that is, here it is irrelevant whether the defendant in the main proceedings was or was not domiciled in the EU. With this rule non-EU defendants lost one of their defenses. Earlier, they could effectively argue before the courts of the country of recognition and enforcement that the courts in the main proceeding had no jurisdiction in an international sense. Nevertheless, today the recognition and enforcement of Member State

1 Article 18(1), Article 21(2), and Articles 24 and 25 of the Brussels I Regulation.

judgments occurs on the basis of the rules of the EU, which, in principle, prevent the court of recognition and enforcement from reviewing the jurisdiction of the court of origin; national exorbitant rules lost their safety valve, and the entire European judicial area's door was opened to them.

The Brussels II Regulation follows a similar approach concerning divorce, legal separation, and marriage annulment, but not regarding parental responsibility; in Article 6, as regards matrimonial matters, it provides that the jurisdictional bases included in the Regulation are exclusive for EU nationals and persons having their habitual residence in the EU; accordingly, national rules remain applicable against non-EU defendants.

The Insolvency Regulation applies if the debtor's center of main interests is in the EU. This follows from Article 3(2) of the Regulation, which provides that where the center of the debtor's main interests is in a Member State, the courts of other Member States can open only territorial insolvency proceedings.

The Maintenance Regulation and the Succession Regulation have universal application.

3.1 *Hungarian Rules of Jurisdiction*

The APIL establishes a set of jurisdictional rules that have general application (Sections 88–91). These rules define those cases where Hungarian courts have exclusive jurisdiction, where their jurisdiction is excluded (the inverse of exclusive jurisdiction), some parallel grounds of jurisdiction, jurisdiction based on appearance, and jurisdiction over interim measures. The APIL establishes no rule of general jurisdiction applicable in all matters.

The APIL establishes separate special regimes on pecuniary matters (Sections 92–100) and family law and personal status matters (Sections 101–108). As Hungary does not take part in the enhanced cooperation concerning the Matrimonial Property Regulation and the Regulation on the Property Consequences of Registered Partnerships, the rules of jurisdiction in these matters are established by the APIL.

The APIL's rules of jurisdiction are generally modeled after EU PIL, most notably the Brussels I Regulation. However, there are some important differences, most notably Section 97 of the APIL, which confers jurisdiction on Hungarian courts in cases where the defendant has assets in Hungary. As the APIL's explanatory memorandum explains, unless there is a compelling policy consideration justifying a divergence, the APIL follows the approach of the EU jurisdiction rules. This implies that, where appropriate, Hungarian courts may take the CJEU's case law into consideration also when interpreting the Hungarian rules of jurisdiction.

3.1.1 Jurisdictional Rules of General Application

Given that the rules on exclusive jurisdiction included in Article 24 of the Brussels I Regulation apply irrespective of the domicile of the parties (they have universal effect), the scope of national jurisdictional rules is limited to cases excluded from the scope of the Brussels I Regulation.

Section 88 of the APIL provides that Hungarian courts alone have jurisdiction over *in rem* rights in and the leasing of immovable property located in Hungary, probate proceedings if the deceased was a Hungarian citizen and the estate is located in Hungary, proceedings for the annulment of documents issued in Hungary, matters concerning entries in Hungarian public registers, and enforcement proceedings carried out in Hungary.

If Hungarian courts have exclusive jurisdiction, the courts of no other state have power to entertain the case. Hungarian rules of jurisdiction are, of course, addressed to the Hungarian judiciary and authorities and are not binding on foreign courts. The practical significance of exclusive jurisdiction in relation to foreign courts lies primarily in the rules on recognition and enforcement. Although foreign courts are not obliged to comply with the Hungarian rules of jurisdiction, Hungary refuses to recognize and enforce judgments that do not comply with these rules.[2] Furthermore, the jurisdiction of a foreign court cannot be stipulated if Hungarian courts have exclusive jurisdiction.[3]

Section 89 of the APIL lists those cases where the jurisdiction of the Hungarian courts is excluded. These provisions mirror the rules of exclusive jurisdiction with the exception of Section 89(d) (foreign industrial property rights) and Section 89(e) (company law disputes concerning entities seated abroad).

Section 90 of the APIL provides for jurisdiction in the case of joinder of parties and counterclaims. Several defendants may be sued jointly before a Hungarian court if at least one of the defendants has his place of living, seat, or central administration in Hungary and there is a close connection between the claims. Jurisdiction over the principal obligor extends to the secondary obligor and, hence, they may be sued jointly if the place of living, seat, or central administration of the principal obligor is in Hungary. Jurisdiction over a claim also extends to the adjudication of the counterclaim.

Section 91 of the APIL deals with jurisdiction based on appearance. It provides that the Hungarian court has jurisdiction if the plaintiff makes submissions on the merits without objecting to jurisdiction. The APIL however

2 Section 109(1)(a) of the APIL.

3 Section 99(2) of the APIL.

establishes exceptions to this rule. If the jurisdiction of the Hungarian court is excluded, jurisdiction cannot be established by appearance. Furthermore, appearance confers no jurisdiction in insolvency, lineage, adoption, parental responsibility, and access (visitation) matters, and matters concerning guardianship over minors, guardianship over adults, and other protective measures, and in matters relating to establishing the fact of death.[4]

The Hungarian court has jurisdiction to adopt provisional measures even in cases where it otherwise has no jurisdiction, provided the measure concerns a person or property located in Hungary.[5] If the foreign court that has jurisdiction delivers a decision on the merits of the case that is recognizable in Hungary, the provisional measure loses its effect. The purpose of this provision is to manage situations where immediate action is necessary to protect a person or property located in Hungary and the court having jurisdiction is not able to take such action. Provisional measures concerning pecuniary matters can be adopted only if the decision of the foreign court that has jurisdiction over the merits of the case is recognizable in Hungary.

3.1.2 Jurisdictional Rules in Pecuniary Matters

The term 'pecuniary matter' (in Hungarian: '*vagyonjogi ügy*') embraces cases where the claim is based on the party's pecuniary rights, or its value can be expressed in monetary terms.[6]

3.1.2.1 *Parallel Bases of Jurisdiction*

As noted above, the APIL does not establish a general jurisdiction, but contains rules of general jurisdiction as to pecuniary matters. According to Section 92, anyone who has his place of living, seat, or central administration[7] in Hungary may be sued there in pecuniary matters, unless the jurisdiction of the Hungarian court is excluded (*actor sequitur forum rei*).

Sections 93–98 of the APIL set out various rules of parallel jurisdiction, Section 99 deals with choice-of-court agreements, and Section 100 with insolvency proceedings.

A good number of the rules of parallel jurisdiction are in accordance with EU PIL, most notably the Brussels I Regulation. The jurisdictional rules on contracts (Section 93 of the APIL) are in line with Article 7(1) of the Brussels I

4 Sections 100(3), 104(2), 105(2), 106(2), 107(3), and 108(2) of the APIL.

5 Section 70 of the APIL.

6 Section 7(1)(18) of the Civil Code.

7 Section 92 of the APIL refers solely to the seat, but Section 90 makes it clear that the term 'seat' embraces both the seat and the place of central administration.

Regulation, with one exception. If the contract is neither a contract of sale, nor a contract for the performance of an activity (provision of a service), the basis of jurisdiction is the place of performance under Hungarian law. On the other hand, under the Brussels I Regulation, the place of performance in the latter case must be determined by the *lex causae*. The rules on non-contractual obligations (Section 94 of the APIL) reflect Article 7(2) of the Brussels I Regulation. Although the latter refers to the place of the 'harmful event', the case law of the CJEU construes this term as embracing both the place of the harmful act or omission (*delictum*) and the place of the loss (*damnum*).[8] Section 94 of the APIL reflects this distinction already in its statutory language. Section 94(3) provides that Hungarian courts have civil jurisdiction over damage caused by a criminal act if they have criminal jurisdiction. This provision accords with Article 7(3) of the Brussels I Regulation with an important difference. Under Section 94(3), criminal jurisdiction entails civil jurisdiction. This implies that if Hungarian criminal courts have jurisdiction over a criminal act, both Hungarian criminal and civil courts can adjudicate on the damage caused. On the other hand, Article 7(3) of the Brussels I Regulation authorizes only the criminal court seised of the criminal proceedings to adjudicate on the civil claims emerging from a prosecuted criminal act and does not give jurisdiction to the the civil courts of the country. Section 96 of the APIL confers jurisdiction on the Hungarian courts over disputes arising out of a foreign undertaking's branch or representation in Hungary.

According to Article 95 of the APIL, Hungarian courts have jurisdiction over matters that have as their object a right *in rem* in movable property located in Hungary.

Section 97 of the APIL contains an exorbitant basis of jurisdiction, which allocates jurisdiction on the basis of the presence of assets.

The Brussels I Regulation rules out the application of this provision with respect to defendants domiciled in the EU. Nonetheless, Section 97 remains applicable outside the scope of the Brussels I Regulation, most notably against non-EU defendants. Hungarian courts have jurisdiction if the defendant has assets in Hungary. Receivables may serve as a basis of Hungarian jurisdiction if the debtor is domiciled in Hungary or if the claim is secured by collateral located in Hungary.

Succession matters are nearly exhaustively regulated by the Succession Regulation, which has universal application. This leaves a very limited practical role to national rules of jurisdiction, which, in essence, have a role to play

---

8 See, e.g., ECJ, Case 21–76, *Mines de potasse d'Alsace* (1976) EU:C:1976:166.

only in cases that do not come within the scope of the Succession Regulation either *ratione temporis* or *ratione materiae*.

In Hungary, succession law is applied in two types of procedures. Probate procedures are carried out by notaries and are aimed at the drawing up of an inventory of the estate and handing it over to the heirs. If there is no dispute between the heirs or if there is a single heir, the estate is transferred by the notary with final effect. In the event of a dispute, the estate may be transferred with only provisional effect. In these cases, the parties may bring actions before the court. Accordingly, the notary's probate procedure is a simplified one and usually closes the succession matter if there is no dispute between the parties.

According to Section 98 of the APIL, the Hungarian notary has jurisdiction to carry out the probate procedure if the deceased was a Hungarian citizen at the time of his death or if the estate (or part of it) is located in Hungary. In contrast, Hungarian courts have jurisdiction in succession proceedings if the deceased was a Hungarian citizen at the time of his death.

3.1.2.2 *Prorogation of Jurisdiction*

Section 99 of the APIL deals with choice-of-court agreements. This provision is modeled on Article 25 of the Brussels I Regulation and has limited practical significance. It applies only if the case falls outside of the scope of the pertinent provisions of the Brussels I Regulation. While the Regulation's jurisdictional rules, in principle, apply only if the defendant is domiciled in the EU, Article 25 of the Regulation applies irrespective of domicile. This implies that Section 99 has relevance in two cases: first, if the matter does not come under the scope of the Brussels I Regulation, for instance, by reason of Article 1(2) of the Regulation; second, Section 99 applies also where the parties stipulate the jurisdiction of the courts of a non-EU country. If an action is launched before a Hungarian court, the latter has to decide whether the choice-of-court agreement excludes the jurisdiction of the Hungarian courts. Notably, Article 25 of the Brussels I Regulation applies only if the parties agree 'that a court or the courts of a Member State are to have jurisdiction'.

3.1.2.3 *Insolvency Proceedings*

The Insolvency Regulation applies if the debtor's center of main interests is in the EU. This follows from Article 3(2) of the Regulation, which provides that where the center of the debtor's main interests is located in a Member State, the courts of other Member States can open only territorial insolvency proceedings. However, if the debtor has its center of main interests outside of the EU, the national rules of jurisdiction apply. According to Section 100 of the APIL, Hungarian courts have jurisdiction if the debtor has its registered office in Hungary or has a place of business (branch, establishment) in Hungary where it carries out non-temporary economic activities. Jurisdiction over insolvency proceedings implies jurisdiction over actions arising out of and closely connected to the insolvency proceedings. A claim qualifies as such if the legal basis of the right or obligation giving rise to the claim is rooted not in the general rules of civil law but in insolvency law.

Although Section 100 of the APIL is not stated to be a rule of exclusive or excluded jurisdiction, in insolvency matters there is no possibility for prorogation of jurisdiction (Section 99) and appearance does not establish jurisdiction (Section 91).

According to Section 67 of the APIL, Hungarian law governs the legal effects of insolvency proceedings launched in Hungary, with the exception of immovable property, a ship, or an aircraft and security subject to public registration.

3.1.3 Jurisdictional Rules in Family Law and Personal Status Matters

The Brussels II Regulation establishes rules of jurisdiction as to divorce, marriage annulment, and legal separation, as well as parental responsibility, but leaves room for national jurisdictional rules in three areas. First, it is uncertain whether the Regulation covers disputes related to the existence and non-existence of marriage. Second, under Article 6 of the Regulation, in matters related to the dissolution of the marital bond, the Regulation's jurisdictional rules are exclusively applicable only if the defendant is habitually resident in or a citizen of a Member State. In other words: in proceedings against a person who is neither habitually resident in the EU nor a citizen of a Member State, the Brussels II Regulation's rules of jurisdiction apply, but they do not exclude the application of national rules. Third, Article 6 of the Brussels II Regulation with regard to matrimonial matters and Article 14 with regard to parental responsibility provide that where no Member State has jurisdiction under the Regulation, 'jurisdiction shall be determined, in each Member State, by the laws of that State'.

As regards disputes concerning the existence and non-existence of marriage, Hungarian courts have jurisdiction if either party is a Hungarian citizen or the defendant is domiciled in Hungary. In addition, the Hungarian legislator has made use of the opportunity offered by Articles 6 and 14 of the Brussels II Regulation: in matrimonial matters to lay down that the Hungarian court has jurisdiction if one of the spouses is a Hungarian citizen; in parental responsibility matters, the Hungarian court has jurisdiction if the child is a Hungarian citizen.[9]

Hungary does not take part in the enhanced cooperation concering the Matrimonial Property Regulation. Hence, the jurisdictional rules in this regard are established by the APIL.

Section 102 of the APIL sets out six parallel grounds of jurisdiction in relation to the personal and property relations of the spouses. Hungarian courts have jurisdiction if the defendant has his/her habitual residence in Hungary; if the last common habitual residence of the spouses was in Hungary, provided that one of the spouses still has habitual residence here; if both spouses are Hungarian citizens; if the property concerned is situated in Hungary; if the dispute emerges in connection with proceedings concerning the matrimonial bond and the latter comes under Hungarian jurisdiction; the dispute emerges in connection with proceedings concerning succession law and the latter comes under Hungarian jurisdiction.

According to Section 103 of the APIL, the Hungarian court has jurisdiction over legal disputes concerning same-sex registered partnerships if either the registered partnership was established in Hungary or at least one of the registered partners is a Hungarian citizen.

According to Section 104 of the APIL, jurisdiction over lineage disputes can be based on the citizenship or domicile of the child or the domicile of the defendant or at least one of the defendants. According to Section 105, Hungarian courts have jurisdiction over the authorization and termination of an adoption if the child or the adoptive person is a Hungarian citizen or is habitually resident in Hungary or if the adoptive person (in case of joint adoption by the spouses, at least one of them) is a Hungarian citizen or has his habitual residence in Hungary. Section 107 provides that the Hungarian court has jurisdiction over proceedings concerning guardianship over adults and other protective measures if the person concerned is a Hungarian citizen or has his habitual residence in Hungary.

Section 108 of the APIL establishes two grounds of jurisdiction with respect to proceedings for a declaration of death or the establishment of the fact of death: Hungarian courts have jurisdiction, first, if the last habitual residence of the missing person was in Hungary and, second, if he or she was a citizen of Hungary and the declaration of death or the establishment of the fact of death is justified by a domestic legal interest.

9 Sections 101 and 106 of the APIL.

3.2 *EU Jurisdictional Rules in the Practice of Hungarian Courts*

3.2.1 Brussels I Regulation

Hungarian courts have been applying the Brussels I Regulation in a large number of cases.[10] Some of these were referred to the CJEU: C-519/12 *Hochtief*,[11] in C-94/14 *Flight Refund Ltd v Deutsche Lufthansa AG*[12] and in C-102/15 *Gazdasági Versenyhivatal v Siemens Aktiengesellschaft Österreich*.

3.2.1.1 *Scope*

The Brussels I Regulation applies, in principle, to civil and commercial matters.

In Case *Gfv.IX.30.186/2010*,[13] the Supreme Court applied the Brussels I Regulation to an administrative authority's termination of a sponsorship contract (which it was a party to), as the authority had not acted in its capacity as a public authority.

In Case *Kf.37137/2019/6*,[14] the Supreme Court applied the CJEU's ruling in C-102/15 *Gazdasági Versenyhivatal v Siemens Aktiengesellschaft Österreich*. According to the Hungarian Competition Act (HCA),[15] the appeal to the court does not suspend the obligation to pay the competition fine, but if the court quashes the fine it must be repaid with interest. In this case, the Hungarian Competition Office (HCO) refunded a fine with interest because its decision was quashed. Nonetheless, the HCO submitted an extraordinary appeal to the Supreme Court, which overturned the judgment of the lower court and reinstated the HCO's decision. Therefore, the defendant paid the fine again, but refused to refund the interest it had earlier received from the HCO, as the HCA contained no provision on that. Given the regulatory gap in the HCA, the HCO sued the defendant before the civil court with reference to the Civil Code's rules on unjust enrichment and claimed that Hungarian courts had jurisdiction under the Brussels I Regulation. Nonetheless, the CJEU held that '[a]n action for recovery of sums not due on the ground of unjust enrichment […] which has its origin in the repayment of a fine imposed in competition law

10 For an overview of the Hungarian case-law on the jurisdictional rules of the Brussels I Regulation, *see* Cs.I. Nagy, "Application of EU Private International Law in Hungary," in Cs.I. Nagy (ed.), *Cross-border litigation in Central-Europe: EU private international law before national courts* (*Kluwer Law International*, The Hague, 2022), 116–123.

11 Case Gf.40560/2011/6 (High Court of Appeal of Budapest).

12 Case Pkk.V.24.731/2016 (Supreme Court), reported as EH 2016.07.P8.

13 Reported as EH 2010.2237.

14 Appealed from Case K.700587/2018/9 (Budapest-Capital Regional Court).

15 Act LVII of 1996 on the prohibition of unfair market conduct and restriction of competition (in Hungarian: '*1996. évi LVII. törvény a tisztességtelen piaci magatartás és versenykorlátozás tilalmáról szóló*').

proceedings does not fall within 'civil and commercial matters' in the application of the Brussels I Regulation. Based on this, the Supreme Court established that the demand to refund the interest paid is an administrative matter and not a 'civil or commercial matter'; hence, the Brussels I Regulation did not apply.[16]

This proposition was confirmed by the Supreme Court also in Case *Kf.37339/2019/8*.[17]

3.2.1.2 *Special Jurisdiction*

The establishment of jurisdiction may involve a vicious circle. The circumstance included in the rule of jurisdiction (the jurisdictional ground) can, at times, be established only after the merits of the case have been examined, while the court can investigate the merits only if it has jurisdiction. Hence, at this stage, courts inquire whether the plaintiff's claim, based on the circumstances alleged by him, comes under one of the heads of jurisdiction. Here, the court does not examine whether the plaintiff's allegations are true but carries out a hypothetical analysis; can jurisdiction be established if one assumes that the plaintiff's allegations are true? Accordingly, the relevant question is whether the plaintiff's allegations satisfy the conditions of the given head of jurisdiction. If the court went beyond the allegations stated in the plaintiff's statement of claim, it would engage in a premature substantive analysis.

In Case *Pfv.I.20.164/2019*,[18] the Supreme Court held that Article 7(1) of the Brussels I Regulation applies and establishes jurisdiction if, after looking into the parties' statements, the court has no well-grounded suspicion about the existence of a contractual relationship. In other words, when deciding on jurisdiction, the court has to proceed from the statements of the parties. Everything that is beyond those and raises questions concerning the existence and validity of the contract goes beyond the application of the rules of jurisdiction and is part of the substantive analysis.

The Brussels I Regulation establishes several grounds of parallel jurisdiction. From these, Hungarian courts have developed a significant amount of case law concerning Article 7(1) (contractual matters) and Article 7(2) (non-contractual matters) of the Regulation. Article 7(1) points to the place of performance of the contract. In the case of a sale of goods, this is the place of delivery. In the case of the provision of services, this is the place where the services were provided or should have been provided. If a contract qualifies as neither a sale of goods nor a provision of services, the contract has no single

---

16 Para. 32.

17 Appealed from Case K.700486/2018/19 (Budapest-Capital Regional Court).

18 Reported as BH 2020.3.78.

place of performance, but jurisdiction is determined by the place of performance of the obligation in question.

In Case *Gfv.IX.30.187/2011*,[19] the Supreme Court interpreted Article 7(1) and (2) of the Brussels I Regulation in the context of precontracts. The Court was not explicit and justified the jurisdiction of the Hungarian courts under Article 7(1) with reference to various circumstances. Nonetheless, its reasoning suggests that the place of performance of the precontract is identical to the place of performance of the final contract the precontract targets, though it also noted that it was not proved that the final contract was supposed to be concluded outside of Hungary. The Court also referred to Article 7(2) of the Brussels I Regulation. In this regard, the damages were defined in part as expenses and in part as loss of profit. The Court noted that the loss of profit occurred in Hungary, as did some of the expenses; hence, the damage also established the jurisdiction of the Hungarian courts.

In Case *16.Gf.40.303/2009/5*,[20] the High Court of Appeal of Budapest encountered a difficult question of characterization concerning Article 7(1) and (2) of the Brussels I Regulation. According to the then-effective rules of company law, the person who acquired controlling influence over a company had to report this to the company registrar. The failure to report entailed the controlling shareholder's subsidiary liability.[21] This raised a question of characterization: was this subsidiary liability contractual or non-contractual? The controlling shareholder's liability was not fault-based, which suggested that it did not rest on a delictual basis. The High Court of Appeal of Budapest held that the subsidiary liability attached to the failure to report the acquisition of direct control is a form of piercing the corporate veil and does not come under the notion of delictual or quasi-delictual liability. Hence, it comes not under Article 7(2) but under Article 7(1) of the Brussels I Regulation. Given that the basis of the plaintiff's claim was a loan contract and the place of performance of the contractual obligation in question was Hungary, Hungarian courts had jurisdiction.

Case *Gf.20003/2015/10*[22] arose out of a contractual dispute concerning the transfer of shares in limited liability companies. The seat of one of the

19 Reported as EH 2011.2416 and BH + 2013.1.33, appealed from Case Pf.21552/2010/3 (High Court of Appeal of Budapest), appealed from Case G.41503/2006 (Budapest-Capital Regional Court).

20 Appealed from Case 12.G.40.835/2008/12 (Budapest-Capital Regional Court).

21 Section 292(3) of Act CXLIV of 1997 on economic companies (in Hungarian: '*1997. évi CXLIV. törvény – a gazdasági társaságokról*').

22 Appealed from Case G.20348/2013/83 (High Court of Appeal of Győr).

defendants was in the Channel Islands. Hence, the Brussels I Regulation was considered inapplicable due to Article 355 TFEU.[23] Accordingly, the court established its jurisdiction on the basis of the Hungarian rules. As for the defendant seated in Luxembourg, the court applied the Brussels I Regulation.

In this case, the parties concluded a share transfer agreement concerning limited liability companies. In Hungarian law, business shares are not negotiable instruments (contrary to shares in stock corporations). The High Court of Appeal of Győr conceived the agreement as a sales contract and defined the place where the goods were to be delivered as the country where the acquisition of the business shares was to be registered. As the transfer of the shares in a company seated in Hungary has to be registered in Hungary, the place of performance was considered to be Hungary and Hungarian courts had jurisdiction under Article 7(1) of the Brussels I Regulation.

In Case *7.G.20.255/2018/92*, the plaintiff claimed compensation for cartel damage by reliance on a decision of the European Commission. The latter established that the competition law violation covered the whole European Economic Area (EEA). The Balassagyarmat Regional Court found that this implied that the harmful event occurred in Hungary, and so Hungarian courts had jurisdiction under Article 7(2) of the Brussels I Regulation. The Court established that the plaintiff had purchased the product concerned by the cartel, paid the price, and traded in his used car in Hungary.

In Case *20.Gf.40.050/2020/36-II*,[24] in the context of a claim for competition damages, the High Court of Appeal of Budapest, referring to the CJEU's case law,[25] held that the place of the harmful event was the relevant market concerned by the violation, that is, the place where the distorted prices were applied and where the victim claimed to have suffered damage, even though the plaintiff had sued a cartelist undertaking it had no contractual relationship with. The Court stressed that as the violation covered the whole EEA and Hungary was part of this, the harmful event occurred in Hungary and, thus, Hungarian courts had jurisdiction.[26]

---

23 '[T]he Treaties shall apply to the Channel Islands and the Isle of Man only to the extent necessary to ensure the implementation of the arrangements for those islands set out in the Treaty concerning the accession of new Member States to the European Economic Community and to the European Atomic Energy Community signed on 22 January 1972'.

24 Appealed from Case 7.G.20.255/2018/92 (Balassagyarmat Regional Court).

25 Paras 55–57. See ECJ, Case C-27/17, *AB 'flyLAL-Lithuanian Airlines' v Starptautiskā lidosta 'Rīga' VAS and 'Air Baltic Corporation' AS* (2018) EU:C:2018:533; ECJ, Case C-352/13, *Cartel Damage Claims (CDC) Hydrogen Peroxide SA v Evonik Degussa GmbH and Others* (2015) EU:C:2015:335; ECJ, Case C-451/18, *Tibor-Trans v DAF TRUCKS* (2019) EU:C:2019:635.

26 Paras 58–59.

The causal reach of the harmful event as a ground of jurisdiction established in Article 7(2) of the Brussels I Regulation may raise questions of interpretation in the event of indirect and consequential damage. In Case *Pf.20539/2017/5*,[27] the Hungarian plaintiff was on holiday in Greece and suffered serious injuries in a traffic accident. He was mistreated in the Greek hospital, was transported to Hungary for further treatment, and had to undergo further operations. The wrongful treatment in the Greek hospital resulted in his permanent bodily injury, the detrimental consequences of which were sustained in Hungary. The Budapest-Capital Regional Court found that the harmful event occurred in Hungary, as the indirect and consequential damage occurred there. This was affirmed by the High Court of Appeal of Budapest.

In Case *Gf.30410/2013/3*,[28] the defendant wanted to set off its claim for compensation for the legal costs it was awarded in proceedings in the Czech Republic against the same plaintiff concerning the same subject-matter. The Hungarian court recognized the Czech decision on legal costs. The plaintiff argued that the Hungarian court had no jurisdiction over the set-off. The High Court of Appeal of Szeged established its jurisdiction on the basis of Article 8(3) of the Brussels I Regulation. Although this provision refers to 'counter-claim[s] arising from the same contract or facts on which the original claim was based' and confers jurisdiction on 'the court in which the original claim is pending', the High Court of Appeal of Szeged held that Article 8(3), as 'from greater to smaller' also covers set-off claims (*argumentum a maiore ad minus*). It has to be noted that the facts of the case suggest that the Czech and Hungarian proceedings concerned the same subject-matter: the plaintiff first tried to enforce its claim in the Czech Republic, where it subsequently withdrew the claim, and then submitted it to the Hungarian court. Hence, the Czech court terminated the procedure and awarded legal costs to the defendant.

3.2.1.3 *Consumer Contracts*

The Brussels I Regulation establishes protective rules of jurisdiction concerning certain contracts that involve a weaker party (insurance, consumer, and employment contracts). The protection in the case of consumer contract consists of the consumer's right to sue in his country of domicile. The cases that arose before Hungarian courts centered mainly around the definition of 'consumer' and the ensuing question whether the protective rules of jurisdiction

27 Appealed from Case P.24487/2012/47 (Budapest-Capital Regional Court).
28 Appealed from Case G.40009/2013/15 (Gyula Regional Court).

applied. The Regulation defines the 'consumer' as a person who acts outside of his trade or profession (Article 17 of the Brussels I Regulation).

In Case *Gf.20062/2015/8*,[29] the High Court of Appeal of Győr interpreted the concept of consumer contract. It held, in the context of a choice-of-court provision in the creditor's standard terms, that a loan contract does not qualify as a consumer contract if its purpose is to build structures on the plots owned by the debtor and its family, including a complex of 18 apartments and a restaurant, which, at the end, became the property of companies.

In Case *P.21044/2015/16*, the Szeged Regional Court dealt with the definition of consumer contract. It held that the party's characteristics and the purpose of the contract must be inspected in this regard. In this case, it established that in relation to the loan contract the plaintiff had adopted the status of his ex-spouse because she was creditworthy due to her job and income, and the purpose of the contract was clearly connected to the planned self-employment activity. Thus, the contract could not be regarded as being concluded outside of the debtor's trade or profession. This was not affected by the circumstance that the agreement fell partly outside of his economic and professional activity; in such a case, the agreement does not qualify as a consumer contract.

3.2.1.4 *Exclusive Jurisdiction*

Article 24 of the Brussels I Regulation establishes grounds of exclusive jurisdiction.

In Case *Gf.I.30.343/2013*,[30] the High Court of Appeal of Szeged held that domain name registration is covered by Article 24(4) of the Brussels I Regulation. The Court considered that the registration of a domain name is similar to that of a trademark, and as Article 24(4) of the Brussels I Regulation refers to 'proceedings concerned with the registration or validity of patents, trademarks, designs, or other similar rights required to be deposited or registered', Hungarian courts have exclusive jurisdiction over domain names registered in Hungary (that is, .hu).

In Case *9.Pkf.25.572/2020/2*,[31] the High Court of Appeal of Budapest highlighted that the exclusive jurisdiction established by Article 24(2) of the Brussels I Regulation concerning immovable property extends solely to *in rem* claims (and tenancy). Hence, this head of jurisdiction does not cover claims under the law of obligations. The term 'rights *in rem*' has an autonomous EU-law meaning and must be interpreted narrowly. Its key element is the *erga*

---

29 Appealed from Case G.20918/2011/115 (Győr Regional Court).

30 Reported as ÍH 2014.58, appealed from Case 7.G.40.061/2013/6 (Szeged Regional Court).

31 Reported as ÍH 2020.116.

omnes effect (while the law of obligations features the principle of privity). Accordingly, not all claims that concern *in rem* rights in immovable property are covered by Article 24(2) of the Regulation. The action in these cases centered around the approval of a disposition over immovable property by a person placed under guardianship. More specifically, the plaintiff sued for a judicial declaration of the contract's invalidity. The Court found that this implied no *in rem* rights and came under the law of obligations. Hence, Article 24(2) of the Regulation did not apply.

3.2.1.5 *Choice-of-Court Agreements*

In Case *Gf.VII.30.228/2013/4*,[32] the parties entered into a distribution contract which, by way of reference to the supplier's standard terms, contained a choice-of-court clause. After a dispute arose, the parties settled this via a memorandum which provided that the supplier would buy back the merchandise as to which the distributor had objections. The Supreme Court held that the choice-of-court agreement covering the distribution contract did not extend to the memorandum, as the latter was not simply the consequence of the distribution contract but created a new contractual obligation (the supplier promised to buy the products it had sold before). Accordingly, the court ignored the stipulation of the jurisdiction of German courts and established that the Hungarian court had jurisdiction, as the place of performance was in Hungary.

Hungarian courts, under Hungarian PIL rules, tend to take a restrictive approach to choice-of-court agreements. According to Section 62/F(1) of the old APIL, the counterpart of Article 25 of the Brussels I Regulation, '[i]n case of pecuniary matters, the parties may stipulate that the courts of a particular state or a particular court has jurisdiction to settle their dispute or their disputes arising from a particular legal relationship'. In the case reported as BH 2004.153, the contract stipulated the exclusive jurisdiction of 'the Brussels courts' ('any legal dispute connected to the contract and/or related to its interpretation, performance, termination or cancellation comes under exclusive Brussels jurisdiction or before the Brussels courts'). The High Court of Appeal of Budapest held that this stipulation was not legally enforceable as it was not in conformity with Section 62/F(1) of the then-effective old APIL, which enabled the parties to choose either the courts of a particular state or a particular court, and the choice of the Brussels courts came under neither of these

32 Appealed from Case 14.Gf.40.512/2012/2 (High Court of Appeal of Budapest), appealed from Case 8.G.40.554/2010/34 (Budapest-Capital Regional Court), tried on remand as Case G.42072/2014/17 (Budapest-Capital Regional Court).

categories. The parties were expected either to choose Belgian courts or to name a specific Belgian court.

It is hoped that Hungarian courts will not follow this approach concerning the Brussels I Regulation, although the statutory language of the two instruments is similar: according to Article 25 of the Brussels I Regulation, the parties may agree 'that a [specific] court or the courts of a Member State are to have jurisdiction'.

An indication of this can be observed in Case *Gfv.30382/2018/8.*[33] Here, the parties stipulated the Szolnok Local Court. However, the plaintiff submitted a claim that, because of its value, came under the subject-matter competence of the Szolnok Regional Court. Hungarian law distinguishes between international jurisdiction, subject matter competence, and venue. The parties may agree to international jurisdiction and venue (domestic territorial jurisdiction) but have no autonomy as to subject-matter competence. High-value claims come under the original (subject-matter) competence of regional courts, and while the parties may choose from the courts located in various parts of the country that have subject-matter competence, the law does not allow them, for instance, to choose a local court in a matter that, due to the value involved, comes under the competence of regional courts. In this sense, the court's power to entertain a case is to be established along three co-ordinates, and party autonomy prevails with respect to international jurisdiction and venue (territorial competence), but not subject-matter competence.

In this case, the Supreme Court emphasized that the Brussels I Regulation deals solely with the question of jurisdiction (in the international sense). To establish jurisdiction, it is necessary and sufficient if it can be established without doubt which country's court or courts the parties chose. The parties' agreement need not extend to the determination of a specific court that has subject-matter and territorial competence (venue), since this is an issue coming under the given Member State's domestic law.[34] The Supreme Court found that when the parties stipulated the Szolnok Local Court, they agreed that the case should be entertained by a Hungarian court located in Szolnok. The agreement cannot be construed narrowly as referring solely to matters coming under the subject-matter competence of the Szolnok Local Court, with the exclusion of matters that come under the subject-matter competence of the

33 Appealed from Case Gf.30270/2017/10 (High Court of Appeal of Szeged), appealed from Case G.21439/2014/63 (Szolnok Regional Court).

34 Para. 39.

Szolnok Regional Court. Such a narrow construction would be irreconcilable with Article 25 of the Brussels I Regulation.[35]

The Supreme Court also noted that the application of Article 25 of the Brussels I Regulation implies the requirement of specificity (that is, the court chosen by the parties should be determinable without doubt) and the parties' agreement did meet this requirement.[36]

In Case *10.Gpkf.44.048/2020/2*,[37] the High Court of Appeal of Budapest established that, given that by means of prorogation of jurisdiction the parties derogate from their rights and the choice may not be equally advantageous for them, the formal requirements set out in Article 25 of the Brussels I Regulation have to be construed rigorously and restrictively. In this case, the choice-of-court clause was part of the defendant's standard terms. However, the framework agreement concluded by the parties did not refer to these. The Court established that the requirement of writing would be met if the framework agreement referred to the standard terms or the parties had signed them separately. The agreement is 'evidenced in writing', as provided in Article 25(1)(a) of the Brussels I Regulation, if one of the parties sends the other a unilateral written confirmatory document and the other party does not object to that within a reasonable time. It does not amount to a confirmation that, after the conclusion of the framework agreement, in connection with the individual orders the defendant sent its standard terms to the plaintiff, because there was no prior agreement the sending of the standard terms could have confirmed.

3.2.1.6 *Parallel Proceedings*

The Brussels I Regulation establishes two sets of rules for parallel proceedings. The rules on *lis pendens* apply if the two matters are, in essence, identical and provide for a mandatory stay. If proceedings involving the same cause of action and between the same parties are brought in the courts of different Member States, the court first seised has priority to decide on its jurisdiction, and if it establishes its jurisdiction the other court or courts have to decline theirs. Where there is a choice-of-court agreement, it is not the court first seised but the chosen one that has priority.[38] The rules on related actions require a less intensive link between the two proceedings and provide for a discretionary stay. Two actions are related if 'they are so closely connected that it is expedient

35 Para. 41.
36 Para. 42.
37 ÍH 2021.19.
38 Articles 29 & 31 of the Brussels I Regulation.

to hear and determine them together to avoid the risk of irreconcilable judgments resulting from separate proceedings'.[39]

In Case *14.Gpkf.43.405/2012/2*,[40] parallel proceedings were pending in Hungary and France. These emerged from a railway accident in Hungary. They concerned different claims and partly different parties (the proceedings in France dealt with damage to the railroad cars, and the action in Hungary with damage to the railroad), so *lis pendens* could not be established. Nonetheless, the two actions did have some overlapping issues, such as who was liable for the accident and responsible for the damage. The High Court of Appeal of Budapest refused to stay the proceedings. However, it based its decision not on Article 30 of the Brussels I Regulation but on the pertinent national rules of civil procedure, which had a narrower scope. According to the latter, if there was no *lis pendens*, the court could stay the proceedings only if the decision in the case before it depended on a preliminary question that was subject to other, parallel proceedings. The Court did not inquire whether the two actions were so closely connected that it was expedient to hear and determine them together to avoid the risk of irreconcilable judgments resulting from separate proceedings.

3.2.1.7 *Relation with Other Instruments*

According to Article 71 of the Brussels I Regulation, the latter does not affect the international treaties which the Member States are parties to, and which govern jurisdiction or recognition and enforcement.

In Case *Gpkf.IV.40.160/2014/2*,[41] the High Court of Appeal of Pécs, based on Article 71 of the Brussels I Regulation, applied the jurisdictional rules of Article 31(1) of the CMR instead of those of the Regulation. The same approach was followed by the High Court of Appeal of Budapest in Case *Gf.40035/2014/7*.

3.2.2 Insolvency Regulation

In Case *12.Fpkf.44.199/2012/3*,[42] the High Court of Appeal of Budapest examined the territorial scope of the Insolvency Regulation and held that it did not apply to enterprises domiciled outside of the EU. Unfortunately, the Court's reasoning conflates the seat and the center of main interests. Although Article 3 of the Insolvency Regulation contains the presumption that the place of the

39 Articles 30 of the Brussels I Regulation.

40 Appealed from Case 25.G.42.229/2009/38 (Budapest-Capital Regional Court).

41 Reported as EBD 2015.12.G3, appealed from Case 4.G.40.017/2014/8 (Zalaegerszeg Regional Court).

42 Reported as ÍH 2013.81.

registered office coincides with the center of main interests, this presumption is rebuttable. The Court reasoned that the EU's legislative powers extend to the Members States and persons domiciled there. Hence, persons domiciled outside of the EU are not covered by the Insolvency Regulation. The jurisdictional rule of Article 3 applies solely to enterprises seated in the EU and the Regulation does not extend to the Seychelles Islands in the Indian Ocean and, hence, in this regard, Article 3 does not establish the jurisdiction of any Member State court. The High Court of Appeal of Budapest established that it was not proved that the debtor had its center of main interests in Hungary and declined jurisdiction.

The principal procedure of C-527/10 *Erste* gave rise to various issues of interpretation.[43] Case *Gfv.XI.30.516/2008/*[44] emerged in an earlier stage of the proceedings. At this stage, the creditor argued that Hungarian courts had jurisdiction to launch a secondary territorial procedure, because the debtor allegedly had an establishment in Hungary. The Supreme Court set out three important principles as regards the notion of establishment and the application of Article 3(2) of the Insolvency Regulation. First, the burden of proof of the existence of an establishment rests on the creditor. If he or she cannot prove that the debtor has an establishment in Hungary, no insolvency proceedings may be opened and pending insolvency proceedings have to be terminated. In this case the creditor failed to meet this burden. Second, the debtor was not established in Hungary merely by acquiring shares in a company seated in Hungary or by opening and maintaining a bank account there. These circumstances are not sufficient to confirm the existence of an establishment. Finally, the Supreme Court noted that the Insolvency Regulation does not require, as an additional pre-requisite, that the establishment exist also at the time the request for the secondary territorial procedure is submitted.

3.2.3 Brussels II Regulation

Hungarian courts have developed a significant amount of case law in parental responsibility matters under the Brussels II Regulation.[45]

43 The request for a preliminary ruling was first submitted to the High Court of Appeal of Budapest, which refused to refer the case to the CJEU. Its order, at this stage, was affirmed by the Supreme Court. See Case Gf.IX.30.324/2009, reported as BH 2010.6.158 and EH 2009.2054.

44 Reported as BH 2010.6.156 and EH 2009.1970, appealed from Case F12.Fpkf.43.856/2008/2 (High Court of Appeal of Budapest), reported as ÍH 2008.122.

45 For an overview of the Hungarian case-law on the jurisdictional rules of the Brussels II Regulation, *see* Cs.I. Nagy, "Application of EU Private International Law in Hungary," in

The notion of 'legal separation' is unknown in Hungarian law.

3.2.3.1 *Scope*

Under Hungarian law, a significant number of family law issues related to children, such as certain issues related to the exercise of access rights, are handled by the Guardianship and Child Protection Office (*'gyámhivatal'*).

In Case *Pfv.II.20.622/2009*,[46] the Supreme Court established that, as the competences concerning access rights are split between the court and the Guardianship and Child Protection Office, the latter must be regarded as a 'court' from the perspective of the Brussels II Regulation.

In Case *Kfv.II.39.412/2007/12*,[47] the plaintiff claimed compensation for the travel costs incurred when exercising his visiting rights in the timeframe set out by the court, because the other parent had failed to inform him that she had moved with the child to Germany and, hence, they could no longer be reached at the earlier address. The Supreme Court held that the claim of reimbursement for the failed visit came within the scope of the Brussels II Regulation. The Court, referring to Articles 1(1)(b) and 2(a) of the Brussels II Regulation, pointed out that the Regulation also applied to the exercise of the right of access, and the claim for reimbursement for the failed visit was part of the exercise of the plaintiff's rights of access.

Hungarian courts have been reluctant to apply the Brussels II Regulation to matters having a significant non-EU element.

In Case *Pfv.II.21.847/2014*,[48] the Supreme Court had to decide whether the Brussels II Regulation applied to a matter with a significant non-EU element. The plaintiff was a Hungarian and the defendant a French citizen. The plaintiff requested the court to dissolve their marriage concluded in Paris, to place their child born in Tokyo (a French-Hungarian dual citizen) with her, and to award maintenance. Before the opening of the Hungarian proceedings, the defendant launched divorce proceedings in Bora Bora (French Polynesia), where the parties allegedly lived at the time the proceedings were launched. While the case centered around the consequences of the Polynesian proceedings in terms of *lis pendens*, the Supreme Court also examined the applicability of the Brussels II Regulation's jurisdictional rules and established, in a summary manner, that they did not apply, since French Polynesia did not come under

---

Cs.I. Nagy (ed.), *Cross-border litigation in Central-Europe: EU private international law before national courts* (*Kluwer Law International*, The Hague, 2022), 137–141.

46 Reported as BH 2009.10.298 and EH 2009.1961.

47 Appealed from Case K.21134/2007/8 (Nyíregyháza Regional Court).

48 Reported as BH + 2016.1.26.

the Regulation's scope of application. Unfortunately, the Supreme Court supported its stance with no detailed analysis, although this construction seems to run counter to Article 6 of the Brussels II Regulation. This provides that a spouse who is habitually resident in or a national of a Member State can be sued only in accordance with the Regulation's jurisdictional rules ('may be sued in another Member State only in accordance with Articles 3, 4 and 5').

As noted above, the reluctance to apply an EU PIL instrument to a matter with a significant non-EU element is not novel in Hungarian case law. In Case *G.20348/2013/83*, the Győr Regional Court indicated that the Rome I Regulation did not apply in a case where one of the contracting parties was Austrian but the other one was from the Cayman Islands, although Article 2 of the Rome I Regulation provides for universal application.

3.2.3.2 *Jurisdictional and Related Procedural Issues in Parental Responsibility Matters*

In parental responsibility matters, the general ground for jurisdiction is the child's habitual residence. In Hungarian judicial practice, habitual residence, as one of the central concepts of the Brussels II Regulation's jurisdictional rules, is treated as a fact-intensive issue and is analyzed on a case-by-case basis. Courts interpret this concept uniformly in the various legal instruments (Brussels II Regulation, Hague conventions, and domestic law). As to the child's habitual residence, courts do not attribute primary relevance to the length of the stay, but instead take into consideration the parents' decision and common will.[49]

In Case *Pfv.II.20.123/2015*,[50] the Supreme Court established that if the parties move with the child to another country for a long period of time, though without the intention to settle, sell their movables in Hungary, and rent out their real estate for an indefinite duration, the child's habitual residence changes.

In Case *Pfv.II.20.910/2011*,[51] the Supreme Court held that the child's place of habitual residence does not shift to Hungary if the parents consider their employment here as provisional and maintain their habitual residence in the other country.

In Case *Pfv.II.21.710/2013*,[52] the Supreme Court examined the reasons for denying validity to a choice-of-court agreement as set out in Article 12(3) of the 2003 Brussels II Regulation. It noted that during the first instance proceedings (where the court rejected the parties' motion) the child's interests would

---

49 *See* Case reported as BH 2014/180.

50 Reported as BH + 2015.11.465.

51 Reported as EH 2011.2318.

52 Reported as BH + 2014.8.352.

have been best served if the first instance court had tried the case and decided on the child's placement, since at that time all interested parties were staying in Hungary. The first instance court, misinterpreting Article 12(3) of the 2003 Brussels II Regulation, erred when it declined jurisdiction and terminated the proceedings. However, due to the change in circumstances, this flawed decision could not be rectified.

In Case *Pfv.II.20.622/2009*,[53] the Supreme Court interpreted Article 8(1) of the Brussels II Regulation in an idiosyncratic manner. Article 8(1) provides that if the child moves lawfully to another Member State, the courts of the previous habitual residence retain jurisdiction 'during a three-month period following the move for the purpose of modifying a judgment on access rights issued in that Member State before the child moved', provided the holder of access rights remains in this country. While the statutory language of Article 8(1) suggests that the starting date of the three-month period is the day of the actual move, as *obiter dicta* the Supreme Court indicated, in a case where the Hungarian court authorized the child's move from Hungary to Italy (i.e., the change of the habitual residence), that the three-month period starts running from the date of the judgment authorizing the move.

Article 11(2) of the 2003 Brussels II Regulation requires the court to ensure 'that the child is given the opportunity to be heard during the proceedings unless this appears inappropriate having regard to his or her age or degree of maturity'. In the 2019 Brussels II Regulation, the child's right to express his views in return proceedings is included in Article 26. The Supreme Court has consistently held that the court does not have to hear the child via a psychologist but may hear him directly and assesses whether the child's declarations should be taken into consideration, having regard to his age and degree of maturity.[54]

In Case *Pfv.II.20.769/2013*,[55] the Supreme Court rejected the plaintiff's allegation of jurisdiction based on appearance, because the defendant objected to the jurisdiction of the Hungarian courts in his very first submission after the delivery of the statement of claim and several times thereafter.

In Case *Pfv.II.22.073/2009*,[56] the Supreme Court established that the defendant had implicitly accepted the jurisdiction of the Hungarian courts by virtue

---

53 Reported as BH 2009.10.298 and EH 2009.1961.

54 Case Pfv.21601/2009/5 (Supreme Court), reported as BH 2010.5.123; Case Pfv.II.20.461/2013 (Supreme Court), reported as BH 2014.3.80; Case Pfv.II.20.461/2013 (Supreme Court), reported as BH 2014.3.80.

55 Reported as BH 2013.12.344.

56 Reported as EH 2010.2141.

of Article 12(3) of the 2003 Brussels II Regulation when he had made submissions as to the merits of the case and before doing so had requested the transfer of the case to another Hungarian court (from the court of the child's habitual residence to the court of his last Hungarian place of living). By objecting to the *situs* of the court and indicating another court the defendant had accepted, tacitly but unequivocally, the jurisdiction of the Hungarian courts, since the question of *situs* arisess only if the Hungarian courts have jurisdiction at all. The defendant had accepted the jurisdiction of the Hungarian courts also when he declared that he was willing to enter into a settlement in accordance with the psychologist's opinion, provided it was not obviously flawed or abusive. The Supreme Court considered that the foregoing two declarations implied that the defendant had accepted the jurisdiction of the Hungarian courts, and this also served the best interests of the child.

In Case *Pfv. II. 20.936/2019*,[57] the Supreme Court interpreted Article 15 of the 2003 Brussels II Regulation, which authorizes the court to transfer the case to a court of another Member State if the latter is better placed to hear the case. According to the Supreme Court, Article 15 sets out three conjunctive conditions: the paramount interests of the child, a close link to the other Member State, and that the other court is better placed to entertain the case.[58] The close link to the other Member State is defined in detail in Article 15(3) of the Regulation, but the other two considerations come under the court's discretion and have to be assessed in light of the purposes of the Regulation.[59] A court is better placed if the transfer of the cases could have real and specific added value. The rules of procedure of the other court may be taken into account, but not its substantive law.[60] The Supreme Court affirmed the lower court's decision that in this case the transfer of the case to the courts of the child's habitual residence was justified, as the German court was better placed to explore the child's circumstances, such as the place of living, school, and out-of-school activities, and had better access to the pertinent evidence (witnesses, deeds).[61] The Supreme Court also stressed that the assessment is based exclusively on the interests of the child, and the interests of the parents play no role here.[62]

Hungarian courts have consistently held that the Brussels II Regulation narrows down the possibility of refusing to return the child. According to Article

57 Reported as BH 2020.2.43.
58 Para. 20.
59 Paras 21 and 26.
60 Para. 28.
61 Paras 29–35.
62 Para. 36.

27(3) of the Regulation (which is the equivalent of Article 11(4) of the 2003 Brussels II Regulation), '[w]here a court considers refusing to return a child solely on the basis of point (b) of Article 13(1) of the 1980 Hague Convention, it shall not refuse to return the child if the party seeking the return of the child satisfies the court by providing sufficient evidence, or the court is otherwise satisfied, that adequate arrangements have been made to secure the protection of the child after his or her return'. The 1980 Hague Convention establishes a presumption that the child's interests are best served if he or she is returned forthwith to the place of habitual residence. This presumption is reinforced by the Brussels II Regulation and can be rebutted only in exceptional cases, if justified by the individual circumstances. The burden of proof rests on the plaintiff. This was confirmed by the Supreme Court in Cases *Pfv.II.22.039/2016/7*,[63] *Pfv.II.20.703/2018/3*[64] and *Pfv.II.21.124/2018/10*.[65]

3.2.4 Maintenance Regulation

In Case *Pfv.II.21.658/2018/16*,[66] the Supreme Court established jurisdiction, under Article 5 of the Maintenance Regulation, on account of the defendant's appearance before the Hungarian court. The defendant had appeared before the court and, thus, tacitly accepted its jurisdiction, when, in his response to the statement of claim, he had asked the court to reject the plaintiff's claim and made submissions on the merits without objecting to the court's jurisdiction.

3.3 *Procedural Issues*

Hungarian courts must decide on their jurisdiction (and lack of it) *ex officio*. However, if the jurisdiction of the Hungarian courts is not excluded, the defendant can establish it by entering an appearance and making a submission on the merits. Hence, the decision on jurisdiction is dependent on the declarations and motions (objection to jurisdiction) of the defendant.

According to Section 170(2) of the Code of Civil Procedure, the plaintiff's statement of claim has to present the facts that establish the court's jurisdiction.

The court rejects the claims as procedurally inadmissible, without further notice and without summoning the defendant (that is, without opening the

63 Para. 27. Appealed from Case 50.Pkf.635.636/2016/2 (Budapest-Capital Regional Court), appealed from Case 2.Pk.500.132/2016/11 (Pest Central District Court).

64 Appealed from Case 50.Pkf.630.055/2018/2 (Budapest-Capital Regional Court), appealed from Case 28.Pk.500.270/2017/27 (Pest Central District Court).

65 Para. 56. Appealed from Case 50.Pkf.631.543/2018/4 (Budapest-Capital Regional Court), appealed from Case 26.Pk.500.277/2017/12 (Pest Central District Court).

66 Reported as BH 2020.4.108.

civil proceedings), if its jurisdiction is excluded or a foreign court has exclusive jurisdiction.[67] Excluded jurisdiction is the mirror image of exclusive jurisdiction.

If the claim was not rejected as procedurally inadmissible and the civil proceedings were opened, the court will terminate them *ex officio* if it lacks jurisdiction. At this stage, the defendant has already been summoned and called to react to the statement of claim, and in the response to the statement of claim he or she has the chance either to object to the jurisdiction of the Hungarian courts or to make a submission on the merits without objecting to jurisdiction, and thus establishing jurisdiction by appearance. At this stage, the court can inquire into all bases of jurisdiction: the ones that cannot be overridden by entering an appearance and those that can.[68]

3.4 *International Service*

In intra-EU matters, international service (both inbound and outbound) is carried out under the Service Regulation. Hungary has concluded numerous international treaties on judicial assistance, which contain provisions on international service and are applied outside of the scope of the Regulation.

If neither the Service Regulation nor an international treaty applies, requests for international service are fulfilled on the basis of reciprocity or individual ministerial decision. The request is declined if to fulfill it violates Hungarian public policy.[69]

3.5 *Rules of Evidence*

In intra-EU matters, the international taking of evidence (both inbound and outbound) is carried out under the Taking-of-Evidence Regulation. Hungary has concluded numerous international treaties on judicial assistance, which contain provisions on the international taking of evidence and are applied outside of the scope of the Regulation.

If neither the Taking-of-Evidence Regulation nor an international treaty applies, requests for the international taking of evidence are fulfilled on the basis of reciprocity or individual ministerial decision. The request is declined if to fulfill it violates Hungarian public policy.[70]

67 Section 176(1)(a) of the Code of Civil Procedure.
68 Section 240(1)(a)-(c) of the Code of Civil Procedure.
69 Section 72 of the APIL.
70 Section 72 of the APIL.

4 Recognition and Enforcement of Foreign Judicial Decisions

Hungarian law's provisions on recognition and the declaration of enforceability (hereafter briefly referred to as 'enforcement') are mainly included in the APIL. Certain procedural rules are to be found in the Enforcement Act. These rules are applicable to recognition and enforcement matters that are not covered by EU PIL or an international treaty. The recognition and enforcement of sister-member-state judgments in civil and commercial matters is governed by the Brussels I Regulation, in divorce (legal separation, marriage annulment) and parental responsibility matters by the Brussels II Regulation, in maintenance and succession matters by the Maintenance and the Succession Regulations. The Insolvency Regulation covers decisions delivered in the context of bankruptcy proceedings by sister-state courts. In practical terms, judgments of Member State courts are, for the most part, covered by EU legislation. Hence, the purview of Hungarian rules is mainly restricted to the recognition and enforcement of non-EU judgments, supplemented with matters excluded from the scope of the foregoing EU-law instruments.

4.1 *Recognition and Enforcement under the* APIL

Recognition of a foreign judicial decision requires no special procedure: if the conditions for recognition are met, the judgment is automatically recognized by virtue of the law and has the same legal effects as Hungarian judgments. The question of recognition is examined by the court or authority in whose proceedings the question of recognition arises, unless otherwise provided by the law. Recognition may be used as a defense (shield) by the defendant in proceedings. In practice, the question of automatic recognition also arises in the case of public registers (e.g., registration of marriage or divorce, registration of transfer of title).[71] On the other hand, a foreign judgment may be enforced in Hungary only if the Hungarian court has declared it enforceable in a separate procedure (*exequatur*).[72]

The APIL's rules on recognition and enforcement differ substantially from their EU counterparts, given that judgments from outside of the EU enjoy a lower level of trust than the judicial decisions of sister member states.

Sections 109–112 of the APIL contain the general rules of recognition and enforcement, which are applicable to all types of cases. Sections 113–115 of the

71 Section 122(1) of the APIL.

72 Section 123 of the APIL.

APIL set out special rules for pecuniary matters, while Section 116–121 do so for matters concerning family law and personal status.

The recognition and enforcement of a foreign judicial decision have three general preconditions (Section 109(1)(a)-(c) of the APIL): the foreign court's jurisdiction was well-grounded in the light of the Hungarian rules (mirror-image principle); the judicial decision has become final (*res judicata*), and there is no ground for refusal. Section 122(5) of the APIL excludes *révision au fond*: the foreign decision may not be reviewed as to its substance.

The jurisdiction of the foreign court is essentially adjudicated upon on the basis of the mirror-image principle. Pursuant to Section 109(2) of the APIL, the jurisdiction of the foreign court is well-founded if the court has acted on the basis of a ground of jurisdiction set out in the APIL. In family and personal status matters, Hungarian citizens with multiple citizenship could be disadvantaged in cases where the foreign court establishes jurisdiction based on foreign nationality, whereas under Hungarian rules the ground of jurisdiction is the person's Hungarian nationality. In light of this, Article 109(3) of the APIL provides that, when assessing the jurisdiction of the foreign court, the other citizenship of the Hungarian citizen also has to be taken into account.

The APIL establishes indirect grounds of jurisdiction. Some EU PIL instruments (such as the Succession Regulation) contain jurisdictional rules of universal application or (like the Brussels II Regulation) leave merely a complementary role to national rules. At the same time, these instruments do not deal with the recognition and enforcement of decisions of courts of third countries, the recognition of which is governed by the APIL. For these cases the APIL sets out indirect grounds of jurisdiction, which are to be considered only in the context of recognition in order to judge whether the jurisdiction of the foreign court was well established. Indirect rules of jurisdiction do not establish the jurisdiction of the Hungarian courts but are used as a yardstick to ascertain if the jurisdiction of the foreign court was well established. The establishment of the jurisdiction of foreign (non-EU) courts cannot be tested under the EU rules, as non-EU courts do not enjoy the same trust as the judiciaries of sister member states.

There are also cases where the APIL establishes both direct and indirect grounds of jurisdiction. In these cases, the reason for establishing indirect grounds of jurisdiction is not the absence of direct rules, but the fact that the legislator intended to establish indirect grounds of jurisdiction more broadly or more narrowly than the direct ones.

According to Section 115 of the APIL, in succession matters the jurisdiction of the foreign court is deemed to be well-founded if it was based on the habitual residence or the citizenship of the decased at the time of death.

As regards proceedings relating to the dissolution of the matrimonial bond, which are governed by the Brussels II Regulation, the APIL lays down the habitual residence of the defendant, the last common habitual residence, and the common citizenship of the spouses as indirect grounds of jurisdiction (Section 116). It is important to stress that only the common citizenship of the spouses constitutes an indirect ground of jurisdiction; the citizenship of one of the spouses does not. This is a reasonable approach, but the non-recognition of a foreign judgment may sometimes put the Hungarian spouse in an unfair position. In view of this, the APIL states that, at the request of the Hungarian spouse, the foreign court's jurisdiction must be considered well-founded, and the decision must be recognized, provided there are no grounds for refusal. In the same vein, the APIL sets out indirect rules of jurisdiction concerning parental responsibility matters. The jurisdiction of the foreign court is well-founded if it is based on the habitual residence of the child or if the case is ancillary to proceedings concerning the matrimonial bond (Section 118).

As regards the existence, validity, and termination of registered partnerships, the APIL provides a wider set of indirect grounds of jurisdiction than of direct ones (Section 117).

Section 119 of the APIL sets out indirect rules of jurisdiction concerning maintenance matters. The jurisdiction of the foreign court is well-founded if it is based on either the defendant's or the maintenance creditor's habitual residence, or if it is ancillary to proceedings concerning personal status, parental responsibility, or guardianship, provided that that foreign court's jurisdiction was well-founded as to the latter.

Section 120 of the APIL deals with adoption, and provides that for the recognition of a foreign decision authorizing the adoption of a child with Hungarian citizenship the adoption must be approved by the Hungarian guardianship authority. This requirement does not apply if the child has multiple citizenships and his habitual residence at the time of the decision was in the state of the other citizenship. This provision aims to prevent limping family statuses, where a child has different family statuses in the countries he or she is a citizen of. Nonetheless, the decision of the foreign court must be recognized if recognition is requested by the adopted person who has come of age according to Hungarian law and who has Hungarian citizenship.

In order to be recognized and enforceable, the foreign judicial decision must be final and conclusive (*res judicata*). This is a major difference from the EU PIL instruments, which, in principle, accord the same status to the foreign judgment in the country of destination that it enjoys in the country of origin. If a judgment is not final but enforceable in the country of origin, these legal effects have to be recognized and enforced in the rest of the Member States. On the other hand, under the APIL a foreign judicial decision that was previously declared enforceable but has not yet become final cannot be recognized and enforced.

The grounds of refusal set out in the APIL include the grounds listed in Article 45(1)(a)-(d) of the Brussels I Regulation (violation of public policy, violation of the right of defense, irreconciliability with a Hungarian final judicial decision, irreconciliability with an earlier final judicial decision of the court of another state). Section 109(4)(c) of the APIL establishes a ground of refusal based on *lis pendens* that has no counterpart in the Brussels I Regulation: if Hungarian court proceedings were instituted before the launch of the foreign proceedings, the ensuing foreign judgment will not be recognizable in Hungary.

In general, the APIL does not require reciprocity for the recognition and enforcement of foreign judgments. Nonetheless, in pecuniary matters reciprocity is a requirement, except for cases where the jurisdiction of the Hungarian courts is excluded and where the jurisdiction of the foreign court was based on the parties' agreement.[73] As a corollary, reciprocity is not a prerequisite of recognition and enforcement in family law and personal status matters.

In the application of the APIL, reciprocity is understood as 'administrative' reciprocity, which exists when the authorities of the two states formally establish the existence of reciprocity. Therefore, the mere fact that the recognition and enforcement of Hungarian decisions would be ensured under the law of a country or that the courts of a country regularly recognize and enforce Hungarian judgments does not suffice in this regard.

Of course, reciprocity is not required where an international treaty provides otherwise. It is important to emphasize that an international treaty extinguishes the requirement of reciprocity only if it establishes enforceability using clear and unambiguous language.[74]

As noted above, reciprocity is not a prerequitite of recognition if the jurisdiction of the Hungarian courts is excluded and if the jurisdiction of the foreign court was based on the parties' agreement. It has to be stressed that only choice-of-court agreements are capable of removing the requirement of reciprocity, whereas jurisdiction based on appearance is not sufficient in this regard.

73 Section 113 of the APIL.

74 Case Pfv.VIII.23.958/1997 (Supreme Court), reported as BH 2000.212.

4.2 *EU Rules on Recognition and Enforcement*

There are fundamental differences between the APIL and EU PIL instruments as regards recognition and enforcement. On the one hand, under the APIL, if an international treaty does not provide otherwise, reciprocity is a precondition of recognition in pecuniary matters, except for cases where the jurisdiction of the Hungarian courts is excluded or where the jurisdiction of the foreign court was based on the parties' agreement. On the other hand, reciprocity plays no role in EU PIL instruments. Furthermore, under the APIL a foreign judicial decision can be recognized only if the foreign court's jurisdiction was well-founded in the light of the jurisdictional grounds used by the APIL. On the other hand, as a general principle, EU PIL instruments, though with some exceptions, prohibit the court of recognition from reviewing the jurisdiction of the court that delivered the judgment. The Insolvency Regulation departs from this principle. In Article 19(1) it provides for the recognition of the judicial decisions of the court that has jurisdiction: '[a]ny judgment opening insolvency proceedings handed down by a court of a Member State which has jurisdiction pursuant to Article 3 shall be recognised in all other Member States from the moment that it becomes effective in the State of the opening of proceedings'.

4.2.1 Brussels I Regulation

In Case *K.27480/2015/26*, the Administrative and Labor Court of Nyíregyháza, in a matter involving the judicial review of an administrative decision taken in a tax matter, established that the recognition of another Member State's judgment under the Brussels I Regulation does not imply that the facts established in the foreign judgment bind the Hungarian court.

In Case *Pfv.21258/2018/3*, the Supreme Court underscored, in the context of the 2001 Brussels I Regulation, that in the first stage of proceedings for a declaration of enforceability the court may examine only the fulfilment of the formal requirements and may not examine the legal and factual elements of the case.

In Case *Pfv.XI.21.581/2008/11*,[75] the applicant sought the enforcement of an Austrian judgment delivered against a Hungarian defendant. The civil proceedings were carried out in German and the court refused to translate the relevant documents (calls, forms, correspondence) into Hungarian, even though the defendant expressly requested that they be translated, because he did not speak German. The Supreme Court found that the enforcement of the judgment violated Hungarian public policy, as the Austrian civil proceedings were

75 Case 42.Pkfv.632.342/2008/2 (Budapest-Capital Regional Court).

irreconcilable with the fundamental principles of Hungarian civil procedure. These fundamental principles include the right to use one's mother tongue. A foreign judgment that does not respect this principle cannot be enforced in Hungary. Given that the defendant could not comprehend the forms, calls, and decisions of the Austrian court, the court had also violated its duty to inform, which was also part of Hungarian civil procedural law and was meant to ensure equal chances.

In Case *P.20071/2014/11*, the Budapest Regional Court dealt with Article 45(1)(b) of the Brussels I Regulation. It established that, at the recognition and enforcement stage, the court may not inquire whether the service of the document instituting the proceedings complied with the applicable rules. Thus, the debtor could not abuse its rights and evade enforcement if there was merely a formal error of service that did not hinder him in exercising his right of defense. If the defendant's right of defense was impaired during the service of the document instituting the proceedings, he was expected to exhaust the legal remedies available to him. If he failed to do so, the error of service did not entail the refusal of recognition. According to the Budapest Regional Court, at the recognition and enforcement stage it is not necessary to examine whether the service complied with the rules; the mere fact that an error has occurred is not susceptible of triggering the refusal of recognition. The court held that at the recognition stage it may be examined only whether the service of the document occurred 'in sufficient time and in such a way' as not to impair the defendant's right of defense. In the case of an error of service, the primary question is whether the error was grave enough to deprive the defendant of the ability to defend himself. In this case, the court answered the question in the negative.

In Case *Pfv.I.20.122/2015*,[76] the Supreme Court held that Article 45(1)(b) of the Brussels I Regulation cannot be applied if the debtor admitted that he received the payment order, which was forwarded to him by the judgment creditor's Italian legal representative, and directed his appeal to this legal representative and not to the court, notwithstanding the information conveyed to him. According to the Supreme Court, in this case the relevant point was that the debtor received the payment order of the court of Pisa and had 50 days to object to it but failed to do so. A formal procedural error that does not impair the right of defense is not sufficient to serve as a ground for refusal.

In Case *Pfv.20128/2016/9*,[77] the plaintiff sued the Hungarian court and claimed damages because he could not have a Hungarian judgment enforced in

76 Reported as BH + 2015.12.519.

77 Appealed from Case Pf.21115/2014/6 (High Court of Appeal of Budapest), appealed from Case P.20071/2014/11 (Budapest Regional Court).

Slovakia due to the Hungarian court's misapplication of the pertinent EU rules, including the Brussels I Regulation. In the earlier proceedings, the Hungarian plaintiff had claimed damages from a Slovak defendant. The Hungarian court decided for the plaintiff, but committed a serious procedural error: it served the Hungarian statement of claim and summons on the defendant without translating them into Slovak. The enforcement of the judgment was refused by the Slovak court with reference to this procedural error. This deprived the judgment of the possibility of being enforced in Slovakia. The Supreme Court held that the plaintiff was entitled to claim compensation from the Hungarian court because the court had violated the law and there was a causal link between the illegal act and the damage. It also noted that the legality of the Slovak decision to refuse enforcement could not be reviewed and that and its fairness could not be questioned.

4.2.2 Insolvency Regulation

In Case *12.Gf.40.010/2008/2*,[78] the High Court of Appeal of Budapest held that the *lex concursus* governs insolvency proceedings' effects on pending civil actions, but only where the latter were launched after the opening of the insolvency proceedings. If the individual civil action was launched before the opening of the insolvency proceedings, it is not the *lex concursus* but the *lex fori* that determines the impact of that opening. While Article 7(2)(f) of the Insolvency Regulation subjects the effects of the insolvency proceedings on proceedings brought by individual creditors' to '[t]he law of the State of the opening of proceedings', it excludes the effects of insolvency proceedings on 'pending lawsuits' from the ambit of the *lex concursus*.

The above approach was confirmed by the High Court of Appeal of Budapest in Case *Gf.40100/2013/8*.

Case *Gfv.VII.30.236/2012*[79] arose in the follow-up proceedings to Case C-527/10 *Erste*. Austrian law, as the law of the main proceedings, provided that all civil actions had to be launched in the context of the insolvency proceedings. This provision, by way of a procedural bar and not an issue of jurisdiction, blocked the enforcement of the creditor's security rights (bond) in Hungary. The question of interpretation was how Article 8 of the Insolvency Regulation affected the application of this rule. According to Article 7 of the Insolvency Regulation, the effects of the insolvency proceedings are, in principle, governed by the law of the Member State within the territory of which such proceedings

78 Reported as ÍH 2008.79.
79 Reported as EH 2013.2.G.4.

are opened. On the other hand, Article 8(1) provides that '[t]he opening of insolvency proceedings shall not affect the rights *in rem*' over assets located in other Member States. The Supreme Court held that the question whether a civil action may be launched for the enforcement of an *in rem* right is governed not by the *lex concursus* but by the *lex rei sitae*. The principle that the opening of the insolvency proceedings has no effect on *in rem* rights over assets located in other Member States implies that it does not affect their creation, validity, and effect, and that the creditor can enforce his right as if no main proceedings had been opened and the debtor was not under the effects of insolvency proceedings. As a corollary, the enforcement of the *in rem* right is not affected by the *lex concurcus* and the restrictions included in it.

4.2.3 Brussels II Regulation

In Case *Pfv.II.21.380/2010*,[80] the Supreme Court established that the recognition and enforcement of a judgment on parental responsibility delivered in another Member State cannot be refused merely because the enforcement of a Hungarian judgment concerning the child's abduction is pending.

In Case *Pfv.II.21.068/2013*,[81] the Supreme Court held that the recognition and enforcement of a judgment delivered in another Member State cannot be rejected if the chance to hear the child was ensured, even though this did not work out because the party concerned obstructed it. In this case the Belgian court established that, while the date of the hearing was carefully selected, the party did not ensure the child's appearance before the court and tried to justify this with a doctor's certificate two weeks thereafter. The Supreme Court held that it was at the Belgian court's discretion to decide whether to accept the certificate and appoint a new date or reject this, if it considered this appropriate to obviate the protraction of the procedure and to serve the best interests of the child. The Belgian court chose the second option.

In this case the Supreme Court also interpreted the concept of public policy as a ground for refusal of recognition and enforcement. It established that it is obviously not counter to Hungarian public policy if the foreign proceedings are based on rules different from the Hungarian ones. Public policy is to be construed narrowly and used exceptionally. Recognition and enforcement can be refused only if the foreign judgment would obviously run counter to Hungarian public policy, that is, if the decision entailed domestic legal consequences that would intolerably infringe the domestic sense of justice. It is

80 Reported as BH 2011.6.167.

81 Reported as BH 2014.8.248.

not sufficient for the foreign procedure and decision to be irreconcilable with domestic mandatory rules.

In Case *Pfv.II.21.594/2014*,[82] the defendant requested the Hungarian court to reject the recognition and enforcement of an Italian judgment because he had not been able to present his case. However, the Supreme Court established that he had had the opportunity to take part in the proceedings. Hence, there was no reason to apply Article 39(1)(b) of the Brussels II Regulation, which provides that the recognition and enforcement of the judgment must be rejected 'where it was given in default of appearance if the person in default was not served with the document which instituted the proceedings or with an equivalent document in sufficient time and in such a way as to enable that person to arrange for his or her defence unless it is determined that such person has accepted the decision unequivocally'. The Court held that the requirement that the document instituting the proceedings has to be served in sufficient time and in an appropriate way implies that the defendant has to have a real chance to appear in person and to hire a local attorney, that is, to defend himself. Accordingly, the primary purpose of the requirement of sufficient time is not to ensure that the defendant learns the date of the trial in time, but to make sure that the defendant has sufficient time to defend himself before the decision ending the proceedings is adopted. The requirement of appropriate way implies that during this time the defendant has the opportunity to defend himself in the proceedings, either personally or through an attorney, and eventually to request a new date for the trial and a personal hearing. The refusal of recognition and enforcement is an exceptional rule, which can be used only if the defendant is not afforded sufficient time between the service of the document instituting the proceedings and the decision ending them to take the necessary measures (e.g., to hire an attorney or to submit a defense as to the merits). In this case, this time was seven months. The Supreme Court noted that the defendant did not take the Italian proceedings seriously. It ignored the call concerning mandatory legal representation and hired no legal representative, thus excluding himself from the chance to protect his legal interests.

4.2.4 Maintenance Regulation

Hungarian law's provision that limits the payment of maintenance to six months' arrears raised questions of interpretation in the context of recognition and enforcement under the Maintenance Regulation. According to Hungarian law, the maintenance creditor may claim maintenance retrospectively for the

82 Reported as BH + 2015.5.211.

period exceeding six months only if the claim's late submission is justifiable; claims for maintenance for a period more than three years old are not legally enforceable.[83]

In Case *Pfv.I.21.308/2017/3*,[84] the maintenance judgment was issued by a French court, and under French law the limitation period was five years. However, in Hungary, the first and second instance courts held that enforcement was governed by local law and, as enforcement was sought in Hungary, the above six-month limitation period applied. The Supreme Court confirmed that, in case of enforcement in Hungary, the limitation period was to be determined by Hungarian law. However, the Court remanded the case because the lower-level courts established the time of the request for enforcement erroneously. While the first and second instance courts considered the request for enforcement submitted to the Hungarian court as relevant, the Supreme Court held that the creditor may claim maintenance as from the time he submitted his request to the French central authority and for the preceding six-months period.

Unfortunately, the Supreme Court's decision seems to be at odds with Article 21 of the Maintenance Regulation. Although Article 21(1) provides that refusal and suspension of enforcement are governed by the law of the Member State where enforcement is sought, Article 21(2) makes clear that enforcement cannot be refused if the claim is not time-barred under either the law of the country of origin or the country of enforcement. Enforcement may be refused 'if the right to enforce the decision of the court of origin is extinguished by the effect of prescription or the limitation of action, either under the law of the Member State of origin or under the law of the Member State of enforcement, whichever provides for the longer limitation period'. In the above case, the limitation period set by French law (country of origin) was five years, while under Hungarian law it was six months (with an objective term of three years). Given that French law provided for a longer limitation period, it should have been applied. Although Section 14 of the Hungarian Act on Court Enforcement (Act LIII of 1994) reproduces the above provision of the Civil Code and specifies the application of the six-month time limit in enforcement proceedings, the fact remains that this is a term of prescription, which, as such, comes under Article 21(2) of the Maintenance Regulation. The concepts of the Maintenance Regulation, in principle, have to be interpreted autonomously, so the characterization under Hungarian law should be of no relevance here.

83 Section 4:208 of the Civil Code.

84 Reported as BH 2018.4.120.

CHAPTER 5

Treaties in the Field of Private International Law and International Civil Procedure

1 Multilateral Treaties

1.1 *Multilateral Treaties Concluded by Hungary*

Treaty name, organization	Accession, entry into force	Hungarian title	Reservations declarations
1954 Convention on civil procedure, The Hague (HCCH)	Accession: May 21, 1965. Entry into force: February 18, 1966.	Promulgated by Law-Decree 8 of 1966 (in Hungarian: 'A polgári eljárásra vonatkozó, Hágában az 1954. évi március hó 1. napján kelt nemzetközi egyezmény kihirdetéséről szóló 1966. évi 8. törvényerejű rendelet')	
1956 Convention on the Recovery Abroad of Maintenance, New York (United Nations)	Accession: July 23, 1957. Entry into force: August 23, 1957	Promulgated by Law-Decree 53 of 1957 (in Hungarian: 'A tartásdíjak külföldön való behajtásáról New Yorkban, az 1956. évi június hó 20. napján kelt nemzetközi egyezmény kihirdetéséről szóló 1957. évi 53. törvényerejű rendelet')	
1958 Convention concerning the recognition and enforcement of decisions relating to maintenance obligations towards children, The Hague (HCCH)	Accession: October 20, 1964. Entry into force: December 19, 1964.	Promulgated by Law-Decree 7 of 1965 (in Hungarian: 'A gyermektartási kötelezettség tárgyában hozott határozatok elismeréséről és végrehajtásáról Hágában, az 1958. évi április hó 15-én aláírt egyezmény kihirdetéséről szóló 1965. évi 7. törvényerejű rendelet')	

 | DOI:10.1163/9789004694569_006

Treaty name, organization	Accession, entry into force	Hungarian title	Reservations, declarations
1958 Convention on the Recognition and Enforcement of Foreign Arbitral Awards, New York (UNCITRAL)	Accession: March 5, 1962. Entry into force: June 3, 1962.	Promulgated by Law-Decree 25 of 1962 (in Hungarian: 'A külföldi választottbírósági határozatok elismeréséről és végrehajtásáról szóló, New Yorkban, 1958. évi június hó 10. napján kelt egyezmény, kihirdette: 1962. évi 25. tvr.')	
1961 Convention Abolishing the Requirement of Legalisation for Foreign Public Documents, The Hague (HCCH)	Accession: April 18, 1972. Entry into force: January 18, 1973.	Promulgated by Law-Decree 11 of 1973 (in Hungarian: 'A külföldön felhasználásra kerülő közokiratok diplomáciai vagy konzuli hitelesítésének (felülhitelesítésének) mellőzéséről Hágában, az 1961. október 5. napján kelt egyezmény kihirdetéséről szóló 1973. évi 11. törvényerejű rendelet')	To Article 13[a]
1961 European Convention on International Commercial Arbitration, Geneva (United Nations, Economic Commission for Europe of the United Nations)	Accession: October 9, 1963. Entry into Force: January 9, 1964.	Promulgated by Law-Decree 8 of 1964 (in Hungarian: 'a nemzetközi kereskedelmi választottbíráskodásról szóló, Genfben 1961. április 21-én kelt Európai Egyezmény kihirdetéséről szóló 1964. évi 8. törvényerejű rendelet')	
1962 Convention on Consent to Marriage, Minimum Age for Marriage and Registration of Marriages,	Accession: November 5, 1975. Entry into force: February 3, 1976.	Promulgated by Law-Decree 7 of 1976 (in Hungarian: 'A házasságkötéshez szükséges kölcsönös beleegyezésről, legalsóbb korhatárról, valamint a házasságkötések anyakönyvezéséről szóló,	

Treaty name, organization	Accession, entry into force	Hungarian title	Reservations, declarations
New York (United Nations)		New Yorkban, 1962. évi december hó 10. napján kelt nemzetközi egyezmény kihirdetéséről szóló 1976. évi 7. törvényerejű rendelet')	
1965 Convention on the Service Abroad of Judicial and Extrajudicial Documents in Civil or Commercial Matters, The Hague (HCCH)	Accession: July 13, 2004. Entry into force: April 1, 2005.	Promulgated by Act XXXVI of 2005 (in Hungarian: 'A polgári és kereskedelmi ügyekben keletkezett bírósági és bíróságon kívüli iratok külföldön történő kézbesítéséről szóló, Hágában, 1965. november 15. napján kelt Egyezmény kihirdetéséről szóló 2005. évi XXXVI. törvény')	To Articles 2, 5, 6, 8, 9, 10, 15, 16
1965 Convention on the Settlement of Investment Disputes between States and Nationals of Other States, Washington	Accession: February 4, 1987. Entry into force: March 6, 1987.	Promulgated by Law-Decree 27 of 1987 (in Hungarian: 'Az Államok és más államok természetes és jogi személyei közötti beruházási viták rendezéséről szóló, Washingtonban, 1965. március 18-án kelt Egyezmény kihirdetéséről szóló 1987. évi 27. törvényerejű rendelet')	
1968 European Convention on Information on Foreign Law, London (Council of Europe)	Accession: November 16, 1989. Entry into force: February 17, 1990.	Promulgated by Governmental Regulation 140 of 1992 (in Hungarian: 'A külföldi jogról való tájékoztatásról szóló, Londonban, 1968. június 7. napján aláírt Európai Egyezmény, valamint a Strasbourgban, 1978. március 15. napján aláírt Egyezmény Kiegészítő Jegyzőkönyv kihirdetéséről szóló 140/1992. (X. 20.) Korm. rendelet')	

Treaty name, organization	Accession, entry into force	Hungarian title	Reservations, declarations
1970 Convention on the Taking of Evidence Abroad in Civil or Commercial Matters, The Hague (HCCH)	Accession: July 13, 2004. Entry into force: September 11, 2004.	Promulgated by Act CXVI of 2004 (in Hungarian: 'A polgári és kereskedelmi ügyekben történő bizonyításfelvételről szóló, 1970. március 17. napján kelt Hágai Egyezmény kihirdetéséről szóló 2004. évi CXVI. törvény')	To Articles 2, 4, 8, 15, 16, 17, 18, 23
1980 Convention on the Civil Aspects of International Child Abduction, The Hague (HCCH)	Accession: April 7, 1986. Entry into force: July 1, 1986.	Promulgated by Law-Decree 14 of 1986 (in Hungarian: 'A Gyermekek Jogellenes Külföldre Vitelének Polgári Jogi Vonatkozásairól szóló, Hágában 1980. október 25-én kelt egyezmény kihirdetéséről szóló 1986. évi 14. törvényerejű rendelet')	
1980 EC Convention on the Law Applicable to Contractual Obligations, Rome (European Community)	Accession: March 9, 2006. Entry into force: June 1, 2006.	Promulgated by Act XXVIII of 2006 (in Hungarian: 'A szerződéses kötelezettségekre alkalmazandó jogról szóló, Rómában, 1980. június 19-én aláírásra megnyitott egyezmény és jegyzőkönyvei, valamint az azokat módosító egyezmények kihirdetéséről szóló 2006. évi XXVIII. törvény')	
1980 European Convention on Recognition and Enforcement of Decisions	Singature: November 14, 2002. Ratification: February 4, 2004. Entry into force: June 1, 2004.	Promulgated by Act LXVIII of 2004 (in Hungarian: 'A gyermekek feletti felügyeleti jogot érintő határozatok elismeréséről és végrehajtásáról, valamint	To Articles 2, 17

Treaty name, organization	Accession, entry into force	Hungarian title	Reservations, declarations
concerning Custody of Children and on Restoration of Custody of Children, Luxembourg (Council of Europe)		a felügyeleti viszonyok helyreállításáról szóló, 1980. május 20. napján Luxemburgban kelt Európai Egyezmény kihirdetéséről szóló 2004. évi LXVIII. törvény')	
1993 Convention on Protection of Children and Co-operation in Respect of Intercountry Adoption, The Hague (HCCH)	Signature: May 25, 2004. Ratification: April 6, 2005 Entry into force: August 1, 2005.	Promulgated by Act LXXX of 2005 (in Hungarian: 'A gyermekeknek a nemzetközi örökbefogadások terén való védelméről és az ilyen ügyekben történő együttműködésről szóló, Hágában, 1993. május 29. napján kelt Egyezmény kihirdetéséről szóló 2005. évi LXXX. törvény')	To Articles 22, 23
1996 Convention on Jurisdiction, Applicable Law, Recognition, Enforcement and Co-operation in Respect of Parental Responsibility and Measures for the Protection of Children, The Hague (HCCH)	Signature: July 4, 2005. Ratification: January 13, 2006. Entry into force: May 1, 2006.	Promulgated by Act CXL of 2005 (in Hungarian: 'A szülői felelősséggel és a gyermekek védelmét szolgáló intézkedésekkel kapcsolatos együttműködésről, valamint az ilyen ügyekre irányadó joghatóságról, alkalmazandó jogról, elismerésről és végrehajtásról szóló, Hágában, 1996. október 19-én kelt Egyezmény kihirdetéséről szóló 2005. évi CXL. törvény')	Declarations to Articles 23, 26, 34, 52, 54, 55

Note:

a "The Republic of Hungary declares that the provisions of Article 13 of the Convention Abolishing the Requirement of Legalisation for Foreign Public Documents, done at The Hague on October 5, 1961, are contrary to resolution 1514/XV on the granting of independence to colonial countries and peoples, adopted by the General Assembly of the United Nations on December 14, 1960."

1.2 *Multilateral Treaties Concluded by the EU and Binding on Hungary*

Treaty name, organization	Accession, entry into force	Promulgation	Reservations, declarations
2005 Convention on Choice of Court Agreements, The Hague (HCCH)	Signature: April 1, 2009 Ratification: June 11, 2015 Entry into force: October 1, 2015	Council Decision 2014/887/EU	Declarations pursuant to Articles 21 & 30
2007 Convention on the International Recovery of Child Support and Other Forms of Family Maintenance, The Hague (HCCH)	Signature: April 6, 2011 Ratification: April 9, 2014 Entry into force: August 1, 2014	Council Decision 2011/432/EU	To Articles 2, 11, 44, 59
2007 Convention on jurisdiction and the recognition and enforcement of judgments in civil and commercial matters, Lugano	Signature: October 30, 2007 Ratification: May 18, 2009 Entry into force: January 1, 2010	Council Decision 2009/430/EC	Declarations pursuant to Article 69(4) and Protocol 1
2007 Protocol on the Law Applicable to Maintenance Obligations, The Hague (HCCH)	Signature: April 8, 2010 Ratification: April 8, 2010 Entry into force: August 1, 2013	Council Decision 2009/941/EC	Declarations pursuant to Articles 24

2 Bilateral Treaties

Albania	Hungarian-Albanian Treaty on legal assistance in civil, family law and criminal matters, signed in Tirana on January 12, 1960 (promulgated by Law-Decree 25 of 1960) (in Hungarian: '*a polgári, családjogi és bűnügyi jogsegély tárgyában Tiranában, az 1960. évi január hó 12. napján aláírt magyar-albán szerződés* (*kihirdette az 1960. évi 25. tvr.*')
Algeria	Hungarian-Algerian Treaty on legal assistance in civil, family law, and criminal matters, signed in Algiers on February 7, 1976 (promulgated by Law-Decree 15 of 1985) (in Hungarian: '*a polgári, családjogi és bűnügyi jogsegélyről szóló, Algírban 1976. február 7. napján aláírt magyar-algériai szerződés* (*kihirdette az 1985. évi 15. tvr.*)')
Australia	Hungarian-British Treaty on legal assistance in civil matters, signed in Budapest on September 25, 1935 (promulgated by Act XIII of 1936) (in Hungarian: '*a polgári jogsegély tárgyában Budapesten, az 1935. évi szeptember hó 25. napján kelt magyar-brit egyezmény* (*kihirdette az 1936. évi XIII. tc.*)')
Austria	Hungarian-Austrian Treaty on mutual legal assistance and deeds, signed in Vienna on April 9, 1965 (promulgated by Law-Decree 24 of 1967) (in Hungarian: '*a kölcsönös polgári jogsegélyforgalomról és az okiratokról Bécsben, az 1965. évi április hó 9. napján aláírt magyar-osztrák szerződés* (*kihirdette az 1967. évi 24. tvr.*)')
	Hungarian-Austrian Treaty on the regulation of probate (inheritance) matters, signed in Vienna on April 9, 1965 (promulgated by Law-Decree 25 of 1967) (in Hungarian: '*a hagyatéki ügyek szabályozásáról Bécsben, az 1965. évi április hó 9. napján aláírt magyar-osztrák szerződés* (*kihirdette az 1967. évi 25. tvr.*)')
Belarus	Hungarian-Soviet Treaty on legal assistance in civil, family law, and criminal matters, signed in Moscow on July 15, 1958, supplemented and amended by the protocol signed in Budapest on October 19, 1971 (promulgated by Law-Decree 38 of 1958) (in Hungarian: '*polgári, családjogi és bűnügyi jogsegély tárgyában Moszkvában, az 1958. évi július hó 15. napján aláírt magyar-szovjet szerződés, valamint az ezt kiegészítő és módosító, Budapesten 1971. évi október hó 19. napján aláírt jegyzőkönyv* (*kihirdette az 1958. évi 38. tvr.*)')

Belgium	Hungarian-Belgian Treaty on the facilitation of the application of the Convention on civil procedure signed in The Hague on March 1, 1954, signed in Brussels on May 11, 1983 (promulgated by Council of Ministers regulation 64/1984 of December 21) (in Hungarian: '*a polgári eljárásról szóló, Hágában az 1954. évi március hó 1. napján kelt Egyezmény alkalmazásának megkönnyítésére irányuló, Brüsszelben 1983. május hó 11. napján aláírt magyar-belga Megállapodás (kihirdette a 64/1984. (XII. 21.) MT rendelet)*')
Bosnia-Herzegovina	Treaty on mutual legal assistance, signed in Belgrade on March 7, 1968, as well as the Hungarian-Yugoslav Treaty, signed in Budapest on April 25, 1986, amending and supplementing it (promulgated by Law-Decree 1 of 1969) (in Hungarian: '*a kölcsönös jogsegélyről szóló, Belgrádban, az 1968. évi március hó 7. napján aláírt szerződés, valamint az ezt módosító és kiegészítő, Budapesten 1986. évi április hó 25. napján aláírt magyar-jugoszláv szerződés (kihirdette az 1969. évi 1. tvr.)*')
Bulgaria	Hungarian-Bulgarian Treaty on legal assistance in civil, family law, and criminal matters, signed in Sophia on May 16, 1966, as well as the Protocol signed in Budapest on September 15, 1981 amending and supplementing it (promulgated by Law-Decree 6 of 1967) (in Hungarian: '*a polgári, családjogi és bűnügyi jogsegély tárgyában Szófiában, 1966. évi május hó 16. napján aláírt magyar-bolgár szerződés, valamint az ezt módosító és kiegészítő Budapesten, 1981. évi szeptember hó 15-én aláírt jegyzőkönyv (kihirdette az 1967. évi 6. tvr.)*')
Canada	Hungarian-British Treaty on legal assistance in civil matters, signed in Budapest on September 25, 1935 (promulgated by Act XIII of 1936) (in Hungarian: '*a polgári jogsegély tárgyában Budapesten, az 1935. évi szeptember hó 25. napján kelt magyar-brit egyezmény (kihirdette az 1936. évi XIII. tc.)*')
China	Hungarian-Chinese Treaty on mutual legal assistance in civil and commercial matters, signed in Beijing on October 9, 1995 (promulgated by Law LXII of 1997); this Treaty does not apply to Macao and Hong-Kong (in Hungarian: '*a polgári és kereskedelmi ügyekben történő kölcsönös jogsegélyről szóló, Pekingben, 1995. év október hónap 9. napján aláírt magyar-kínai szerződés (kihirdette az 1997. évi LXII. tv.)*')

Croatia	Treaty on mutual legal assistance, signed in Belgrade on March 7, 1968, as well as the Hungarian-Yugoslav Treaty, signed in Budapest on April 25, 1986, amending and supplementing it (promulgated by Law-Decree 1 of 1969) (in Hungarian: '*a kölcsönös jogsegélyről szóló, Belgrádban, az 1968. évi március hó 7. napján aláírt szerződés, valamint az ezt módosító és kiegészítő, Budapesten 1986. évi április hó 25. napján aláírt magyar-jugoszláv szerződés* (*kihirdette az 1969. évi 1. tvr.*)')
Cuba	Hungarian-Cuban Treaty on legal assistance in civil, family law, and criminal matters, signed in Havana on November 27, 1982 (promulgated by Law-Decree 4 of 1984) (in Hungarian: '*a polgári, családjogi és bűnügyi jogsegély tárgyában Havannában, az 1982. évi november hó 27. napján aláírt magyar-kubai szerződés* (*kihirdette az 1984. évi 4. tvr.*)')
Cyprus	Hungarian-Cyprian Treaty on legal assistance in civil and criminal matters, signed in Budapest on November 30, 1981 (promulgated by Law-Decree 19 of 1983) (in Hungarian: '*polgári és bűnügyi jogsegélyről szóló, Budapesten 1981. november 30-án aláírt magyar-ciprusi szerződés* (*kihirdette az 1983. évi 19. tvr.*)')
Czech Republic	Hungarian-Czechoslovakian Treaty on legal assistance, as well as on the regulation of the legal relations concerning civil, family law, and criminal matters, signed in Bratislava on March 28, 1989 (promulgated by Law LXI of 1991) (in Hungarian: '*a jogsegélyről, valamint a polgári jogi, családjogi és a büntetőügyekre vonatkozó jogi kapcsolatok szabályozásáról szólóan létrejött, Bratislavában, az 1989. évi március hó 28. napján aláírt magyar-csehszlovák szerződés* (*kihirdette az 1991. évi LXI. tv.*)')
Egypt	Hungarian-Egyptian Treaty on legal assistance in civil and commercial matters signed in Cairo on March 26, 1996 (promulgated by Law CII of 1999) (in Hungarian: '*a polgári és kereskedelmi jogsegélyről szóló Kairóban, 1996. március 26. napján aláírt magyar-egyiptomi egyezmény* (*kihirdette az 1999. évi CII. tv.*)')
Fiji	Hungarian-British Treaty on legal assistance in civil matters, signed in Budapest on September 25, 1935 (promulgated by Act XIII of 1936); see decision 28/1974 of September 29 of the Presidential Council of the People's Republic (in Hungarian: '*a polgári jogsegély tárgyában Budapesten, az 1935. évi szeptember hó 25. napján kelt magyar-brit egyezmény* (*kihirdette az 1936. évi XIII. tc.*)*; lásd 28/1974.* (*IX.29.*)*. NET határozat.*')

Finland	Hungarian-Finnish Treaty on legal protection and legal assistance in civil, family law, and criminal matters, signed in Budapest on May 22, 1981 (promulgated by Law-Decree 25 of 1982) (in Hungarian: '*a polgári, családjogi és büntetőügyekben nyújtandó jogvédelemről és jogsegélyről szóló Budapesten, az 1981. évi május hó 22-én aláírt magyar-finn szerződés* (*kihirdette az 1982. évi 25. tvr.*)')
France	Hungarian-French Treaty on legal assistance, recognition and enforcement of decisions in civil and family law matters, as well as on criminal legal assistance and extradition, signed in Budapest on July 31, 1980 (promulgated by Law-Decree 3 of 1982) (in Hungarian: '*a polgári és a családjogi jogsegélyről, a határozatok elismeréséről és végrehajtásáról, valamint a bűnügyi jogsegélyről és a kiadatásról szóló Budapesten, az 1980. évi július 31. napján aláírt magyar-francia szerződés* (*kihirdette az 1982. évi 3. tvr.*)')
Germany	Reciprocity for the recognition and enforcement of judicial decisions that became final and conclusive (*res judicata*) after February 26, 1992 concerning property claims [claims having a monetary value] in civil and commercial matters, see Regulation 36 of 2017 of the Ministry of Justice (in Hungarian: '*36/2017. (XII. 29.) IM rendelet a nemzetközi jogsegélyre és a külföldi határozatok elismerésére és végrehajtására vonatkozó viszonosság megállapításáról*')
Greece	Hungarian-Greek Treaty on legal assistance in civil and criminal matters signed in Budapest on October 8, 1979 (promulgated by Law-Decree 21 of 1981) (in Hungarian: '*a polgári és bűnügyi jogsegélyről szóló Budapesten, az 1979. október hó 8. napján aláírt magyar-görög szerződés* (*kihirdette az 1981. évi 21. tvr.*)')
Iraq	Hungarian-Iraqi Treaty on the provision of legal assistance signed in Budapest on March 4, 1977 (promulgated by Law-Decree 11 of 1978) (in Hungarian: '*a jogsegély nyújtásáról Budapesten, az 1977. évi március hó 4. napján aláírt magyar-iraki szerződés* (*kihirdette az 1978. évi 11. tvr.*)')
Italy	Treaty on mutual legal assistance in civil matters concluded by the People's Republic of Hungary and the Italian Republic, signed in Budapest on May 26, 1977 (promulgated by Law-Decree 11 of 1981) (in Hungarian: '*A Magyar Népköztársaság és az Olasz Köztársaság között Budapesten az 1977. évi május hó 26. napján aláírt, a kölcsönös polgári jogsegélyről szóló egyezmény* (*1981. évi 11. tvr.*)')
	Reciprocity for the mutual recognition and enforcement of judicial decisions concerning property claims [claims

having a monetary value] in civil and commercial matters that became final and conclusive (res judicata) on April 1, 2003 or afterwards, see Regulation 36 of 2017 of the Ministry of Justice (in Hungarian: '*36/2017. (XII. 29.) IM rendelet a nemzetközi jogsegélyre és a külföldi határozatok elismerésére és végrehajtására vonatkozó viszonosság megállapításáról*')

Kenya	Hungarian-British Treaty on legal assistance in civil matters, signed in Budapest on September 25, 1935 (promulgated by Act XIII of 1936); see decision 14/1967 of May 16 of the Presidential Council of the People's Republic. (in Hungarian: '*a polgári jogsegély tárgyában Budapesten, az 1935. évi szeptember hó 25. napján kelt magyar-brit egyezmény (kihirdette az 1936. évi XIII. tc.); lásd 14/1967. (V. 16.) NET határozat.*')
Korea People's Republic	Treaty between the Hungarian People's Republic and the Korean People's Republic on legal assistance in civil, family law, and criminal matters, signed in Phenjan on October 5, 1970. (in Hungarian: '*a Magyar Népköztársaság és a Koreai Népi Demokratikus Köztársaság között a polgári, családjogi és bűnügyi jogsegélyről szóló, Phenjanban az 1970. évi október hó 5. napján aláírt szerződés kihirdetéséről*')
Kosovo	Treaty on mutual legal assistance, signed in Belgrade on March 7, 1968, as well as the Hungarian-Yugoslav Treaty, signed in Budapest on April 25, 1986, amending and supplementing it (promulgated by Law-Decree 1 of 1969) (in Hungarian: '*a kölcsönös jogsegélyről szóló, Belgrádban, az 1968. évi március hó 7. napján aláírt szerződés, valamint az ezt módosító és kiegészítő, Budapesten 1986. évi április hó 25. napján aláírt magyar-jugoszláv szerződés (kihirdette az 1969. évi 1. tvr.)*')
Lesotho	Hungarian-British Treaty on legal assistance in civil matters, signed in Budapest on September 25, 1935 (promulgated by Act XIII of 1936); see decision 29/1974 of September 29 of the Presidential Council of the People's Republic. (in Hungarian: '*a polgári jogsegély tárgyában Budapesten, az 1935. évi szeptember hó 25. napján kelt magyar-brit egyezmény (kihirdette az 1936. évi XIII. tc.); lásd 29/1974. (IX.29.) NET határozat.*')
Moldova	Hungarian-Soviet Treaty on legal assistance in civil, family law, and criminal matters, signed in Moscow on July 15, 1958, supplemented and amended by the protocol signed in Budapest on October 19, 1971 (promulgated by Law-Decree 38 of 1958) (in Hungarian: '*polgári, családjogi és bűnügyi jogsegély tárgyában x*

	having a monetary value] in civil and commercial matters that became final and conclusive (res judicata) on April 1, 2003 or afterwards, see Regulation 36 of 2017 of the Ministry of Justice (in Hungarian: '*36/2017. (XII. 29.) IM rendelet a nemzetközi jogsegélyre és a külföldi határozatok elismerésére és végrehajtására vonatkozó viszonosság megállapításáról*')
Mongolia	Hungarian-Mongolian Treaty on legal assistance in civil, family law, and criminal matters, signed in Budapest on November 22, 1968 (promulgated by Law-Decree 11 of 1969) (in Hungarian: '*a polgári, családjogi és bűnügyi jogsegély tárgyában Budapesten, az 1968. évi november hó 22. napján aláírt magyar-mongol szerződés (kihirdette az 1969. évi 11. tvr.)*')
Montenegro	Treaty on mutual legal assistance, signed in Belgrade on March 7, 1968, as well as the Hungarian-Yugoslav Treaty, signed in Budapest on April 25, 1986, amending and supplementing it (promulgated by Law-Decree 1 of 1969) (in Hungarian: '*a kölcsönös jogsegélyről szóló, Belgrádban, az 1968. évi március hó 7. napján aláírt szerződés, valamint az ezt módosító és kiegészítő, Budapesten 1986. évi április hó 25. napján aláírt magyar-jugoszláv szerződés (kihirdette az 1969. évi 1. tvr.)*') Remark: it is unclear whether this treaty is applicable in respect of Montenegro.[a]
New-Zealand	Hungarian-British Treaty on legal assistance in civil matters, signed in Budapest on September 25, 1935 (promulgated by Act XIII of 1936) (in Hungarian: '*a polgári jogsegély tárgyában Budapesten, az 1935. évi szeptember hó 25. napján kelt magyar-brit egyezmény (kihirdette az 1936. évi XIII. tc.)*')
North Macedonia	Treaty on mutual legal assistance, signed in Belgrade on March 7, 1968, as well as the Hungarian-Yugoslav Treaty, signed in Budapest on April 25, 1986, amending and supplementing it (promulgated by Law-Decree 1 of 1969) (in Hungarian: '*a kölcsönös jogsegélyről szóló, Belgrádban, az 1968. évi március hó 7. napján aláírt szerződés, valamint az ezt módosító és kiegészítő, Budapesten 1986. évi április hó 25. napján aláírt magyar-jugoszláv szerződés (kihirdette az 1969. évi 1. tvr.)*')
Poland	Hungarian-Polish Treaty on legal assistance in civil, family law, and criminal matters, signed in Budapest on March 6, 1959, as well as the Protocol signed in Warsaw on September 18, 1980, supplementing and amending it (promulgated by Law-Decree 5 of 1960) (in Hungarian: '*polgári családjogi és bűnügyi jogsegély tárgyában Budapesten, az 1959. évi március hó 6. napján aláírt*

	magyar-lengyel szerződés, valamint az ezt kiegészítő és módosító, Varsóban 1980. évi szeptember hó 18. napján aláírt, jegyzőkönyv (kihirdette az 1960. évi 5. tvr.)')
Romania	Hungarian-Romanian Treaty on legal assistance in civil, family law, and criminal matters, signed in Bucharest on October 7, 1958 (promulgated by Law-Decree 19 of 1959) (in Hungarian: '*a polgári, családjogi és bűnügyi jogsegély tárgyában Bukarestben, az 1958. évi október hó 7. napján aláírt magyar-román szerződés (kihirdette az 1959. évi 19. tvr.)*')
Russian Federation	Hungarian-Soviet Treaty on legal assistance in civil, family law, and criminal matters, signed in Moscow on July 15, 1958, supplemented and amended by the protocol signed in Budapest on October 19, 1971 (promulgated by Law-Decree 38 of 1958) (in Hungarian: '*polgári, családjogi és bűnügyi jogsegély tárgyában Moszkvában, az 1958. évi július hó 15. napján aláírt magyar-szovjet szerződés, valamint az ezt kiegészítő és módosító, Budapesten 1971. évi október hó 19. napján aláírt jegyzőkönyv (kihirdette az 1958. évi 38. tvr.)*')
Serbia	Treaty on mutual legal assistance, signed in Belgrade on March 7, 1968, as well as the Hungarian-Yugoslav Treaty, signed in Budapest on April 25, 1986, amending and supplementing it (promulgated by Law-Decree 1 of 1969) (in Hungarian: '*a kölcsönös jogsegélyről szóló, Belgrádban, az 1968. évi március hó 7. napján aláírt szerződés, valamint az ezt módosító és kiegészítő, Budapesten 1986. évi április hó 25. napján aláírt magyar-jugoszláv szerződés (kihirdette az 1969. évi 1. tvr.)*')
Slovakia	Hungarian-Czechoslovakian Treaty on legal assistance, as well as on the regulation of the legal relations concerning civil, family law, and criminal matters, signed in Bratislava on March 28, 1989 (promulgated by Law LXI of 1991) (in Hungarian: '*a jogsegélyről, valamint a polgári jogi, családjogi és a büntetőügyekre vonatkozó jogi kapcsolatok szabályozásáról szólóan létrejött, Bratislavában, az 1989. évi március hó 28. napján aláírt magyar-csehszlovák szerződés (kihirdette az 1991. évi LXI. tv.)*')
Slovenia	Treaty on mutual legal assistance, signed in Belgrade on March 7, 1968, as well as the Hungarian-Yugoslav Treaty, signed in Budapest on April 25, 1986, amending and supplementing it (promulgated by Law-Decree 1 of 1969) (in Hungarian: '*a kölcsönös jogsegélyről szóló, Belgrádban, az 1968. évi március hó 7. napján aláírt szerződés, valamint az ezt módosító és kiegészítő, Budapesten 1986. évi április hó 25. napján aláírt magyar-jugoszláv szerződés (kihirdette az 1969. évi 1. tvr.)*')

Syria	Hungarian-Syrian Treaty on legal assistance in civil and criminal matters, signed in Damascus on May 1, 1986 (promulgated by Law-Decree 9 of 1988) (in Hungarian: '*a polgári és bűnügyi jogsegélyről szóló, 1986. május 1. napján, Damaszkuszban aláírt magyar-szíriai egyezmény* (*kihirdette az 1988. évi 9. tvr.*)')
Tonga	Hungarian-British Treaty on legal assistance in civil matters, signed in Budapest on September 25, 1935 (promulgated by Act XIII of 1936); see decision 30/1974 of September 29 of the Presidential Council of the People's Republic (in Hungarian: '*a polgári jogsegély tárgyában Budapesten, az 1935. évi szeptember hó 25. napján kelt magyar-brit egyezmény* (*kihirdette az 1936. évi XIII. tc.*); *lásd 30/1974.* (*IX.29.*) *NET határozat.*')
Tunisia	Hungarian-Tunisian Treaty on legal assistance in civil and crimnal matters, on the recognition and enforcement of judicial decisions, as well as on extradition, signed in Budapest on December 6, 1982 (promulgated by Law-Decree 2 of 1985) (in Hungarian: '*a polgári és bűnügyi jogsegély, a bírói határozatok elismerése és végrehajtása, valamint a kiadatás tárgyában Budapesten, az 1982. évi december hó 6. napján aláírt magyar-tunéziai szerződés* (*kihirdette az 1985. évi 2. tvr.*)')
Turkey	Hungarian-Turkish Treaty on legal assistance in civil and commercial matters, signed in Ankara on June 6, 1988 (promulgated by Law LVII of 1992) (in Hungarian: '*a polgári és kereskedelmi ügyekben jogsegélyről szólóan létrejött, Ankarában 1988. évi június hó 6-án kelt magyar-török szerződés* (*kihirdette az 1992. évi LVII. tv.*)')
Ukraine	Treaty on legal assistance between the Hungarian Republic and Ukraine in civil matters, signed in Budapest on August 2, 2001 (promulgated by Law XVI of 2002) (in Hungarian: '*a Magyar Köztársaság és Ukrajna között a polgári ügyekben történő kölcsönös jogsegélyről szóló, Budapesten, 2001. augusztus 2-án aláírt szerződés* (*kihirdette a 2002. évi XVI. tv.*)')
United Kingdom	Hungarian-British Treaty on legal assistance in civil matters, signed in Budapest on September 25, 1935 (promulgated by Act XIII of 1936) (in Hungarian: '*a polgári jogsegély tárgyában Budapesten, az 1935. évi szeptember hó 25. napján kelt magyar-brit egyezmény* (*kihirdette az 1936. évi XIII. tc.*)')

United States of America	Reciprocity between the United States of America and Hungary regarding the enforcement of decisions on child and spousal maintenance, see Regulation 36 of 2017 of the Ministry of Justice (in Hungarian: '*36/2017. (XII. 29.) IM rendelet a nemzetközi jogsegélyre és a külföldi határozatok elismerésére és végrehajtására vonatkozó viszonosság megállapításáról*')
Vietnam	Agreement between Hungary and the Socialist Republic of Viet Nam on mutual legal assistance in civil matters, signed in Budapest on September 10, 2018 (promulgated by Act LXXXVII of 2018) (in Hungarian: '*2018. évi LXXXVII. törvény a Magyarország és a Vietnami Szocialista Köztársaság között a polgári ügyekben nyújtandó kölcsönös jogsegélyről szóló megállapodás kihirdetéséről*')

Note:

a Note that Montenegro was part of the State Union of Serbia and Montenegro, which was dissolved in June 2006 (Montenegro declared its independence on June 3, 2006, while Serbia declared its independence on June 5, 2006).

Annex: Act XXVIII of 2017 on Private International Law

Chapter 1: General Provisions[1]

1 *Scope of Application of the Act*

Section 1

Concerning private law relationships involving a foreign element, this Act determines:

a) the law of which state is to be applied,
b) the rules based on which Hungarian courts establish their jurisdiction and the procedural rules to be followed, and
c) the conditions for the recognition and enforcement of decisions rendered by foreign courts.

Section 2

The provisions of this Act shall apply to questions which do not fall under the scope of application of a legal act of the European Union which has general application and is directly applicable or an international treaty.

2 *Definitions*

Section 3

For the purpose of this Act,

a) court duly means also any other authority proceeding in private law matters, unless otherwise provided,
b) an individual's place of habitual residence is the place where, taking all the circumstances of the given legal relationship into account, the actual center of his life is located; in determining this, the facts referring to the intention of the person concerned must be also taken into consideration,

1 The translation of the APIL was prepared by Professor Tamás Szabados and first published as T. Szabados, "Hungary: Act XXVIII of 2017 on Private International Law," 82(4) *Rabels Zeitschrift für Ausländisches und Internationales Privatrecht* 1004–1045 (2018). This is an unofficial translation of the APIL's original version, as promulgated in *Magyar Közlöny* 2017, No. 54, 6527, as adopted by the Hungarian Parliament on April 4, 2017 and entered into force on January 1, 2018. It does not include the amendments that have been made to the act since then. The author of the present monograph is most grateful to Professor Tamás Szabados for his kind and generous permission to republish his translation in this monograph.

 | DOI:10.1163/9789004694569_007

c) domicile is the place where a person lives permanently or with the intention of settling there definitively.

3 *Qualification*

Section 4

(1) In deciding which choice-of-law rule will determine the law applicable to the facts, the concepts of Hungarian law shall govern.

(2) The qualification of a legal institution which is unknown in Hungarian law shall be carried out based on the foreign law regulating the legal institution, with special regard to its function and purpose in that foreign law.

(3) If a legal institution is not unknown in Hungarian law, but its function or purpose differs from the one it has in the foreign law, in the course of qualification the foreign law shall also be taken into consideration.

(4) Subsections (1)–(3) shall duly apply in the course of the establishment of jurisdiction as well as the recognition and enforcement of foreign decisions.

4 *Renvoi*

Section 5

(1) If the choice-of-law rules of this Act which determine the applicable law refer to a foreign law, the substantive provisions of that foreign law which directly decide the issue shall apply.

(2) If, pursuant to this Act, citizenship determines the applicable foreign law and the choice-of-law rule of that foreign law

a) refers back to Hungarian law, the substantive rules of Hungarian law shall apply;

b) refers to another foreign law, the substantive rules of this law shall apply.

5 *States with More Than One Legal System*

Section 6

(1) If, pursuant to this Act, the law of a state with more than one territorial unit applies to the facts, and these territorial units have their own legal system, the interstate choice-of-law rules of the given state determine the law of which territorial unit shall apply.

(2) If, pursuant to this Act, the law of a state which has various legal systems concerning various groups of persons applies to the facts, the interpersonal choice-of-law rules of the given state determine which law shall apply.

(3) If the applicable law does not contain interstate or interpersonal choice-of-law rules or their content cannot be established or if these rules do not lead to the designation of a single applicable law, that legal system of the given state shall apply which is most closely connected to the facts.

6 *Application and Establishment of the Content of Foreign Law*

Section 7

(1) The court shall apply foreign law ex officio.

(2) The court shall interpret the foreign law in accordance with the rules and practice of that law.

Section 8

(1) The court shall establish the content of foreign law ex officio.

(2) To establish the content of foreign law, the court may have recourse to any means, in particular the submissions of the parties, an expert opinion or the relevant information provided by the minister in charge of justice (hereinafter: the minister).

(3) If the content of foreign law cannot be established within a reasonable time, Hungarian law shall apply. If the facts concerned cannot be decided based on the rules of Hungarian law, the foreign law which is closest to the applicable law shall apply.

7 *Choice of Law*

Section 9

(1) Unless otherwise provided by this Act,

a) the choice of law must be made expressly,

b) the existence and validity of the choice-of-law agreement are governed by the law of that state whose law would apply to the legal relationship concerned in the case of the existence and validity of the agreement; however, the choice of law shall be also considered as existing and valid if it complies with the law of the state where the agreement was made.

(2) The choice of law may not prejudice the acquired rights of third parties.

8 *General Escape Clause*

Section 10

(1) If, based on the circumstances of the case, it is obvious that the case is substantially more closely connected to a law other than the law governing under this Act, this law may exceptionally apply. The court shall decide on this at the latest within thirty days after the defendant's counterplea has been received by the court.

(2) Subsection (1) cannot be applied if the governing law was determined by choice of law.

9 *General Subsidiary Choice-of-Law Rule*

Section 11

If this Act does not contain any rule for a legal relationship that falls under its scope of application, the law of that state to which the legal relationship is most closely connected shall apply.

10 *Public Policy Clause*

Section 12

(1) The application of the foreign law governing under this Act breaches Hungarian public policy and therefore shall be disregarded if the result thereof in the given case obviously and seriously violated the fundamental values and constitutional principles of the Hungarian legal system.

(2) If the violation of public policy cannot be prevented in any other way, the provisions of Hungarian law shall apply instead of the disregarded provision of foreign law.

11 *Overriding Mandatory Provisions*

Section 13

(1) Those provisions of Hungarian law whose content and purpose unequivocally establish their mandatory application in the legal relationships falling under the scope of application of this Act shall apply irrespective of the law governing under this Act (overriding mandatory provisions).

(2) The overriding mandatory provisions of another state may be taken into consideration if they are closely connected to the facts and they have decisive significance as to the determination of the case.

12 *Change of Status*

Section 14

A change in the circumstances determining the applicable law shall impact legal relationships which validly came into existence in accordance with the law applicable before the change only if this Act expressly so provides.

Chapter 2: Persons

13 *Human Being as Subject of Law*

Section 15

(1) An individual's legal capacity, disposing capacity and personal rights shall be adjudged according to his personal law.

(2) An individual's personal law is the law of the state of his citizenship.

(3) If a person has multiple citizenships and one of his citizenships is Hungarian, his personal law is Hungarian law, unless he is more closely connected to his other citizenship.

(4) The personal law of a person who has multiple citizenships, none of which is Hungarian, is the law of the state of his citizenship to which he is most closely connected, taking the relevant circumstances of the case into account.

(5) The personal law of a person who has multiple citizenships, none of which is Hungarian, and who is not more closely connected to any of his citizenships, and of a person whose citizenship may not be established as well as of a stateless person, is the law of the state where his place of habitual residence is located.

(6) If an individual's personal law cannot be established on the basis of subsections (2)–(5), Hungarian law shall apply.

(7) Hungarian law shall apply to the legal relationships specified in subsection (1) for a person enjoying the right of asylum in Hungary and for a person admitted to Hungary.

Section 16

(1) Regarding the bearing of a name, the individual's personal law or, at his request, Hungarian law shall apply.

(2) Regarding the bearing of his birth name, a person having multiple citizenships may choose the law of any of his citizenships.

(3) Regarding the bearing of the married name, at the parties' joint request, the law of the citizenship of either of the spouses or Hungarian law shall apply. In the absence of a joint request, section 27 applies.

(4) Regarding the bearing of a name, the law of the state based on which the married name came into existence shall apply in the case of the dissolution or the establishment of the invalidity of the marriage.

(5) The birth name as well as the married name of a Hungarian citizen which has been validly registered under the law of another state must be recognized in Hungary if the person concerned having Hungarian citizenship or his spouse is also a citizen of this other state or if the place of habitual residence of the Hungarian citizen concerned is located in that state. A name which violates Hungarian public policy may not be recognized.

Section 17

(1) A person who has no disposing capacity or who has restricted disposing capacity under his personal law shall be regarded as a person having disposing capacity in terms of contracts of minor significance

that are concluded and performed in Hungary and which take place in large numbers in everyday life and which would not require any particular consideration if this person had disposing capacity under Hungarian law.

(2) A person who has no disposing capacity or has restricted disposing capacity under his personal law but who would have disposing capacity under Hungarian law shall be regarded as a person having disposing capacity also in terms of this person's other property transactions if the legal consequences of the transaction arise in Hungary.

Section 18

(1) Regarding the conditions, existence, modification, termination, and legal consequences of being placed under conservatorship or of other protective measures not affecting an adult's disposing capacity and the legal relationships arising from this, the law of that state shall apply where the place of habitual residence of the person concerned is located at the time of the adjudication of the underlying facts.

(2) If it is justified by the interests of the adult concerned, the court seised may exceptionally apply or take into account the law of another state to which the case is more closely connected.

Section 19

(1) Section 18 shall duly apply also to the existence, validity, scope, modification, and withdrawal of a legal declaration, made by an adult having disposing capacity for the case of a future limitation of his disposing capacity or the absence of his capacity to protect his interests, so that the law of the state of the place of habitual residence existing at the time of making the legal declaration shall apply to these isues.

(2) Irrespective of subsection (1), an adult who has disposing capacity can choose by written declaration: a) the law of the state of his citizenship, b) the law of that state where he previously had his place of habitual residence, c) regarding a specified object of property, the law of that state in whose territory the object of property is located.

Section 20

Regarding the legal representation of a person prevented from managing his own affairs and regarding ad hoc conservatorship, the law of the state of the appointing court shall apply.

Section 21

(1) Regarding a declaration of death or a missing person as well as in regards to establishing the fact of death, the missing person's personal law shall apply.

(2) If the missing person's personal law is not Hungarian law, Hungarian law shall apply in the case of the existence of any domestic legal interest.

14 *Legal Persons*

Section 22

(1) The personal law of a legal person is the law of that state in whose territory the legal person was incorporated.

(2) If a legal person is incorporated under the laws of more than one state, or no incorporation is required under the law applicable at the place of the seat indicated in the statute, its personal law shall be the law of that state where its seat as indicated in its statute is located.

(3) If a legal person has no seat under its statute, or has several such seats and is not incorporated in accordance with the law of any of these states, its personal law shall be the law of that state in whose territory its place of central administration is located.

(4) The legal status of a legal person, in particular

a) its legal capacity,

b) its formation and termination,

c) its legal and organizational representation,

d) its personality rights,

e) its organization,

f) the legal relationships between its members,

g) the legal relationships between the members and the legal person, and

h) the responsibility of the legal person, its members, and its executive officers for the obligations of the legal person shall be adjudged according to the personal law of the legal person.

(5) The provisions contained in this section shall duly govern entities which do not have legal personality.

15 *Violation of Personality Rights*

Section 23

(1) Regarding the violation of personality rights, the law of the place of habitual residence of the injured party – in the case of a legal person that of its seat as indicated in the statute – shall apply. It must be adjudged under this law whether any violation of law occurred and the

consequences of the violation of law shall be established in accordance with this same law.

(2) A person whose personality rights have been violated can choose at the latest within the deadline set by the court in the pleading phase: a) the law of that state where the center of his interests is located, b) the law of that state where the wrongdoer has his place of habitual residence – in the case of a legal person the seat indicated in the statute, or c) Hungarian law. (3) Subsections (1)–(2) shall also apply in cases where there is a risk of a violation of personality rights.

Chapter 3: Family Law

16 *General Rules*

Section 24

The common citizenship of spouses is the citizenship both possess. If spouses have more than one common citizenship, for the purpose of this Chapter, that common citizenship shall be taken into account to which they are most closely connected considering all the circumstances of the case.

Section 25

Regarding family law relationships concerning a child, Hungarian law shall apply provided that it is more favorable to the child.

17 *Special Rules on Marriage*

Section 26

(1) A marriage is valid only if the substantive law conditions thereof are satisfied under the personal law of both intended spouses at the time of concluding the marriage.

(2) Regarding the formal requirements of the validity of marriage, the law in force at the place and date of the celebration of marriage shall apply.

(3) The provisions on the conclusion of marriage and the validity thereof shall duly apply also to the question of establishing the existence or non-existence of marriage.

(4) The marriage may not be celebrated in Hungary if there is an unavoidable impediment to the celebration of the marriage under Hungarian law.

Section 27

(1) Regarding the personal and property relationships of the spouses – subject to the deviations laid down in section 16 (3)–(5) – the law of that

state of which both spouses possess citizenship at the time of adjudication shall apply.

(2) If the personal laws of the spouses are different at the time of adjudication, the law of that state shall apply in whose territory the spouses' common place of habitual residence is located, or in the absence of this their last common place of habitual residence.

(3) If the spouses had no common place of habitual residence, the law of the state of the court seised shall apply.

Section 28

(1) The spouses may choose the law applicable to their property relationships, provided that this is one of following laws:

a) the law of that state the citizenship of which one of the spouses possesses at the time of concluding the agreement,

b) the law of that state in whose territory one of the spouses has his place of habitual residence at the time of concluding the agreement,

c) the law of the state of the court seised.

(2) Parties intending to marry are also entitled to choose the applicable law.

(3) The choice of law is possible at the latest within the deadline set by the court in the pleading phase.

(4) If the spouses do not agree otherwise, the choice of the law applicable to the property relationships of the spouses has legal effect only prospectively.

Section 29

A matrimonial property contract is formally valid also if it complies with the law of the place of its conclusion.

Section 30

The spouses may choose the applicable law in accordance with Articles 5–7 of Council Regulation (EU) No 1259/2010 at the latest within the deadline set by the court in the pleading phase.

18 *Family Status*

Section 31

(1) On questions regarding the establishment of paternity or maternity and the rebuttal of the presumption of paternity, the personal law of the child prevailing at the time of his birth shall apply.

(2) The recognition of a child by the father shall be adjudged under the personal law of the child prevailing at the time of recognition; the recognition of a child already conceived but not yet born shall be adjudged under the personal law of the mother prevailing at the time of recognition. The recognition may not be considered as invalid for formal reasons if it is formally valid either under Hungarian law or under the law in force at the place and time of recognition.

Section 32

If the status of the father is not filled under the law applicable based on section 31, the law of another state closely connected to the case shall apply if it is more favorable to the child in this regard.

19 *Adoption*

Section 33

(1) An adoption is valid only if the conditions thereof are met under the personal law of both the adoptive parent and the person intended to be adopted at the time of adoption.

(2) Regarding the legal effects of an adoption, the termination of an adoption, and the legal effects thereof, the personal law of the adoptive parent at the time of the adoption or the termination thereof shall apply.

(3) If the adoptive parents are spouses, the law to be applied regarding the legal effects of the adoption, the termination of the adoption, and the legal effects thereof shall be

a) the law of the state of the common citizenship of the spouses prevailing at the time of the adoption or the termination thereof; in the absence of this,

b) the law of the state in whose territory the spouses had a common place of habitual residence at the time of the adoption or the termination thereof; in the absence of this,

c) the law of the state of the court seised.

20 *Legal Relationship between Parent and Child, Guardianship*

Section 34

(1) Regarding the legal relationship between parent and child and regarding guardianship – with the exceptions of becoming of full age and bearing a name – the law of the state of the court seised shall apply.

(2) If it is justified by the interests of the child, the court seised may exceptionally apply or take into account the law of another state to which the case is closely connected.

Chapter 4: Partners, Registered Partners

21 *Partners*

Section 35

(1) Regarding the existence, termination, and legal effects of a partnership, the law of the state of the common citizenship of the partners shall apply.

(2) If the citizenships of the partners are different, the law of that state shall apply in whose territory the place of habitual residence of the partners is located, or in the absence of this their last common place of habitual residence.

(3) If the common place of habitual residence of the partners cannot be established, the law of the state of the court seised shall apply.

(4) The provisions of section 24 shall duly apply to the common citizenship of the partners.

Section 36

Partners may choose the law applicable to their property relationships. Section 28 shall duly apply to the choice of law by the partners.

22 *Registered Partners*

Section 37

(1) Regarding the existence, validity, and legal effects of a registered partnership, not including the bearing of a name, the provisions of sections 26–29 shall duly apply, subject to the exceptions specified in this section.

(2) It is not an impediment to the conclusion of a registered partnership and the validity thereof is not affected if the personal law of the intended registered partner does not provide for the legal institution of registered partnership of same-sex couples, provided that

a) the intended registered partner not having Hungarian citizenship proves that there would be no impediment to the conclusion of marriage under his personal law, and

b) at least one of the intended registered partners is a Hungarian citizen or has his place of habitual residence in Hungary.

(3) Regarding the legal effects of a registered partnership, Hungarian law shall apply in the cases specified in subsection (2).

(4) The provisions of section 24 shall duly apply to the common citizenship of the registered partners.

Section 38

(1) Regarding the termination of a registered partnership, the law of that state shall apply

a) in whose territory the place of habitual residence of the registered partners is located at the time of filing the action or request for the termination of the registered partnership; in the absence of this

b) in whose territory the last place of habitual residence of the registered partners is located if this place of habitual residence was terminated no more than one year before filing the action or request, provided that one of the registered partners still resides in this state at the time of filing the action or request; in the absence of this

c) of which both registered partners were citizens at the time of filing the action or request.

(2) If the applicable law cannot be determined based on subsection (1), as well as in the cases specified in section 37(2), the court seised shall apply the law of its own state.

Chapter 5: Rights in Rem

23 *General Rules*

Section 39

(1) Unless otherwise provided by this Act, the law applicable at the place of the location of a thing shall apply to the property right and other rights in rem, including pledge and possession.

(2) The law applicable at the place of the location of a thing is the law of that state in whose territory the thing is located at the time of the emergence of the fact giving rise to the legal effect.

(3) If a thing is a component part or accessory of another thing, the law of the place of the location of the main thing shall apply; regarding other connections between things or an aggregate of things, the law which is most closely connected to it shall apply.

Section 40

The applicable law determines, in particular

a) the legal characteristics of the thing,

b) the content of the right in rem,

c) the order of the charges encumbering the thing,

d) the holder of the right in rem,
e) the coming into existence, the existence, and the termination of the right in rem, and
f) the effect of the right in rem towards third parties.

Section 41

(1) If, after a change in the right in rem, the movable thing is relocated to the territory of another state permanently, the rights acquired previously may be recognized in accordance with the law of the new place of location of the thing.
(2) If the legal effect of the acquisition of a right in rem did not take place at the previous place of location and the movable thing is relocated to the territory of another state permanently, the law of this latter state shall apply to the acquisition of rights.
(3) Regarding adverse possession of a movable thing, the law of that state shall apply in whose territory the thing was located at the time of the expiry of the period of adverse possession.
(4) Adverse possession shall not be interrupted by a change in the location of the thing.

24 *Special Rules*

Section 42

(1) Regarding rights in rem related to a registered watercraft or aircraft, the law of that state shall apply under whose flag or other insignia the vehicle is operating.
(2) Regarding rights in rem related to a railway vehicle, the law of that state shall apply where it was put into operation.

Section 43

(1) The law of the state of destination shall apply to rights in rem related to a movable thing in transit. Regarding the in rem legal effects related to the sale, storage, or pledging of a movable thing in transit, if this takes place beyond the will of the owner or the person entitled to dispose over it, the law applicable at the place of the location of the thing at the time of the measure shall apply.
(2) The personal law of a passenger shall apply to the rights in rem related to objects taken along for the purpose of personal use.

Section 44

(1) Regarding a security in rem which comes into existence with its registration, the law of the state where the register of securities is kept shall apply.

(2) If the coming into existence of a security in rem does not require registration or the applicable law cannot be established in accordance with subsection (1), the personal law of the security debtor shall apply to the security in rem.

(3) Regarding a movable thing transferred with reservation of title, the law of the state of the place of the location of the thing shall apply to the legal effects of the reservation of title, except if the parties choose the law of the destination of the movable thing transferred.

(4) Regarding a security related to a payment account, bank deposit, or dematerialized securities, the law of that state shall apply in which the register or the account containing the security is kept or in which the central depository system operates.

(5) Regarding a security over a claim, the law chosen by the parties shall apply; in the absence of this, the law of the state where the security was registered, or, in the case of a security which was not registered, the personal law of the security debtor shall apply.

Section 45

(1) In their contract transferring ownership of a movable thing, the parties may choose the law of the state of the place of location or the destination of the thing specified in the contract as regards the in rem legal effects.

(2) If the assets of an undertaking (business) are transferred as a whole, with the exception of the immovable property, the parties may choose the personal law of the legal predecessor as regards the in rem legal effects.

(3) The choice of law is possible at the latest within the deadline set by the court in the pleading phase.

Section 46

(1) If a thing deemed by a state as belonging to its own cultural goods leaves the territory of that state in a way which is illegal under the laws of that state at the time of export, regarding the property claim brought by that state, at the choice of the state bringing the claim, either the law of this state or the law of that other state, in whose territory the thing concerned is located at the time of adjudication of the property claim, shall apply.

(2) If the law of the state which deems the illegally exported thing as belonging to its own cultural goods does not provide protection for a bona fide possessor, this person may claim protection in accordance with the law of that state in whose territory the thing concerned is located at the time of adjudication of the property claim.

Section 47

(1) Regarding a property claim related to a thing taken illegally from the possession of the original owner, at the choice of the original owner, either the law of that state in whose territory the thing was located at the time of its disappearance or the law of that state in whose territory the thing is located at the time of adjudication of the property claim shall apply.

(2) If the law of the state in whose territory the thing was located at the time of disappearance does not provide protection for a bona fide possessor, this person may claim protection in accordance with the law of that state in whose territory the thing concerned is located at the time of adjudication of the property claim.

Chapter 6: Intellectual Property Rights

25 *Copyrights and Industrial Property Rights*

Section 48

Regarding the existence, content, termination, and enforcement of copyrights, the law of that state shall apply for whose territory the protection is claimed.

Section 49

Regarding the existence, content, termination, and enforcement of industrial property rights, the law of that state shall apply in which the protection was granted or where the application was made.

Chapter 7: The Law of Obligations

26 *Contractual Obligations*

Section 50

(1) The law chosen by the parties shall apply to a contract. If the choice has not been made expressly, it must be clearly demonstrated by the terms of the contract or the circumstances of the case. By their choice, the parties can select the law applicable to the whole contract or to only a part of the contract.

(2) The choice of law is possible at the latest within the deadline set by the court in the pleading phase.

(3) Without prejudice to subsection (2), the parties may agree that instead of the law which – based on choice of law under this section or in the absence of this based on the provisions of this Act – previously governed the contract, another law shall apply. Any amendment to the provisions of the contract on the applicable law that is made after the conclusion of the contract does not affect the validity of the contract in accordance with the law governing validity as to form.

(4) If the contract is connected to the law of a single state, the choice of law may not prejudice those provisions of this law which cannot be derogated from by agreement.

(5) Sections 53–54 shall duly apply to the existence and validity of the agreement of the parties as to the choice of the applicable law.

Section 51

In the absence of a choice of law, the law of that state to which the contract is most closely connected based on the relevant elements of the given legal relationship shall apply.

Section 52

(1) The parties may choose the law applicable to an arbitration agreement.

(2) In the absence of a choice of law, the law chosen to govern the underlying legal relationship shall apply to an arbitration agreement, or in the absence of this the law governing the underlying legal relationship in the absence of a choice of law shall apply.

(3) If the parties have designated the place of the arbitration proceedings, the law of the state of the place of the proceedings shall apply to the arbitration agreement, provided that this law is more closely connected to the agreement than the law specified in subsection (2).

(4) An arbitration agreement may not be deemed to be formally invalid if it complies with the formal requirements of any of the laws specified in this section or of the law of the state of the court seised.

Section 53

The existence and validity of a contract, or of any term of a contract, shall be determined by the law which would be applicable based on this Act if the contract or the contract term were valid.

Section 54

(1) A contract is formally valid between those persons who are, or whose agents are, in the same state at the time of the conclusion of the contract if the contract complies with the formal requirements of the law applicable under this Act or of the law of the state where it is concluded.

(2) A contract is formally valid between those persons who are, or whose agents are, in different countries at the time of its conclusion if the contract complies with the formal requirements of the law applicable under this Act or of the law of that state where either of the parties or his agent is present at the time of the conclusion of the contract, or where either of the parties had his place of habitual residence at the given time.

(3) A unilateral legal declaration intended to have legal effect regarding an existing or contemplated contract is formally valid if it complies with the formal requirements of the law applicable to the contract under this Act or of the law which would be applicable to the contract, or if it complies with the formal requirements of the law of the state where the legal declaration was made, or of the state where the person by whom the legal declaration was made had his place of habitual residence at the time of making the legal declaration.

(4) Notwithstanding subsections (1)–(3), the formal requirements provided by the law of the state where the property is located shall govern a contract the subject matter of which is a right in rem in immovable property or the renting of immovable property if: a) these requirements shall apply mandatorily irrespective of the place of contracting and the law governing the contract, and b) these requirements cannot be derogated from by agreement.

Section 55

(1) For the purpose of this subchapter, the place of central administration shall be considered as the place of habitual residence of a legal person or an entity which does not have legal personality. The place of habitual residence of a natural person acting in the course of his business activity shall be his principal place of business.

(2) In the case of a contract concluded in the course of the operation of a branch, agency, or any other establishment, or if a branch, agency, or any other establishment is obliged to perform under the contract, the state where the branch, agency, or any other establishment is located shall be considered as the place of habitual residence.

(3) For the purpose of determining the place of habitual residence, the time of the conclusion of the contract is relevant.

Section 56

Unless otherwise provided by this Act, the rules on contracts shall duly apply to unilateral declarations.

27 *Securities*

Section 57

(1) Regarding the formalities and nature of a security, including whether it is a bearer or registered security, the law of that state shall apply whose law applies to the right incorporated in the security.

(2) The provisions on rights in rem in this Act shall duly apply to the in rem legal effects of the disposition of a security.

(3) Regarding the legal effects of the disposition of a dematerialized security, beyond the right incorporated in the security, the law of that state shall apply which carries out state supervision over the provider of the securities account, or in the absence of this, where the securities account is kept. If the application of more than one law arises according to this, the law of that state shall apply which ensures the acquisition of rights by the right holder.

Section 58

(1) Regarding a right under the law of obligations based on a security, the law chosen by the parties shall apply; in the absence of this the place where the security was issued; if this cannot be established, the personal law of the issuer shall apply.

(2) Regarding a membership right incorporated in a security, the personal law of the issuer shall apply.

(3) Regarding a right in rem incorporated in a security, the law of the state of the place where the security was issued shall apply.

(4) If a security embodies more than one right, in the absence of a choice of law the provisions governing the right constituting the central element of the security shall apply.

28 *Non-contractual Obligations*

Section 59

The person seeking damages may choose the law of the place in which the event giving rise to the damage occurred in accordance with the second branch of Article 7 of Regulation (EC) No. 864/2007 of the European Parliament and of the Council, at the latest within the deadline set by the court in the pleading phase.

Section 60

Regarding non-contractual obligations, the law of that state shall apply in whose territory the effect of the legal fact giving rise to the obligation occurred.

Section 61

If the obligee and the obligor of a non-contractual legal relationship both have their place of habitual residence – or in the case of a legal person, its seat as indicated in its statute – in the same state at the time when the effect of the legal fact giving rise to the obligation occurs, the law of this state shall apply.

Section 62

If the non-contractual legal relationship is closely connected to another legal relationship already existing between the parties when the non-contractual legal relationship comes into existence, the law governing this other legal relationship shall apply also to the non-contractual legal relationship.

Section 63

(1) The parties may choose the applicable law subsequent to the emergence of the non-contractual obligation. If the choice has not been made expressly, it must be clearly demonstrated by the circumstances of the case.

(2) The choice of law is possible at the latest within the deadline set by the court in the pleading phase.

(3) If the legal relationship is connected to the law of a single state, the choice of law may not prejudice those provisions of this law which cannot be derogated from by agreement.

Chapter 8: Law of Succession

29 *Oral Will, Inheritance by the State*

Section 64

An oral will and its revocation are formally valid if they comply with

a) Hungarian law,

b) the law in force at the place and time of the will's making and revocation,

c) the law which was the personal law of the deceased at the time of making or revoking the oral will or at the time of the deceased's death,

d) the law in force at the deceased's domicile or place of habitual residence at the time of making or revoking the oral will or at the time of the deceased's death, or
e) in the case of an oral will concerning immovable property, the law prevailing at the location of the immovable property.

Section 65

If, under the law applicable to succession, an estate located in Hungary does not have an heir, the rules of Hungarian law governing succession by the Hungarian State shall apply to the inheritance of the estate located in Hungary.

Chapter 9: Procedural Provisions

30 *General Rules*

Section 66

Unless otherwise provided by this Act, Hungarian law shall apply to the proceedings of a Hungarian court.

Section 67

(1) Regarding the legal effects of insolvency proceedings initiated before a Hungarian court, Hungarian law shall apply.
(2) Regarding the effects of insolvency proceedings on the rights of a debtor in immovable property, a ship, or an aircraft and in security subject to registration in a public register and on contracts concerning the acquisition or the alienation of such rights for consideration, the law of the state of the location of the immovable property or in which the register is kept shall apply.

Section 68

(1) Regarding the legal capacity and disposing capacity of a party in a lawsuit, his personal law shall apply.
(2) A person who has no disposing capacity or who has restricted disposing capacity under his personal law but who would have disposing capacity under Hungarian law shall be considered as having disposing capacity in proceedings before a Hungarian court.
(3) Subsection (2) does not exclude that a legal representative entitled to act in accordance with his personal law shall proceed in place of a person having no disposing capacity or having restricted disposing capacity under his personal law.

(4) The capacity to be party to legal proceedings of a legal person or an entity not having legal personality that is registered abroad must be presumed until proven to the contrary.

Section 69

(1) If between the parties, at the time of instituting the proceedings, proceedings stemming from the same facts and for the same claim has been brought previously before a foreign court, the Hungarian court may stay the procedure, ex officio or upon request, provided that the recognition of the decision of the foreign court in Hungary is not excluded.

(2) The Hungarian court shall continue the proceedings if the proceedings were terminated before the foreign court without a decision on the merits. The Hungarian court may continue the proceedings if the foreign proceedings were stayed or it considers that the foreign proceedings cannot be expected to be concluded within a reasonable time. If a circumstance giving cause to the continuation of the proceedings takes place, the parties are obliged to notify the court of this without delay. The court may at any time review the justification for staying proceedings; for this purpose it may call upon the parties by setting a deadline to make a declaration on the procedural acts done before a foreign court.

(3) Subsections (1)–(2) shall also apply if an action which is related to an action that has been brought before a foreign court is brought before a Hungarian court.

(4) If the foreign court issued a decision on the merits of the case which is capable of recognition in Hungary, the Hungarian court shall terminate the proceedings.

(5) For the purpose of this Act, the proceedings shall be considered as instituted

a) at the time when the document instituting the proceedings is lodged with the court, provided that the claimant has not subsequently failed to take the steps he was required to take to have service effected on the defendant, or

b) if the document has to be served before being lodged with the court, at the time when it is received by the authority responsible for service, provided that the claimant has not subsequently failed to take the steps he was required to take to have the document lodged with the court.

Section 70

(1) A Hungarian court may adopt a provisional measure, including a protective measure, in accordance with Hungarian law concerning a person

or property located in Hungary even if it does not have jurisdiction as to the merits of the case. The condition for adopting a provisional measure concerning property is that there is a possibility to recognize in Hungary the decision on the merits of the case rendered by the foreign court having jurisdiction.

(2) The provisional measure shall be ordered by the court competent according to the place of habitual residence of the person concerned or the location of the property concerned.

(3) If Hungarian law requires for the maintenance of the effect of the provisional measure the institution of proceedings on the merits of the case, the proceedings before a foreign court which has jurisdiction on the merits of the case shall be taken into consideration for this purpose.

(4) If the foreign court having jurisdiction renders a decision concerning the subject matter of the measure adopted based on subsection (1) that is capable of being recognized in Hungary, the provisional measure loses its effect.

Section 71

The minister shall issue a certificate on Hungarian law and on the practice followed in the course of application thereof.

31 *General Rules of International Legal Assistance*

Section 72

(1) A Hungarian court shall provide legal assistance at the request of a foreign court, on the basis of an international treaty, a directly applicable legal act of the European Union, or in case of reciprocity.

(2) In the absence of reciprocity, the legal assistance may be performed in the case of agreement between the minister and the minister in charge of foreign affairs and, if necessary, the minister competent pursuant to the subject matter of the case.

(3) The performance of legal assistance shall be denied if it would violate Hungarian public policy.

32 *Service of Documents*

Section 73

(1) A document to be served abroad by an authority of the requested state shall be sent to the minister for adoption of a measure.

(2) If an international treaty allows the service of a document by post, the court may send it directly to the addressee.

(3) Where the conditions specified in an international treaty are met, the document may also be served through the foreign representation of Hungary competent in accordance with the place of residence of the addressee. In this case, it must be sent to the minister in charge of foreign affairs for adoption of a measure.

(4) The service abroad must be considered as legal if it complies with either Hungarian law or the law governing at the place of service. If the service took place based on subsection (2), the fiction of service shall not be applied.

Section 74

(1) The minister shall forward the request for legal assistance for the service of a document issued in foreign proceedings in accordance with its content to the court specified in subsection (2) or – through the Hungarian Chamber of Court Bailiffs – to an independent court bailiff (hereinafter: bailiff).

(2) The service shall be effected in accordance with the request for legal assistance by the district court (by the Central District Court of Pest in Budapest) or by the bailiff competent in accordance with the address of the addressee indicated in the request for legal assistance.

(3) The court or bailiff shall adopt measures within eight days upon receipt of the request for legal assistance to effect the service.

Section 75

(1) In the course of the service of a document issued in foreign proceedings, subject to subsections (2)–(5), Hungarian laws on the service of official documents shall apply.

(2) If the document to be served is not provided with an official Hungarian translation or a Hungarian translation deemed appropriate for the purpose of the proceedings by the law of the requesting state, it may be served only if it is accepted voluntarily by the addressee. Receipt of such a document by the addressee does not mean its definite acceptance; the addressee may return the document to the domestic court or bailiff performing the request for service within fifteen days from the date of receipt or post it on the understanding that he refuses acceptance.

(3) If the service of the document not provided with a translation as specified in subsection (2) has been ineffective because the addressee did not accept the document (it was returned to the court with the indication 'unclaimed'), the fiction of service specified in section 137(2) of Act

CXXX of 2016 on Civil Procedure (hereinafter: Code of Civil Procedure) shall not apply.

(4) If the addressee refuses to accept the document in accordance with subsection (2), or it was not served on the grounds specified in subsection (3), the court or bailiff performing the request for service shall establish the result of the service so that the document may not be considered as served under Hungarian law.

(5) In performing the service, a foreign procedural rule shall be applied at the request of the requesting foreign court if it does not violate Hungarian public policy.

Section 76

(1) The court or bailiff performing the request for service shall notify the minister of the performance of the service and the date thereof, or any obstacle to the service and its grounds, within eight days.

(2) If the Convention on the Service Abroad of Judicial and Extrajudicial Documents in Civil or Commercial Matters promulgated by Act XXXVI of 2005 applies to the service, the minister shall issue a certificate in accordance with Article 6 of the Convention based on the data provided by the court or bailiff.

Section 77

(1) The functions of the transmitting agency specified in Article 2(1) of Regulation (EC) No 1393/2007 of the European Parliament and of the Council (hereinafter in this section: the regulation) are performed: a) in the case of court documents by the court in whose proceedings the document to be served was issued, b) in the case of documents issued in notary public proceedings by the notary public in whose proceedings the document was issued, c) in the case of other extrajudicial documents by the minister.

(2) The functions of the receiving agency specified in section 2(2) of the regulation are performed: a) by the district court competent in accordance with the address of the addressee indicated in the request for legal assistance (the Central District Court of Pest in Budapest) and b) by the Hungarian Chamber of Court Bailiffs; in the case of point b) the service is performed by the bailiff competent in accordance with the address of the addressee.

(3) In the course of the performance of the request for legal assistance made based on the regulation, section 74(3) shall duly apply.

(4) The functions of the central body under Article 3 of the regulation are performed by the minister.

(5) Based on Article 4(2) of the regulation, the receiving agency shall accept the documents to be served by post, fax and electronic means. The transmitting or receiving agency shall accept the standard forms introduced by the regulation in the Hungarian, English, German, or French language.

(6) If the result of the service has been established by the application of the fiction of service under section 137(2) of the Code of Civil Procedure, the receiving agency shall notify the transmitting agency of the fact that the service and its date were established based on this fiction of service and the addressee is entitled to raise an objection against it under section 138 of the Code of Civil Procedure. If the court later accepts the objection of the addressee, it shall simultaneously notify the foreign transmitting agency of the fact that the legal consequences related to the service are ineffective under Hungarian law.

(7) The receiving agency shall notify the transmitting agency of the service and the date thereof, or any obstacle to it and its grounds, within eight days.

(8) The means of service under Article 13 of the regulation may be applied in Hungary only if the addressee is a citizen of the transmitting Member State.

(9) In the case of the application of the means of service under Article 13 of the regulation, the document to be served abroad shall be transmitted in accordance with section 73(3).

(10) The means of service under Article 15 of the regulation may be applied in Hungary in accordance with the laws on service by the bailiff.

33 *Taking Evidence*

Section 78

(1) A request for legal assistance concerning the taking of evidence to be submitted to a foreign court shall be sent to the minister.

(2) If the taking of the evidence may also take place through a diplomatic or consular agent based on an international treaty, the court may contact the competent Hungarian foreign representation through the minister in charge of foreign affairs for the purpose of taking evidence.

(3) In a case specified by international treaty, a Hungarian court may take evidence directly abroad for the purpose of proceedings pending before it. In this case, the general rules on taking evidence shall apply under the condition that coercive measures shall not be applied.

(4) In the absence of an international treaty or reciprocity, the court may set a deadline for the party upon his request to present an authentic instrument on the taking of the evidence which complies with the law of the foreign state and has been endorsed as necessary.

(5) The lawfulness of taking evidence abroad shall be adjudged according to the law of the place of the taking of the evidence, but it shall be also considered as lawful if it complies with Hungarian law.

Section 79

(1) Except as provided in subsection (2), the minister shall forward the request made by a foreign court for legal assistance in taking evidence in Hungary to the court specified in subsection (3).

(2) If the request for legal assistance concerns the provision of data which may be obtained directly from a public register, the minister may contact the organ keeping the register concerned to secure provision of the data requested.

(3) Performance of a request for legal assistance in taking evidence falls within the cognizance and territorial competence of the district court (the Central District Court of Buda in Budapest) in the territory of which a) the domicile or the place of habitual residence of the person to be heard is located, b) the object to be inspected is located, or c) the taking of the evidence can otherwise be executed most expeditiously, in particular when the domicile or the place of habitual residence of more than one person to be heard or where several objects concerned by the inspection are located in the territory of different courts.

(4) In the course of performing a request for legal assistance concerning the taking of evidence, Hungarian law shall apply. A foreign procedural rule may be applied only at the request of the requesting foreign court, unless it violates Hungarian public policy.

(5) If the requesting foreign court has indicated that its member, the parties concerned by the foreign proceedings, or the representatives of those parties intend to be present for the performance of the request for legal assistance, the court performing the legal assistance shall set the date of performance of the legal assistance taking this into consideration. The court shall notify the minister without delay of the date, the place of the taking of the evidence, and other circumstances concerning the attendance.

Section 80

(1) Based on an international treaty, the minister may permit in accordance with this section that the person designated as commissioner by the

foreign court for this purpose or the member of the foreign court shall directly perform an act of taking evidence in Hungary for the purpose of the foreign proceedings.

(2) The request for the permission specified in subsection (1) shall be submitted to the minister in the Hungarian, English, French, or German language. The request shall include the following particulars:

a) the name of the foreign court seised and the number of the case,
b) the names and addresses of the parties concerned in the proceedings and of their representatives,
c) the subject matter of the proceedings,
d) a short description of the facts of the case,
e) the name and contact details of the person who intends to perform an act of taking evidence in Hungary as commissioner or the member of the court,
f) the act of taking evidence to be performed in Hungary,
g) the name and address of the person whose participation is necessary for the performance of the taking of the evidence.

(3) The commissioning decision of the foreign court or an equivalent document on behalf of the person acting as commissioner performing the taking of evidence shall be attached to the request.

(4) The minister shall not grant the request if the act of taking evidence would violate Hungarian public policy.

(5) If the minister grants the request, he shall notify the district court specified in section 79(3), unless the performance of the act of taking evidence does not require the participation of the court.

(6) If the act of taking evidence aims at the hearing of a person, before the hearing

a) this person shall be notified that
   aa) his participation is voluntary; no negative legal consequence may be effected against him for the denial thereof,
   ab) he is entitled to use his mother tongue in the course of the hearing, and
   ac) his legal counsel may be present in the course of the hearing, and
b) in the case of this person's being heard as a witness, he shall be advised in accordance with the rules on advising a witness as specified in the Code of Civil Procedure.

(7) The notification under subsection (6) shall be provided by the court acting under subsection (5). If no such court exists, the minister shall prescribe the notification by the requesting court and the proof of this

notification for the minister as a condition for granting permission for the taking of the evidence.

(8) If the performance of a hearing requires the participation of an interpreter, the requesting court shall provide for the advance on and payment of the interpreter's fee.

(9) When permitting the taking of evidence in accordance with this section, the minister may establish additional conditions.

Section 81

(1) The functions of the central body under Article 3(1) and (3) of Council Regulation (EC) No 1206/2001 (hereinafter in this section: regulation) shall be performed by the minister.

(2) The performance of the request for legal assistance under Article 1(1) point a) falls within the cognizance and territorial competence of the court specified in section 79(3). If the court accepting the request for legal assistance establishes that its performance falls within the cognizance or territorial competence of another court, it shall forward it to this court within eight days.

(3) The minister shall accept and decide upon a request made by a court of another Member State under Article 17(1) of the regulation; in the course of this, section 80(5)–(9) shall duly apply.

(4) The court shall accept the standard forms specified by the regulation by post, fax, and electronic means in the Hungarian, English, or German language.

(5) A Hungarian court may take evidence directly in another Member State of the European Union, with the exception of Denmark, for the purpose of proceedings pending before it also outside the manner specified in Article 17 of the regulation. In such a case, the general rules on taking evidence shall apply under the condition that coercive measures shall not be applied.

34 ***Provisions Related to Immunity***

Section 82

For the purpose of this subchapter, a reference to the state involves:

a) the state,

b) the organs of the state exercising public power, when they act in this capacity, and

c) persons acting as representatives of the state, when they act in this capacity.

Section 83

(1) Subject to the exceptions specified in this Act, exclusively Hungarian courts shall have jurisdiction in proceedings against the Hungarian state.

(2) Subject to the exceptions specified in this Act, a Hungarian court may not undertake proceedings against a foreign state.

Section 84

(1) A state cannot claim immunity irrespective of the subject matter of the proceedings

a) if it has expressly waived its immunity,

b) if it has itself instituted the proceedings, if it intervened in the proceedings, or if it took any step in the proceedings relating to the merits of the case, or

c) in respect to a counterclaim submitted in proceedings instituted by the state, if it is based on the legal relationship which is the subject matter of the legal dispute.

(2) A state cannot claim immunity if the subject matter of the proceedings is

a) a right or obligation of the state stemming from a contract under civil law, unless the other party is another state or if the parties agreed otherwise,

b) a right or obligation stemming from a contract of employment or another legal relationship for carrying out work entered into between the state and a natural person, provided that the place of employment is or was in the territory of the state where the proceedings are conducted, unless the employee is a citizen of the employing state or performed a function of public power,

c) a claim brought against the state on the grounds of injury caused to life, health, physical integrity, or property, provided that the event or omission giving rise to the damage occurred in the territory of the state where the proceedings are conducted and the person sustaining the damage was in that state at that time,

d) any right, interest of the state in or its possession of immovable property located in the territory of the state where the proceedings are conducted or the use of the immovable property by the state or the obligations arising out of these,

e) the membership, share, or interest of a state in a legal person or an entity without legal personality registered or seated or having its place of central administration in the territory of the state where the proceedings are conducted, or any right or obligation stemming therefrom,

f) a legal relationship of succession of the state related to an estate opened in the territory of the state where the proceedings are conducted,

g) the granting, the content, or the termination of an intellectual property right in the state where the proceedings are conducted,

h) any right or interest of the state concerning the treatment of property under insolvency proceedings in the state where the proceedings are conducted, or

i) the validity, interpretation, or application of an arbitration agreement concluded by the state for the purpose of the settlement of a legal dispute related to a private law contract, the arbitration procedure conducted based on such an agreement or the setting aside of the award rendered in it, unless the arbitration agreement provides otherwise.

Section 85

(1) For the purpose of this section, enforcement also involves any provisional or protective measure restraining the right of disposal.

(2) The waiver of immunity in accordance with section 84(1) does not also mean a waiver of immunity from enforcement.

(3) No enforcement may be levied on the property of a foreign state located in Hungary, unless

a) the foreign state has expressly consented to it,

b) the foreign state has separated the property for the satisfaction of the given claim, or

c) the property serves a purpose other than non-commercial governmental activity.

(4) For the purpose of subsection (3) point c), in particular

a) property serving the operation of diplomatic missions of the state,

b) property serving the use of military functions,

c) property of the central bank or other financial authority,

d) property belonging to the cultural heritage or archives of the state which is not intended to be alienated,

e) objects of property forming part of a scientific, cultural, or historical exhibition which are not intended to be alienated serve a purpose of non-commercial governmental activity.

Section 86

(1) Exclusively Hungarian courts may proceed in proceedings brought against a Hungarian citizen acting as a diplomatic representative abroad or otherwise enjoying jurisdictional immunity, unless the Hungarian state or the employing international organization has expressly waived immunity.

(2) A Hungarian court may not proceed in proceedings brought against a foreign citizen acting as a diplomatic representative in Hungary or otherwise enjoying jurisdictional immunity, unless the foreign state or the employing international organization has expressly waived immunity.

Section 87

(1) Regarding the service of documents for a foreign state, a legal act of the European Union which has general application and is directly applicable or an international treaty which regulates the legal assistance for service in respect of the given state shall apply; in the absence of this the document shall be served through the minister in charge of foreign affairs.

(2) Documents may not be served for a foreign state directly by post.

(3) Documents shall be served for an international organization or a natural person enjoying immunity through the minister in charge of foreign affairs.

Chapter 10: Jurisdiction

35 *General Rules*

Section 88

Irrespective of the other jurisdictional rules of this Act, exclusively Hungarian courts may proceed

a) in proceedings, the subject matter of which is a right in rem in immovable property located in Hungary or the renting and leasing of such immovable property,

b) in probate proceedings concerning the estate located in Hungary of a deceased person having Hungarian citizenship,

c) in proceedings concerning the annulment of a document issued in Hungary,

d) in proceedings concerning the entry of rights, facts, and data in a public register kept in Hungary,

e) in proceedings concerning an enforcement in Hungary.

Section 89

Irrespective of the other jurisdictional rules of this Act, the jurisdiction of Hungarian courts is excluded

a) in proceedings, the subject matter of which is a right in rem in immovable property located abroad or the renting and leasing of such immovable property,
b) in probate proceedings concerning an estate located abroad of a deceased person not having Hungarian citizenship,
c) in proceedings concerning the annulment of a document or security issued abroad,
d) in proceedings related to the granting, the content, and the termination of a foreign industrial property right,
e) in proceedings related to the formation or termination of a legal person or an entity not having legal personality (for the purpose of this point, hereinafter collectively: legal person) seated abroad; in proceedings concerning the validity of the contract or statute on the basis of which the legal person is registered; and in proceedings concerning the review of decisions passed by the organs of the legal person,
f) in proceedings concerning the entry of rights, facts, and data in public registers kept abroad,
g) in proceedings concerning an enforcement abroad.

Section 90

(1) In the case of an action brought against more than one defendant, a Hungarian court may proceed against all of the defendants if the domicile or the seat or the place of central administration (of a legal person or of an entity not having legal personality (for the purpose of this chapter, hereinafter collectively: seat)) of at least one of the defendants is located in Hungary, provided that the claims are so closely connected that it is expedient to hear and determine them together to avoid the risk of irreconcilable judgments resulting from separate proceedings.

(2) In the case of a joint claim brought against both the principal and the secondary obligor, a Hungarian court may proceed irrespective of the domicile or seat of the secondary obligor if the domicile or seat of the principal obligor is located in Hungary.

(3) If a Hungarian court has jurisdiction for the adjudication of a claim, it may also proceed in respect of the counterclaim.

Section 91

Subject to the exceptions laid down in this Act, the jurisdiction of a Hungarian court is also established if the defendant makes a counterplea without contending a lack of jurisdiction (jurisdiction by appearance).

36 *Matters Involving an Economic Interest*

Section 92

A Hungarian court may proceed in all matters involving an economic interest if the defendant's domicile or seat is located in Hungary.

Section 93

A Hungarian court may also proceed in a legal dispute related to a contract if the place of performance of the disputed obligation is located in Hungary. In applying this section, the place of performance of the disputed obligation is

a) the place that was stipulated by the parties in the contract as the place of performance; in the absence of this

b) in the case of a contract for the sale of a movable thing, the place where the movable thing was delivered or should have been delivered under the contract,

c) in the case of the provision of a service, the place where the service was provided or should have been provided under the contract, or

d) in the case of other contracts, the place determined by Hungarian law as the place of performance of the disputed claim.

Section 94

(1) A Hungarian court may also proceed in a legal dispute related to non-contractual obligations if the legal fact giving rise to the obligation was realised or may be realized in Hungary, or if its result occurred or may occur in Hungary. This provision shall duly apply also to claims stemming from a violation of personality rights.

(2) In respect of a claim brought for the compensation of damage caused by crime or a private law claim enforced in criminal proceedings, a Hungarian court may proceed if the criminal act constituting the grounds for the procedure falls under Hungarian criminal jurisdiction.

(3) In a lawsuit brought for establishing or increasing compensation payments, a Hungarian court may also proceed if the domicile of the person entitled thereto is located in Hungary.

Section 95

A Hungarian court may proceed in a procedure the subject matter of which is a right in rem in a movable thing located in Hungary at the time of instituting the procedure.

Section 96

In a lawsuit brought against an undertaking seated abroad, a Hungarian court may also proceed if the undertaking has a branch or agency located in Hungary and the legal dispute concerns the activity of the latter, including a case where the contract was concluded in Hungary on behalf of the undertaking seated abroad.

Section 97

In a lawsuit concerning matters involving an economic interest, a Hungarian court may also proceed against a defendant who has no domicile or seat in Hungary, provided that the defendant has property located in Hungary on which enforcement may be levied. Any claim due to the defendant shall also be considered as the defendant's property located in Hungary if the debtor of the claim is domiciled in Hungary or if the claim is secured by a thing located in Hungary.

Section 98

(1) In a succession lawsuit, a Hungarian court may also proceed if the deceased had Hungarian citizenship at the time of his death.

(2) A Hungarian notary public may proceed in probate proceedings if the deceased had Hungarian citizenship at the time of his death or if the estate is located in Hungary.

Section 99

(1) In respect of matters involving an economic interest, the parties may stipulate the jurisdiction of the courts or one or more specific courts of a state for a legal dispute which has arisen or which may arise in the future in connection with a particular legal relationship.

(2) An agreement conferring jurisdiction is null and void

a) where the parties stipulate the jurisdiction of a foreign court in respect of any case for which the jurisdiction of Hungarian courts is exclusive, or

b) where the parties stipulate the jurisdiction of a Hungarian court in respect of any case for which the jurisdiction of Hungarian courts is excluded.

(3) Parties may make an agreement conferring jurisdiction

a) in writing,

b) verbally with written confirmation,

c) in a form which accords with practices which the parties have established between themselves, or

d) in international commerce, in a form which accords with the commercial usages of which the parties are or ought to have been aware and which are widely known of and regularly observed by parties to contracts of the type involved in the particular commerce concerned.

(4) An agreement conferring jurisdiction shall be considered as concluded in writing if it came into existence through an exchange of messages by means which provide a durable record of the legal declaration of the parties.

(5) Regarding the existence and validity of an agreement conferring jurisdiction, in the questions not regulated by this Act, the law of the state of the court or courts stipulated in the agreement conferring jurisdiction shall apply.

(6) If the parties made an agreement conferring jurisdiction as part of another contract, the agreement conferring jurisdiction shall be treated as an agreement independent of the other terms of the contract as regards its existence and validity.

(7) Unless the parties agree to the contrary, the jurisdiction stipulated by a choice-of-court agreement shall be exclusive. However, if the parties stipulated the jurisdiction of a foreign court and this court declares that it has no jurisdiction, a Hungarian court may establish its jurisdiction according to the general rules.

Section 100

(1) A Hungarian court shall have jurisdiction to conduct insolvency proceedings if the debtor legal person has its seat as indicated in the statute in Hungary or has a place of operations (branch or other establishment) in Hungary where it carries out non-transitory activity.

(2) If a Hungarian court has jurisdiction to conduct insolvency proceedings, it may proceed concerning actions which derive from the insolvency proceedings and are closely linked with them.

(3) In insolvency proceedings, sections 91 and 99 shall not be applied.

37 *Matters Concerning Family Law and Personal Status*

Section 101

(1) For the case specified in Article 7 of Council Regulation (EC) No 2201/2003, a Hungarian court shall have jurisdiction if one of the spouses is a Hungarian citizen.

(2) Regarding the establishment of the existence or non-existence of a marriage, a Hungarian court shall have jurisdiction if one of the parties is a Hungarian citizen or the place of habitual residence of the defendant is located in Hungary.

Section 102

(1) For proceedings on the personal and property relationships of the spouses, a Hungarian court shall have jurisdiction if a) the place of habitual residence of the defendant spouse is located in Hungary, b) the last common place of habitual residence of the spouses was located in Hungary, provided that the place of habitual residence of one of the spouses is still located in Hungary at the time of bringing the action, c) both spouses are Hungarian citizens.

(2) For proceedings concerning a matrimonial property relationship, a Hungarian court shall have jurisdiction also if the property constituting the subject matter of the proceedings is located in Hungary.

(3) If a legal relationship specified in subsection (1) is settled within the framework of proceedings concerning the matrimonial ties, a Hungarian court may also proceed if it has jurisdiction for those proceedings.

(4) If a Hungarian court has jurisdiction for proceedings concerning an inheritance relationship, its jurisdiction extends to the adjudication of any legal issue regarding matrimonial property related to the inheritance.

Section 103

Regarding proceedings related to the existence, validity, termination, and legal effects of a registered partnership, a Hungarian court shall have jurisdiction if a) the partnership was entered into in Hungary, or b) at least one of the registered partners is a Hungarian citizen.

Section 104

(1) In proceedings for the establishment of origin, a Hungarian court shall have jurisdiction if

a) the child is a Hungarian citizen,

b) the child has his place of habitual residence in Hungary, or

c) in the case of the obligatory involvement in the lawsuit of the defendant or more than one person, at least one of the defendants has his place of habitual residence in Hungary.

(2) In matters on the establishment of origin, section 91 shall not apply.

Section 105

(1) In proceedings for the authorization or termination of adoption, a Hungarian court shall have jurisdiction if a) the child to be adopted or the adopted child is a Hungarian citizen or has his place of habitual residence in Hungary, or b) the adoptive parent or in the case of adoption

by spouses at least one of them is a Hungarian citizen or has his place of habitual residence in Hungary.

(2) In adoption matters, section 91 shall not apply.

Section 106

(1) For the case specified in Article 14 of Council Regulation (EC) No 2201/2003, a Hungarian court shall have jurisdiction in proceedings concerning parental custody, contact, and guardianship if the child is a Hungarian citizen.

(2) In matters concerning parental custody, contact, and guardianship, section 91 shall not apply.

Section 107

(1) In proceedings related to conservatorship, a Hungarian court shall have jurisdiction if the person to be placed or being under conservatorship is a Hungarian citizen or has his place of habitual residence in Hungary.

(2) Subsection (1) shall duly apply also to proceedings related to other protective measures.

(3) In matters related to conservatorship and other protective measures, section 91 shall not apply.

Section 108

(1) Regarding proceedings for the declaration of a person as dead or the establishment of the fact of death, a Hungarian court shall have jurisdiction if the missing person

a) had his last known place of habitual residence in Hungary, or

b) was a Hungarian citizen and some domestic legal interest – in particular, the existence of a marriage or registered partnership of the missing person with a spouse or registered partner having Hungarian citizenship or a domicile in Hungary, or the settlement of the legal fate of his property located in Hungary – renders it necessary to declare him dead or to establish the fact of his death.

(2) In matters for the declaration of a person as dead or for the establishment of the fact of death, section 91 shall not apply.

Chapter 11: Recognition and Enforcement of Foreign Decisions

38 *General Rules*

Section 109

(1) The decision of a foreign court shall be recognized if

a) the jurisdiction of the foreign court seised was founded based on this Act,
b) the decision became final or has an equivalent legal effect under the law of the state in which it was rendered, and c) none of the grounds for denial specified in subsection (4) apply.

(2) If this Act does not provide otherwise, for the purpose of subsection (1) point a), the jurisdiction of the foreign court seised shall be considered as founded if it proceeded based on a ground of jurisdiction which would establish the jurisdiction of a Hungarian court based on this Act.

(3) Regarding the recognition of decisions in matters concerning family law and personal status, any other citizenship of a Hungarian citizen shall be taken into consideration in the course of the examination of whether the jurisdiction of the foreign court seised was founded.

(4) A foreign decision may not be recognized if
a) the recognition thereof would violate Hungarian public policy,
b) the party against whom the decision was rendered did not participate in the proceedings either in person or by representative, because the summons and the statement of claim or other document on the basis of which the proceedings were instituted was not served on him at his domicile or place of habitual residence in such a way and at such a time as to allow him to prepare for his defence,
c) proceedings were instituted before a Hungarian court for the same right stemming from the same facts between identical parties before instituting foreign proceedings,
d) a Hungarian court previously rendered a final decision on the merits concerning the same right stemming from the same facts between identical parties, or
e) a court of a foreign state other than the state of the court rendering a decision previously rendered a final decision concerning the same right stemming from the same facts between identical parties which complies with the conditions for recognition in Hungary.

Section 110

A settlement made in proceedings of a foreign court or another authority may be recognized and enforced in Hungary in accordance with the conditions governing decisions.

Section 111

If a foreign decision does not comply with the conditions for recognition and enforcement specified by an international agreement entered into by Hungary which is applicable under section 2, it may also be recognized and enforced if it complies with the conditions determined by this Act. For the purpose of this provision, the existence of reciprocity with the state concerned shall be presumed.

Section 112

Regarding the recognition of foreign decisions on the legal relationships regulated in subchapters 39–40, the general rules of recognition shall apply subject to the deviations contained in subchapters 39–40.

39 *Matters Involving an Economic Interest*

Section 113

(1) In matters involving an economic interest, a further condition for the recognition of decisions is the existence of reciprocity between Hungary and the state of the court rendering the decision.

(2) A decision may be recognized even in the absence of reciprocity if
  - a) the jurisdiction of Hungarian courts was excluded in the case, or
  - b) the jurisdiction of the foreign court seised was based on an agreement of the parties which complies with the provisions of Hungarian law.

Section 114

(1) A further condition for the recognition of decisions rendered in insolvency proceedings is the existence of reciprocity between Hungary and the state of the court rendering the decision.

(2) The recognition of foreign main insolvency proceedings does not preclude the opening of secondary insolvency proceedings before a Hungarian court.

(3) A decision opening foreign insolvency proceedings has the legal effects determined by the law of the state of the place of the opening of proceedings in Hungary only if no secondary insolvency proceedings are opened in Hungary.

(4) Regarding the recognition of specific legal effects related to foreign main insolvency proceedings, further conditions and a special procedural order may be established by law.

Section 115

In proceedings related to succession, the jurisdiction of the foreign court seised shall be considered as founded if it was based on

a) the deceased person's place of habitual residence at the time of his death or

b) the deceased person's citizenship.

40 *Matters Concerning Family Law and Personal Status*

Section 116

(1) In proceedings related to the existence, validity, and dissolution of marriage, the jurisdiction of the foreign court seised shall be considered as founded if it was based on

a) the place of habitual residence of the defendant spouse,

b) the last common place of habitual residence of the spouses, or

c) the common citizenship of the spouses.

(2) A decision of a foreign court, which is final or has equivalent legal effect under the law of the state of that court, on the existence, validity, and dissolution of marriage shall also be recognized if the spouse having Hungarian citizenship himself requests the recognition and neither of the grounds for denial specified in section 109(4) applies even if the jurisdiction of the foreign court was not founded according to this Act.

(3) In derogation from section 109(4), points c)–e), the recognition of a decision specified in subsection (1) or related to the personal relationships of the spouses may be denied if

a) proceedings were instituted before a Hungarian court for the same right stemming from the same facts before instituting foreign proceedings,

b) a Hungarian court previously rendered a final decision on the merits concerning the same right stemming from the same facts, or

c) a court of a foreign state other than the state of the court rendering the decision previously rendered a final decision concerning the same right stemming from the same facts which complies with the conditions for recognition in Hungary.

Section 117

(1) In proceedings related to the existence, validity, and termination of a registered partnership, the jurisdiction of the foreign court seised shall be considered as founded if it was based on

a) the place of habitual residence of the defendant registered partner,
b) the last common place of habitual residence of the registered partners,
c) the common citizenship of the registered partners, or
d) the place where the registered partnership came into existence.

(2) Regarding decisions related to the existence, validity, and termination of a registered partnership, section 116(2)–(3) shall duly apply.

Section 118

In proceedings related to parental custody, contact, and guardianship, the jurisdiction of the foreign court seised shall be considered as founded if

a) it was based on the place of habitual residence of the child, or
b) the decision was rendered by the court seised in the matter of the matrimonial ties of the parents of the child, provided that its jurisdiction for the proceedings related to the marriage was founded based on section 101.

Section 119

In proceedings related to the maintenance arising from a family law relationship or registered partnership, the jurisdiction of the foreign court seised shall be considered as founded if

a) it was based on the place of habitual residence of the defendant,
b) it was based on the place of habitual residence of the person entitled to maintenance, or
c) if the decision was rendered by the court seised in a matter of personal status, parental custody, or guardianship, provided that its jurisdiction was founded based either on section 101 or 103 regarding proceedings concerning personal status or on section 106 regarding proceedings concerning parental custody or guardianship, and the claim for maintenance was accessory.

Section 120

(1) In addition to the conditions specified in section 109, a decision related to the adoption of a child having Hungarian citizenship may be recognized only if the adoption was approved by the Hungarian public guardianship authority. The approval of the Hungarian public guardianship authority is not required in the case of a child having more than one citizenship if one of his citizenships is Hungarian and his place of habitual residence was located in the state of his other citizenship at the time

the decision was rendered, provided that the adoption has already been approved by the court of the state of his other citizenship.

(2) In derogation from subsection (1), a decision of a foreign court, which is final or has equivalent legal effect under the law of the state of that court, shall be recognized if recognition is requested by the adopted person, who has reached the age of legal majority according to Hungarian law and who has Hungarian citizenship, and neither of the grounds for denial specified in section 109(4) applies, even if the Hungarian public guardianship authority did not approve the adoption or the jurisdiction of the foreign court is not founded under this Act.

Section 121

Derogating from section 109(4) c)–e), the recognition of decisions related to a) origin, b) adoption, c) parental custody, contact, and guardianship, d) conservatorship and other protective measures, e) declaration of death and establishing the fact of death, and f) bearing a name, may be denied in the cases specified in section 116(3) a)–c).

41 *Procedural Provisions*

Section 122

(1) No special procedure is required for the recognition of a foreign decision. Unless otherwise provided by law, the question of recognition is examined by the court hearing the procedure in which it arises.

(2) The party concerned may also request the court to establish in a special procedure that the foreign decision may be recognized in Hungary. The court shall decide on such a request in a non-litigious procedure.

(3) This procedure falls under the cognizance and exclusive territorial competence of

a) the district court operating at the seat of the regional court in accordance with the adverse party's domicile (seat) – and in the absence of this his place of habitual residence – in Hungary (the Central District Court of Buda in Budapest); in the case of a foreign arbitral award, the regional court (the Budapest Regional Court in Budapest),

b) in the absence of this, the district court operating at the seat of the regional court in accordance with the claimant's domicile (seat) – and in the absence of this his place of habitual residence – in Hungary (the Central District Court of Buda in Budapest); in the case of a foreign arbitral award, the regional court (the Budapest Regional Court in Budapest), or

c) if the claimant has neither domicile (seat) nor place of habitual residence in Hungary, the Central District Court of Buda; in the case of a foreign arbitral award the Budapest Regional Court.

(4) Regarding this procedure, including the available legal remedies, the provisions of the Act on Judicial Enforcement on the issuance of the certificate of enforcement shall duly apply.

(5) A foreign decision shall not be subject to review on the merits. The existence of the conditions specified in section 109(1) points a)–b), section 113(1), section 114(1), and section 120(1) which are required for the recognition of a decision in Hungary and the absence of a ground for the denial specified in section 109(4) a) shall be examined ex officio, while the absence of any of the grounds for denial specified in section 109(4) b)–e) shall be presumed until the contrary is proved.

(6) If the conditions for the recognition of the decision are fulfilled, the court shall order a protective measure at the request of the interested party in accordance with the provisions of the Act on Judicial Enforcement. The ordering of a protective measure does not prevent the issuance of the certificate of enforcement.

Section 123

A foreign decision declared enforceable under the Act on Judicial Enforcement may be enforced in Hungary in accordance with the provisions of the relevant law.

Chapter 12: Final Provisions

42 *Authorizing Measure*

Section 124

The minister shall be authorized to establish in a regulation the existence of reciprocity concerning international legal assistance and the recognition and enforcement of foreign decisions.

43 *Provision on Entry Into Force*

Section 125

This Act shall enter into force on January 1, 2018.

44 *Transitional Provisions*

Section 126

(1) The provisions of subchapters 31–33 shall apply also to pending proceedings.

(2) The provisions of subchapters 38–40 shall apply to decisions rendered after the entry into force of this Act.

(3) In derogation from subsection (2), a foreign decision concerning the personal status and family law relationships of a Hungarian citizen which complies with the provisions of sections 109–111 and sections 116–121 shall be recognized also if it was rendered before the entry into force of this Act.

45 *Provisions Referring to the Requirements of the European Union*

Section 127

(1) Section 44(4) of this Act serves the compliance with Article 9 of Directive 2002/47/EC of the European Parliament and of the Council of 6 June 2002 on financial collateral arrangements.

(2) The following sections of this Act establish implementing provisions:

a) section 81 regarding Council Regulation (EC) No 1206/2001 of 28 May 2001 on cooperation between the courts of the Member States in the taking of evidence in civil or commercial matters,

b) section 101(1) and section 106 regarding Council Regulation (EC) No 2201/2003 of 27 November 2003 concerning jurisdiction and the recognition and enforcement of judgments in matrimonial matters and matters of parental responsibility, repealing Regulation (EC) No 1347/2000,

c) section 59 regarding Regulation (EC) No 864/2007 of the European Parliament and of the Council of 11 July 2007 on the law applicable to non-contractual obligations (Rome II),

d) section 77 regarding Regulation (EC) No 1393/2007 of the European Parliament and of the Council of 13 November 2007 on the service in the Member States of judicial and extrajudicial documents in civil or commercial matters (service of documents), and repealing Council Regulation (EC) No 1348/2000,

e) section 30 regarding Council Regulation (EU) No 1259/2010 of 20 December 2010 implementing enhanced cooperation in the area of the law applicable to divorce and legal separation,

f) section 3 point c) regarding Regulation (EU) No 1215/2012 of the European Parliament and of the Council of 12 December 2012 on jurisdiction and the recognition and enforcement of judgments in civil and commercial matters.

46 ***Amending Provisions***

Section 128

(1) Section 136(1) of Act XLI of 1991 on Public Notaries (hereinafter: Act on Public Notaries) shall be supplemented with the following point j): (The public notary shall issue a certificate) 'j) on an extrajudicial oath or vow made for the purpose of foreign proceedings.'

(2) The Act on Public Notaries shall be supplemented with the following section 146/A: 'Section 146/A (1) Before a public notary, for the purpose of foreign proceedings, an extrajudicial oath or vow may be made (hereinafter collectively in this section: oath). With the oath, the party confirms that the content of the document containing the text of the oath (hereinafter: certificate of oath) corresponds to reality or his will. (2) The public notary shall certify the oath by a clause written on or attached to the certificate of oath subsequent to the reading of that part of the certificate of oath which contains the oath or the oral presentation of the oath regarding the certificate of oath by the person taking the oath. Regarding the preparation of the clause, section 139 shall duly apply. (3) The public notary may also certify the oath by taking minutes of the text of the oath word by word. The minutes shall be signed by the person taking the oath. The certificate of oath shall constitute an annex to the minutes. (4) In the document issued by a public notary which certifies the oath, reference shall be made to the fact that the oath was taken for the purpose of use in foreign proceedings.'

Section 129

Act LIII of 1994 on Judicial Enforcement shall be supplemented with the following section 186(5): '(5) The court rendering a decision concerning the certificate of enforcement may order protective measures if a certificate of enforcement could be issued in accordance with section 208.'

Section 130

In section 10 point f) of Act LXXV of 1996 on Labour Inspection, the text 'the Labour Code, Act on Labour Protection and Decree-Law on Private International Law' shall be replaced by the text 'the Labour Code and Act on Labour Protection'.

Section 131

Section 3 of Act CXVI of 2004 on the Promulgation of the Convention on the Taking of Evidence Abroad in Civil or Commercial Matters concluded in the Hague on March 17, 1970 shall be replaced by the following provision: 'Section 3

Hungary makes the following declarations and reservations to the Convention: a) reservations based on Article 33 of the Convention: – to the second subsection of Article 4: Hungary excludes the application of the second subsection of Article 4 of the Convention. – to Article 16: Hungary excludes the application of Article 16. – to Article 18: Hungarian authorities do not provide assistance in obtaining evidence by compulsion by a diplomatic officer or consular agent based on Article 15 or by a commissioner based on Article 17. b) declarations to the Convention: – to Article 2: In Hungary, the functions of the Central Authority under Article 2 of the Convention shall be performed by the ministry headed by the minister in charge of justice. – to Article 8: The members of the requesting court may be present at the execution of acts conducted by the requested court for taking evidence subject to the prior authorisation of the Hungarian Central Authority. – to Article 15: Based on Article 15 of the Convention, a diplomatic officer or consular agent of another Contracting State may take evidence in the territory of Hungary without prior authorisation of the Hungarian authorities in aid of proceedings pending in the Contracting State which he represents, provided that it concerns a person who is exclusively a citizen of the State sending the diplomatic or consular agent. Taking the evidence may not involve the application or threat of compulsion or any negative legal consequence. – to Article 17: The permission specified by the second subsection of Article 17 of the Convention may be granted in Hungary by the Central Authority. – to Article 23: Hungarian authorities shall not execute requests on procedures known as "pre-trial discovery of documents" unless the request for legal assistance precisely specifies the document which shall be rendered available by the person who possesses it and the document is directly connected to the purpose of the proceedings.'

Section 132

Section 3 of Act XXXVI of 2005 on the Promulgation of the Convention on the Service Abroad of Judicial and Extrajudicial Documents in Civil or Commercial Matters concluded in the Hague on November 15, 1965 shall be replaced by the following provision: 'Section 3 Hungary makes the following declarations and reservations to the Convention: – to Article 2: In Hungary, the functions of the Central Authority under Article 2 of the Convention shall be performed by the ministry headed by the minister in charge of justice. – to the third subsection of Article 5: The manners of service specified in the first subsection of Article 5 of the Convention may be applied in Hungary only if the document to be served was provided with an official Hungarian translation or a Hungarian translation deemed appropriate for the purpose of court proceedings under the law of the requesting state. – to Article 6: The certificate specified in Article

6 of the Convention shall be issued in Hungary by the Central Authority. – to Article 8: Hungary opposes the direct serving of documents within the territory of Hungary by diplomatic or consular agents of foreign states, unless the addressee is a citizen of the state sending the diplomatic or consular agent. – to Article 9: Documents forwarded through consular channels and to be served pursuant to Article 9 of the Convention shall be accepted by the Central Authority in Hungary. – to Article 10: Hungary opposes the application of the manners of service specified in Article 10 of the Convention in its territory. – to Article 15: Hungary declares that Hungarian courts may decide a legal dispute, provided that all the conditions specified in the second subsection of Article 15 of the Convention have been fulfilled. – to Article 16: Hungary declares that an application for relief as specified in Article 16 of the Convention will not be entertained if it is filed more than one year after the date of the decision.'

Section 133

In Annex No. 5, point 2), subpoint a) of Act CLIII of 2010 on the Amendment of Certain Acts Establishing the Budget of 2011 of the Republic of Hungary, the text 'Decree-Law 13 of 1979 on Private International Law (hereinafter: PIL Decree-Law) or an international treaty mentioned in section 2 of the PIL Decree-Law' shall be replaced by the text 'private international law rules'.

47 *Repealing Provisions*

Section 134

a) Decree-Law 13 of 1979 on Private International Law, and
b) section 4 of Act CXVI of 2004 on the Promulgation of the Convention on the Taking of Evidence Abroad in Civil or Commercial Matters concluded in The Hague on March 17, 1970 are repealed.

Selected Bibliography

Books

In Hungarian

Bánrévy, G. *A nemzetközi gazdasági kapcsolatok joga* (Szt. István Társulat, Budapest, 2009) (The Law of International Economic Relations).

Burián, L., D.T. Czigler, L. Kecskés & I. Vörös, *Európai és magyar nemzetközi kollíziós magánjog* (Krim Bt., Budapest, 2010) (European and Hungarian International Conflict Private Law).

Csőke, A. *A határokon átnyúló fizetésképtelenségi eljárások problémai* (Hvg-Orac, Budapest, 2008) (The Problems of Cross-Border Insolvency Procedures).

Horváth, É. *Nemzetközi eljárások joga – a kereskedelmi választottbíráskodás* (Szent István Társulat, Budapest, 2003) (The Law of International Procedures – Commercial Arbitration).

Kengyel, M. *Európai polgári eljárásjog* (Osiris, Budapest, 2009) (European Civil Procedural Law).

Mádl, F. *Nemzetközi magánjog és nemzetközi gazdasági kapcsolatok joga* (ELTE Eötvös Kiadó, Budapest, 2018) (Private International Law and the Law of International Economic Relations).

Nagy, Cs.I. *Az Európai Unió nemzetközi magánjoga. Határon átnyúló jogviták az EU-ban* (HVG-Orac, Budapest, 2006) (The Private International Law of the EU. Cross-border Legal Disputes in the EU).

Nagy, Cs.I. *Nemzetközi magánjog* (HVG-Orac, Budapest, 2017) (Private International Law).

Ottóné. Brávácz *Jogviták határok nélkül. Joghatóság, külföldi határozatok elismerése és végrehajtása polgári ügyekben* (HVG-Orac, Budapest, 2003) (Legal Disputes Without Borders. Jurisdiction, Recognition and Enforcement of Foreign Decisions in Civil Matters).

Vékás L., L. Osztovits A. & Nemessányi Z. (eds.), *Nemzetközi magánjogi rendeletek az Európai Unió Bírósága gyakorlatában* (HVG-Orac, Budapest, 2021) (Private International Law Regulations in the Practice of the Court of Justice of the European Union).

Vékás, L., Z. Nemessányi & A. Osztovits (eds.), *A nemzetközi magánjogról szóló törvény kommentárja* (HVG-Orac, Budapest, 2020) (The Commentary of the Act on Private International Law).

Wopera Zs. & L. Wallacher (eds), *Polgári eljárásjogi szabályok az Európai Unió jogában* (Complex, Budapest, 2006) (Civil ProceduralRules in the Law of the European Union).

In English

Kecskés L. (ed.), *Business Law in Hungary* (Közgazdasági és Jogi Könyvkiadó, Budapest, 1998).

Mádl F. & L. Vékás, *The Law of Conflicts and of International Economic Relations* (Akadémiai Kiadó, Budapest, 1998).

Nagy, Cs.I. (ed.), *Cross-border litigation in Central-Europe: EU private international law before national courts* (Kluwer Law International, The Hague, 2022).

Nagy, Cs.I. *Private International Law in Hungary* (Kluwer Law International, The Hague, 2012).

Articles

In Hungarian

Bán, T. "Új távlatok a külföldi ítéletek elismerése és végrehajtása előtt," (6) *Magyar Jog* (1993), 332–342.

Bánrévy, G. "A nemzetközi magánjog fogalmának meghatározása hazai jogunkban," in Gy. Bándi (ed.), *Ünnepi kötet Boytha Györgyné tiszteléré* (PPKE Jog-és Államtudományi Kar, Budapest, 2002), 26–35.

Bauer, M. "Választottbíráskodás és mediáció. Kiköthet-e magyar fél külföldi székhelyű választottbíróságot?" (12) *Jogtudományi Közlöny* (2005), 489–501.

Benke, G. "A nemzetközi választottbírósági klauzula kikötése szerződésekben." (3) *Gazdaság és Jog* (2001), 11–15.

Bodzási, B. "A határon átnyúló jelzáloghitelezés nemzetközi magánjogi problémái," (4) *Magyar Jog* (2009), 237–249.

Bóka, J. "Családjog és öröklési jog az új nemzetközi magánjogi törvényben," 74(3) *Jogtudományi Közlöny* (2019), 93–103.

Boóc, Á. "Észrevételek az új Polgári Törvénykönyv tervezetéhez nemzetközi magánjogi szempontból," (3) *Polgári Jogi Kodifikáció* (2008), 3–8.

Boytha, Gy. "A szerzői jogok átruházására irányadó jog meghatározásának és alkalmazásának kérdései," in G. Faludi (ed.), *Liber amicorum. Ünnepi dolgozatok Gyertyánfy Péter tiszteletére* (ELTE, Budapest, 2008), 101–138.

Bruhács, J. "A határon túli környezeti károk orvoslásának problémája: nemzetközi magánjogi egyezmények." (1) *Jura* (2005), 48–60.

Burián, L. "A deliktuális felelősség a magyar nemzetközi magánjogban," (3) *Jogtudományi Közlöny* (1990), 150–161.

Burián, L. "A fogyasztóvédelem az új nemzetközi magánjogi szerződési szabályok tükrében," (1) *Magyar Jog* (1999), 16–23.

Burián, L. "A lex mercatoria alkalmazása nemzetközi kereskedelmi jogvitákban." (8) *Magyar Jog* (1996), 490–503.

Burián, L. "A magyar nemzetközi magánjog a rendszerváltás után," (12) *Magyar Jog* (1992), 712–719.

Burián, L. "A Római Egyezmény alkalmazásának elméleti és gyakorlati kérdései, valamint az Egyezmény várható reformja," (3) *Közjegyzők Közlönye* (2008), 3–19.

Burián, L. "A szerződésen kívüli károkozásért fennálló felelősség nemzetközi magánjogi szabályainak gyakorlati és elméleti kérdései néhány európai ország jogában," (1)-(4) *Állam-és Jogtudomány* (1990), 143–168.

Burián, L. "Fogyasztóvédelem és nemzetközi magánjog," (7)-(8) *Jogtudományi Közlöny* (1994), 307–313.

Császár, M. "Szerződésen kívüli kötelmek kollíziós joga: Róma II. v. magyar Kódex." (2) *Európai Jog* (2008), 18–27.

Csehi, Z. "A nemzetközi kereskedelmi választottbíróság eljárására alkalmazandó szabályok meghatározása," (7) *Magyar Jog* (1995), 431–448.

Csőke, A. "A határokon átnyúló fizetésképtelenségi eljárás az Európai Közösségben," (2) *Gazdaság és Jog* (2002), 3–7.

Csöndes, M. "Jogválasztás a Római Egyezménytől a Róma I. rendelet tervezetéig," (5) *Jogtudományi Közlöny* (2008), 239–250.

Czékmány O. & D.T. Ziegler, "Az állampolgárság nemzetközi magánjogi kérdései," 58 (11)-(12) Külgazdaság (2014), 116–123.

Czigler, D.T. "A szerződésekre alkalmazandó jog jövőbeni meghatározása az európai közösségben: a Róma I. rendelet szabályai," (1) *Állam-és Jogtudomány* (2009), 73–110.

Czigler, D.T. "A szerződésekre alkalmazandó jogról szóló Róma I. rendelet a praktikum tükrében," (9)-(10) *Külgazdaság Jogi Melléklete* (2009), 103–125.

Czigler, D.T. "A szerződésen kívüli kötelmi jogviszonyra alkalmazandó jog meghatározása az Európai Közösségben: a Róma II. rendelet szabálya," (8)-(9) *Külgazdaság Jogi Melléklete* (2008), 125–146.

Czigler, D.T. "Az első Brüsszel IIa. rendelettel kapcsolatos ügyek az Európai Bíróság előtt," (9) *Jogtudományi Közlöny* (2008), 449–455.

Czigler, D.T. "Európai családi jog – Az Európai Unió és a Hágai Nemzetközi Magánjogi Konferencia családjogi rendszerének össszefüggései," (3) *Állam-és Jogtudomány* (2007), 411–439.

Dámosy, B. "Az Európai Unió a szerződésen kívüli kötelmi jogviszonyokra alkalmazandó jogról szóló Róma II rendelet tervezete," (11) *Magyar Jog* (2005), 681–690.

Darázs, L. "A fogyasztói szerződések új kollíziós jogi szabályozórendszere," (2) *Magyar Jog* (2010), 116–128.

Darázs, L. "Törekvések az európai fizetésképtelenségi jog egységesítésére," (9) *Magyar Jog* (1993), 549–555.

Gombos, K. "Joghatóság, külföldi határozatok elismerése és végrehajtása az új nemzetközi magánjogi törvényben," 74(4) *Jogtudományi Közlöny* (2019), 141–149.

Gyertyánfy, P. "A szerzői jog átruházhatóságára és a felhasználási szerződésekre irányadó jog," in F. Mádl & L. Vékás (eds.), *Nizsalovszky Endre emlékkönyv* (ELTE, Budapest, 1994), 93–104.

Gyertyánfy, P. "Az alkalmazandó jog kérdése az internettel kapcsolatos jogvitákban," (8) *Magyar Jog* (2000), 491–494.

Harsági, V. "A házassági ügyekben, valamint a szülői felelősségre vonatkozó eljárásokban hozott határozatok elismerése az Európai Unióban," (3) *Magyar Jog* (2006), 169–176.

Horváth, É. "A (nemzetközi) kereskedelmi választottbíráskodásról," (7) *Jogtudományi Közlöny* (1992), 314–320.

Kecskés, L. "Lehet-e közrendbe ütköző, ami nem jogellenes?," (9) *Magyar Jog* (2007), 531–536.

Kecskés,L. "A civilisztikai jogalkalmazást érintő újabb EU jogalkotással kapcsolatos néhány elméleti kérdés," (5) *Európai Jog* (2006), 3–13.

Kengyel, M. "A 'polgári és kereskedelmi' ügyek fogalma az európai polgári eljárásjogban," (8) *Magyar Jog* (2005), 485–494.

Kengyel, M. "A határon átívelő jogviták és a nemzetközi jogfejlődés," (1) *Közjegyzők Közlönye* (2008), 3–12.

Király, M. "A személyek és a felek autonómiája az új nemzetközi magánjogi törvényben," 73(12) *Jogtudományi Közlöny* (2018), 509–516.

Köblös, A. "Joghatósági és illetékességi kikötés a 2000. évi CX. törvény után az európai szabályozás tükrében," (7) *Magyar Jog* (2002), 385–396.

Köblös, A. "Joghatósági szabályok Európában és Magyarországon. A kizárólagos és az általános joghatóság," (6) *Jogtudományi Közlöny* (2003), 266–275.

Köblös, A. "Joghatósági szabályok Európában és Magyarországon. A vagylagos joghatóság," (7)-(8) *Jogtudományi Közlöny* (2003), 311–321.

Köblös, A. "Perfüggőség és összefüggő eljárások a Brüsszeli Konvencióban és a 44/2001. EK tanácsi rendeletben," (2) *Collega* (2002), 27–33.

Kőrös, A. "A közjegyzői gyakorlatot érintő jogi esetek. Nemzetközi családjogi kérdések az Európai Unióban. – Joghatóság és az alkalmazandó jog a bontóperben viszontkeresettel érvényesített tartási igény tekintetében," (1) *Közjegyzők Közlönye* (2010), 12–23.

Kovács, K. "Előrelépés a közösségi nemzetközi magánjogi harmonizációban," (1) *Európai Tükör* (2008), 132–137.

Kozák, H. "Gyermek jogellenes elvitele miatti eljárás a határok nélküli Európában," (1) *Családi Jog* (2009), 25–29.

Metzinger, P. "A bejegyzés elve és a Gt. hatálya, avagy a bilaterális és az unilaterális kollíziós szabályozás kollíziója," (5) *Gazdaság és Jog* (2007), 19–21.

Metzinger, P. "A de facto külföldi irányítású magyar társaságok székhelye és honossága az európai jog tükrében (de lege lata és de lege ferenda)," (3) *Európai Jog* (2006), 17–26.

Nagy, Cs.I. "A jogellenes károkozás kollíziós szabályai a Róma II Rendeletben," (8) *Magyar Jog* (2008), 542–549.

Nagy, Cs.I. "A joghatósági megállapodás magyar és európai szabályozásának értelmezési kérdéseiről," (12) *Jogtudományi Közlöny* (2009), 505–517.

Nagy, Cs.I. "Application of EU Private International Law in Hungary," in Nagy, Cs.I. (ed.), *Cross-border litigation in Central-Europe: EU private international law before national courts* (Kluwer Law International, The Hague, 2022), 113-166.

Nagy, Cs.I. "A Róma II rendelet és a közlekedési balesetek: egységes kollíziós szabályok egy kis forum-shoppinggal fűszerezve. Hogy is van ez?" (4) *Magyar Jog* (2009), 250–256.

Nagy, Cs.I. "A szerződéses kötelezettségekre alkalmazandó jogról szóló rendelet hatálya," in G. Palásti & I. Vörös (eds.), *Európai kollíziós kötelmi jog* (Krim Bt., Budapest, 2009).

Nagy, Cs.I. "Az egységes fogalomértelmezés követelménye a formálódó közösségi nemzetközi magánjogban, különös tekintettel a polgári és kereskedelmi ügy, a szerződés és szerződésen kívüli kötelem fogalmára," (2) *Európai Jog* (2008), 3–12.

Nagy, Cs.I. "Jogválasztás az új nemzetközi magánjogi törvényben," 74(5) *Jogtudományi Közlöny* (2019), 189–196.

Nagy, Cs.I. "Külföldi-e a fióktelep: ki lehet-e kötni külföldi jogot a külföldi vállalkozás magyarországi fióktelepével kötött szerződésekben?," (1) *Magyar Jog* (2011), 52–57.

Osztovits, A. "Az Európai Közösségek Bíróságának joggyakorlata a szülői felelősséggel kapcsolatos perek joghatósági kérdéseiben," (3) *Családi Jog* (2009), 25–30.

Palásti, G. "A joghatóság kikötésének és a jogválasztásnak a kapcsolata," (11) *Cég és Jog* (2003), 33–38.

Palásti, G. "Dépecage és tronc commune a nemzetközi magánjogban," (3) *Jogtudományi Közlöny*, (2006), 83–90.

Palásti, G. "Közrendi, imperatív, kógens és diszpozitív szabályok," (2) *Magyar Jog* (2006), 65–76.

Palásti, G. "Lex mercatoria, a nemzetközi jog elvei és hasonló kikötések a jogválasztó klauzulában," (11)-(12) *Külgazdaság Jogi Melléklete* (2005), 133–148.

Palásti, G. "Micsoda madár ez? Néhány minősítéssel kapcsolatos észrevétel a Róma II. rendelet kapcsán," (6) *Jogtudományi Közlöny* (2009), 249–258.

Palásti, G. "Nemzetközi magánjog az Európai Unióban. A szerződésen kívüli kötelmekre alkalmazandó jogról szóló 864/2007/EK sz. rendelet a magyar jogrendszerben," (7)-(8) *Jogtudományi Közlöny* (2009), 341–351.

Palásti, G. "Speciális jogválasztási modellek – a méltányosság választása," (3) *Gazdaság és Jog* (2006), 11–15.

Palásti, G. "Speciális jogválasztási modellek – az önszabályozó szerződés," (2) *Gazdaság és Jog* (2006), 7–10.

Raffai, K. "A közrend a kereskedelmi választott bíráskodásban," (1)-(2) *Külgazdaság Jogi Melléklete* (2007), 1–12.

Szabados, T. "A jogi státusz elismerése a magyar nemzetközi magánjogban," in Z. Nemessányi (ed.), *Nemzetközi magánjogi évkönyv 2022* (HVG-ORac, Budapest, 2022), 40–56.

Szabados, T. "A jogi személyek a nemzetközi kollíziós magánjogban," in B. Berke & Z. Nemessányi (eds.), *Az új nemzetközi magánjogi törvény alapjai: Kodifikációs előtanulmányok* (HVG-Orac, Budapest, 2016), 114–135.

Szabados, T. "A jogi személyek személyes joga," in A. Jakab, M. Könczöl, A. Menyhárd & G. Sulyok (eds.), *Internetes Jogtudományi Enciklopédia* (Pázmány Péter Katolikus Egyetem, Jog-és Államtudományi Kar, Budapest, 2018).

Szabados, T. "Nemzetközi magánjogi tényállás," in A. Jakab, M. Könczöl, A. Menyhárd & G. Sulyok (eds.), *Internetes Jogtudományi Enciklopédia* (Pázmány Péter Katolikus Egyetem, Jog-és Államtudományi Kar, Budapest, 2018).

Szabados, T. "Vívódás a valósággal a nemzetközi magánjogban. Akkor és ma," in M. Király (ed.), *A titokzatos kastély. Ünnepi tanulmányok Mádl Ferenc emlékére* (ELTE Eötvös Kiadó, Budapest, 2022), 79–90.

Szabó, S. "Az új nemzetközi magánjogi törvény egyes általános részi kérdéseiről," 73(11) *Jogtudományi Közlöny* (2018), 449–463.

Szécsényi, L. "Lex mercatoria – a nemzetközi kereskedelem autonóm joga," (5) *Jogtudományi Közlöny* (1995), 201–212.

Szőcs, T. "Bírósági határozatok külföldön történő végrehajthatóvá nyilvánítása Európában, különös tekintettel a Luganoi Egyezményre," (4) *Magyar Jog* (1997), 238–243.

Vékás, L. "A „külföldi elem" a nemzetközi magánjogi tényállásban," 74(10) *Jogtudományi Közlöny* (2019), 377–386.

Vékás, L. "Az új nemzetközi magánjogi törvényről," 73(10) *Jogtudományi Közlöny* (2018), 413–421.

Vékás, L. "Nemzetközi kollíziós szerződési jogunk reformjához," (12) *Magyar Jog* (1999), 705–717.

Vígh, J.F. "A jogválasztási kikötést nem tartalmazó franchise szerződések nemzetközi magánjogi megítéléséről," (10) *Külgazdaság Jogi Melléklete* (1995), 145–155.

Ziegler, D.T. "Nemzetközi öröklési jog az Európai Unióban," in B. Fekete, B. Horváthy & B. Kreisz, *A világ mi magunk vagyunk ... : Liber Amicorum Imre Vörös* (HVG-Orac, Budapest, 2014), 612–635.

In English

Burián, L "Private International Law," in L. Kecskés (ed.), *Business Law in Hungary. Handbook for Investors, Managers and Lawyers* (KJK, Budapest, 1998), 489–506.

Burián, L. "Hungarian Private International Law at the End of the 20th Century," in S.C. Symeonides (ed.), *Private International Law at the End of the 20th Century. Progress or Regress?* (Kluwer Law International, The Hague, 1999), 263–277.

Burián, L. "Private International Law in Hungary," in P. Sarcevic & P. Volken (eds.), *Yearbook of Private International Law*. I. 1999 (Kluwer Law International, The Hague, 2000), 157–188.

Burián, L. "The impact of Community law on the determination of the personal law of companies," in P. Hay et al. (eds.), *Resolving international conflicts. Liber amicorum Várady Tibor* (Central European University Press, Budapest, 2009), 67–81.

Czigler D.T. & I. Takács, "The Quest to Find a Law Applicable to Contracts in the European Union – A Summary of Fragmented Provisions," 12(2) *Global Jurist* (2012), 1–46.

Czigler, D.T. "Choice-of-Law in the Internet Age – US and European Rules," 53(3) *Acta Juridica Hungarica* (2012), 193–203.

Gombos, K. "Rules of jurisdiction in the new Hungarian private international law," 61(1) *Hungarian Journal of Legal Studies* (2021), 52–70.

Harmathy, A. "Questions of arbitration and the case law of the European Court of Justice," in P. Hay et al. (eds.), *Resolving international conflicts. Liber amicorum Várady Tibor* (Central European University Press, Budapest, 2009), 135–142.

Kecskés, L. "European Union legislation and private international law: a view from Hungary," in P. Hay et al. (eds.), *Resolving international conflicts. Liber amicorum Várady Tibor* (Central European University Press, Budapest, 2009), 165–186.

Nagy Cs.I. & S. Szabó, "A way ahead toward a deeper integration of EU PIL: the unification of the rules on violation of privacy and rights relating to personality," in R. Somssich & T. Szabados (eds.), *Central and Eastern European Countries After and Before the Accession. Vol 1.* (ELTE – Jean Monnet Center of Excellence, Budapest, 2011), 191–211.

Nagy, Cs.I. "The Rome II Regulation and Traffic Accidents: Uniform Conflict Rules with Some Room for Forum Shopping – How So?" 6(1) *Journal of Private International Law* (2010), 93–108.

Oláh Zs. & Cs.I. Nagy, "Enforcement of contracts in Hungary," in S. Messmann & T. Tajti (eds.), *The Case Law of Central and Eastern Europe. Enforcement of Contracts. Volume 1.* (European University Press, Bochum, 2009), 215–315.

Palásti, G. "The future impact of the Rome Convention on Hungarian conflict rules," 3(1) *European Integration Studies* (2004), 57–67.

Szabados T. & Cs. Merkel, "The application of overriding mandatory rules in Hungarian Private International law," (1) *ELTE Law Journal* (2020), 113–122.

Szabados, T. "Challenges of the Codification of the Law Applicable to Legal Persons from the Perspective of Recodifying Hungarian Private International Law," 3(2) *ELTE Law Journal* (2015), 81–98.

Szabados, T. "Constitutional identity and judicial cooperation in civil matters in the European Union – An ace up the sleeve?" 58(1) *Common Market Law Review* (2021), 71–98.

Szabados, T. "EU Private International Law in Hungary: An Overview on the Occasion of the 15th Anniversary of Hungary's Accession to the EU," 6(2) *ELTE Law Journal* (2018), 41–64.

Szabados, T. "In Search of the Holy Grail of the Conflict of Laws of Cultural Property: Recent Trends in European Private International Law Codifications," 27(3) *International Journal of Cultural Property* (2020), 323–347.

Szabados, T. "Overriding mandatory provisions in Private International Law and Arbitration: Introduction by the guest editor," (1) *ELTE Law Journal* (2020), 7–8.

Szabados, T. "Overriding mandatory provisions in the autonomous private international law of the EU member states: General report," (1) *ELTE Law Journal* (2020), 9–35.

Szabados, T. "Recognition of a status acquired abroad," 14(1) *Cuadernos de Derecho Transnacional* (2022), 1210–1225.

Szabados, T."The New Hungarian Private International Law Act: New Rules, New Questions," 82(4) *Rabels Zeitschrift für Ausländisches und Internationales Privatrecht* (2018), 972–1003.

Szabó S. & K. Raffai, "Selected Issues on Recent Hungarian Private International Law Codification," 51(2) *Acta Juridica Hungarica* (2010), 136–155.

Takács I. & D.T. Czigler, "The Law Applicable to Contracts in the European Union: A Competition Between Rome I Regulation, Other Sources of EU Law And Directive Law As Implemented," 20 (1)-(2) *California International Law Journal* (2012), 21–53.

Vékás, L. "About the Rome II Regulation: the European unification of the conflict rules to torts," in P. Hay et al. (eds.), *Resolving international conflicts. Liber amicorum Várady Tibor* (Central European University Press, Budapest, 2009), 267–281.

Vékás, L. "Private international law in Hungary," in J. Basedow et al. (eds.), *Encyclopedia of Private International Law* (Edward Elgar, Cheltenham, 2017), 2138–2147.

Ziegler, D.T. "International child abduction cases in Hungary: A comprehensive summary of statistics, legal framework and important case law," 56(4) *Acta Juridica Hungarica* (2015), 317–342.

Ziegler, D.T., V. Vadasz & S. Szabó, "The New Hungarian Private International Law Code – A Mixture of Modern and Traditional Solutions," in A. Bonomi & P.R. Gian (eds.), *Yearbook of Private International Law 2017/2018* (Verlag Dr. Otto Schmidt, Cologne, 2018), 333–364.

In French

Szabados, T. "La nouvelle loi hongroise de droit international privé," (1) *Revue critique de droit international privé* (2019), 87–109.

In German

Burián, L. "Das ungarische internationale Schuldrecht nach dem Inkrafttreten von Rom I und Rom II," in L. Burián et al. (eds.), *Öffnung und Wandel Die internationale Dimension des Rechts II: Festschrift für Willibald Posch zum 65. Geburtstag* (LexisNexis, Vienna, 2011), 101–108.

Burián, L. "Die Neukodifikation des ungarischen internationalen Privatrechts – Probleme des Allgemeinen Teils," in P. Maksymilian et al. (eds.), *Rozprawy z prawa prywatnego. Księga jubileuszowa dedykowana Profesorowi Wojciechowi Popiołkowi* (Warsaw, 2017), 27–36.

Burián, L. "Die Partieautonomie im neuen ungarischen Gesetz über das Internationale Privatrecht," in A. Homicskó et al. (eds.), *Studia in honorem Péter Miskolczi-Bodnár 60* (Károli Gáspár Református Egyetem, Budapest, 2017), 83–93.

Burián, L. "Internationales Vertragsrecht – Römisches Übereinkommen und ungarisches IPR," in G. Hamza, *Symposion Hundert Jahre BGB: Entwicklung des Privatrechts im deutschen und mittel-osteuropäischen Sprachraum seit dem Inkrafttreten des BGB* (ELTE, Budapest, 2006), 13–19.

Burián, L."Drittstaatliche Eingriffsnormen in der Theorie des ungarischen internationalen Privatrechts und die Neukodifizierung des IPR," in R. Somssich (ed.), *Ratio et mensura. Studia M. Király dedicata* (ELTE, Budapest, 2021), 129–138.

Harsági, V. "Gerichtsbarkeit, internationale Zuständigkeit und Rechtshängigkeit im ungarischen IPR nach der Reform 2018," in R. Schütze et al. (eds.), *Usus atque scientia* (De Gruyter, Berlin, 2020), 313–329.

Szabados, T."Bestimmung des Personalstatuts in den postsozialistischen Staaten," 24(1) *Zeitschrift für europäisches Privatrecht* (2016), 278–299.

Szabó, S."Das Verhältnis des UN-Kaufrechts und der Regelungen des Gerichtsstandes in der Gemeinschaft," (2) *Magyar kereskedelmi jog évkönyve* (2010), 76–134.

Vékás, L. "Die Reform des internationalen Zivilverfahrensrechts in Ungarn," (2) *IPRAX* (2002), 142–145.

Vékás, L. "Wertorientierung und ihre Grenzen im IPR," in W. Holl (ed.), *Internationales Privatrecht, internationales Wirtschaftsrecht* (Carl Heymanns Verlag, München, 1985), 145–159.

Vékás, L."Autonome Angleichung an das Gemeinschaftsprivatrecht und das EUR-IPR in Ungarn," in F. Glatz (ed.), *Europa und „wir": 10 Jahre Europa Institut Budapest* (Europa Institut Budapest, Budapest, 2000), 187–194.

Vékás, L."Über die Ergebnisse der IPR-Wissenschaft im 20. Jahrhundert," in I. Schwenzer (ed.), *Festschrift für Peter Schlechtriem zum 70. Geburtstag* (Mohr Siebeck, Tübingen, 2003). 42–42.

Index